RADIO
ASTRONOMY

THE CRAB NEBULA.

Photograph from the Mount Wilson and Palomar Observatories,
Copyright 1963 by California Institute of Technology.
Anscochrome Film.

RADIO ASTRONOMY

J. L. STEINBERG and **J. LEQUEUX**
radio astronomy division   paris-meudon observatory

translated by **R. N. BRACEWELL**   stanford university

McGRAW-HILL BOOK COMPANY, INC.

new york   san francisco   toronto   london

RADIO ASTRONOMY

Library of Congress Catalog Card Number 62–21905
61115

First published in the French language under the title *Radioastronomie* and
copyright © 1960 by Dunod, Paris, France.

234567890(HD)72106987

FOREWORD

Since the start of modern times, advances in astronomy have closely followed advances in methods of observation. The discoveries of Kepler and Newton were the direct consequence of improvements introduced by Tycho Brahe into the measurement of angular distances. Physical astronomy was created by Cassini, thanks to telescopes whose construction had been greatly improved by Huyghens. Later, the use of the first large reflectors by Sir William Herschel marked the beginnings of galactic astronomy, just as the invention of photography and spectroscopy brought about the onset of stellar astronomy.

Among the methods that have become available to astronomers in the past 20 or 30 years, those which bring electronic techniques to bear have been the most fruitful. In particular, they have permitted the extension of astronomical observation to radio frequencies and the discovery of the low-frequency emissions of celestial bodies and interstellar matter, where formerly only the light detected by ordinary optical methods was known.

The investigators who first succeeded in identifying the radio waves coming from the heavens had been working for several years, in the midst of general indifference, when war broke out in 1939. The radio emission of the sun soon posed a problem of considerable military importance by virtue of its effects on communications. Astronomers were alerted in 1946 by the publication of results which until then had been subject to secrecy restrictions imposed by the military authorities. Optical astronomers and radio astronomers then learned to know and to cooperate with each other. France very quickly set a good example, and the radio groups soon merged into preexisting organizations such as the Meudon Observatory and the Institute of Astrophysics, in Paris. Solar physics has greatly benefited from day-to-day comparison of the data furnished by the spectroheliograph, monochromatic filter, coronameter, radio telescope, and radio interferometer.

At first the scientific public, always eager for novelty, seemed somewhat disconcerted by the effervescent development of radio astronomy. Publications placed much more emphasis on details of the electronic equipment used than on the results, which were still fragmentary and sometimes contradictory. But since then great strides have been taken, and radio astronomy is no longer in the groping stage. Techniques have been established, and the solid results of the most recent years have brought a priceless contribution to astrophysics. The emission mechanism of solar, galactic, and extragalactic radio waves is becoming clear, and the boundaries of the space accessible to the new techniques are receding steadily.

This work of Messrs. Steinberg and Lequeux is written by two experts whose research brings them into almost daily contact with the equipment problems of the technician; but it is not written for experts or technicians, and the reader who wishes to survey this very new field of astronomy, without struggling through the undergrowth, will be grateful to the two young authors. (If Dr. Steinberg has the appearance of a veteran, it is simply because he was one of the original workers and one of the most active organizers of the Nançay Radio Astronomy Station.)

In only a few years, the Meudon-Nançay radio astronomy group, under the direction of Prof. J. F. Denisse, has made notable achievements, which do them honor and have brought them a well-deserved reputation abroad. They are now proceeding with the construction of great projects: great, but costly, needless to say. The present work, which I warmly commend to the reader's attention, thus comes at an opportune moment to clarify the value of radio astronomy and the place it must occupy in the science of today and of tomorrow.

A. Danjon

PREFACE

The present work is devoted to the study of radio waves of extra-terrestrial origin, which is the objective of radio astronomy. At the time of the discovery of these waves, and until recently, this new branch of astronomy was dominated by instrumental problems and tended to develop independently of classical astronomy. The situation is changing rapidly: while we have given considerable space to the new techniques of radio astronomy, we have presented its results in close conjunction with the results of optical observation; now that most of the original technical problems have been solved, the two kinds of observation should contribute jointly to the study of the universe.

The mathematical equipment needed to understand the text has been reduced to a minimum, except that we have resorted to the language of mathematics in a few rare cases, where a formula could advantageously replace a page of explanation. We felt we should devote a sizable chapter to the mechanisms of emission of radio waves. The reader may find these pages hard going, but they contain the basic foundation of our science and the most important part of its contribution to astrophysics.

We wish to thank Professor Danjon, Director of the Observatories of Paris and Meudon and member of the Institut National, who kindly agreed to present our work to the public. We also wish to thank all our friends in the Radio Astronomy Group at Meudon Observatory, who have constantly helped us with advice and criticism, as well as our colleagues, both in France and abroad, who have kindly provided the photographs that illustrate this work.

We wish to acknowledge the very efficient cooperation of Dr. R. N. Bracewell in producing the English edition of this book. Dr. Bracewell is well known as a radio astronomer and a physicist. He has made a large number of outstanding contributions in this field and is the author, in cooperation with Dr. J. L. Pawsey, of one of the few radio astronomy textbooks.

He is also an excellent linguist and has done much more than a translation in criticizing, improving, and bringing up to date the original French text. If the English version is somewhat improved as compared with the French original, it is largely through his friendly cooperation.

J. L. Steinberg
J. Lequeux

CONTENTS

FOREWORD   v

PREFACE   ix

INTRODUCTION   1

1 THE ROLE OF THE ATMOSPHERE   6
   Bibliography   9

2 THERMAL RADIATION   11
   Energy transferred by radiation   11
   Brightness of a black body and brightness temperature   14
   Gray-body radiation   15
   Origin of thermal radiation   16
   Practical construction of a black body   17
   Bibliography   19

3   SIMPLE RADIO TELESCOPES   20

Background noise   21
Noise thermometer and effective temperatures   22
Origin of the thermal noise of resistances   23
The antenna   24
The thermodynamic properties of the antenna   27
Gain and collecting area   30
Observation of a localized source   31
Case of extended brightness distribution   32
Role of sidelobes   33
Gain measurement   35
Signal measurement   36
Transmission of noise through an amplifier   37
Noise measurement and statistical fluctuations   37 ⌐
The role of detection   40
Frequency changing and superheterodyne receivers   40
Receiver sensitivity and receiver noise   42 ⌐
Gain stability and switched receivers   43
Maser amplifiers   47
Parametric amplifiers   51
Polarization and its measurement   53
Antennas for polarization measurement   54
Calibration equipment for receivers   56
Bibliography   57

4   INTERFEROMETERS AND APERTURE SYNTHESIS   58

The two-antenna interferometer   59
Measurement of position of sources   61
Various types of two-antenna interferometer   63
Construction of two-antenna interferometers   65
Extended sources, aperture synthesis   68
Multielement interferometers, gratings   74
Reception pattern of gratings   75
Synthesis of arbitrary antennas   79
Correlation systems   82
Interferometry and integrators   85
Number of sources observable by a given radio telescope   86
Bibliography   88

5   SPECTRAL OBSERVATIONS   89

The 21-cm line   89
Swept-frequency receivers for 21 cm   90
Multichannel receivers for 21 cm   93
Solar radiospectrographs   93
Bibliography   95

6   MECHANISMS OF EMISSION OF RADIO WAVES   96

General laws of emission and absorption   97
Radiation transfer in a gas   101
The 21-cm line of neutral hydrogen   104
Thermal emission of radio waves by ionized gases   106
Plasma oscillations   109
Gyromagnetic emission   110
Synchrotron radiation   111
Čerenkov radiation   114
Bibliography   116

7   RADIO EMISSION FROM THE SUN   117

Introduction   117
The radio emission of the quiet sun   119
The slowly varying component   127
Chromospheric flares   132
The first phase: bursts of type III and V   137
The second phase: type II and type IV bursts   141
Radio noise storms   149
Radio astronomy and solar-terrestrial relations   154
Bibliography   159

8   RADIO EMISSION FROM THE SOLAR SYSTEM   161

The thermal radiation from the moon   161
Thermal emission from the planets   163
Nonthermal emission from planets   164
Radar echoes from the moon, meteor trails, and the aurora   165
Bibliography   167

9   GALACTIC RADIO EMISSION   168

Galactic structure   *169*
The 21-cm line and spiral structure of the galaxy   *176*
Continuous galactic emission   *182*
The center of the galaxy   *189*
Bibliography   *198*

10   GALACTIC RADIO SOURCES   200

Galactic sources of thermal radiation   *202*
The Crab nebula   *209*
Nonthermal radio sources in the galaxy   *216*
Galactic radio sources and the 21-cm line   *221*
Bibliography   *225*

11   EXTRAGALACTIC RADIO SOURCES   226

Normal galaxies   *226*
The 21-cm line in external galaxies   *229*
Radio galaxies   *233*
  Virgo A   *236*
  Cygnus A   *238*
  NGC 1275   *240*
  Centaurus A   *240*
  Fornax A (NGC 1316)   *243*

Radio emission from clusters of galaxies   *244*
Radio astronomy and the structure of the universe   *248*
Bibliography   *250*

12   CONCLUSION   252

INDEX   255

INTRODUCTION

Radio astronomy is a recent branch of astronomy whose aim is to study the celestial bodies by radio techniques. Two kinds of technique are involved, the study of the radio emission of the bodies and the study of the echoes received from them following the transmission of radio impulses generated on the earth. The second technique is essentially that of radar. It has led to the determination of the orbits of meteorites, most of which are invisible, as they enter the earth's atmosphere; to high-precision determinations of the distance to the moon and Venus; and to the first tentative probing of the outer atmosphere of the sun. No mass of astrophysical knowledge comparable in importance with that yielded by studies of natural radio emission has yet emerged from the radar side, but we look forward with interest to the coming developments.

Radio astronomy is a very young science, the first observations dating from 1932. Like many sciences, radio astronomy is an offspring of technology, brought forth by the demand for progress in commercial radio communication. When K. G. Jansky undertook the work that was to make him famous, it was with a view to improving the range and reliability of radio communication. Jansky was an engineer in a big organization, the Bell Telephone Laboratory, devoted to all scientific and technical aspects of radio. In 1929 he was asked to find out the cause of the background noise that limits the range of short-wave communication in the 15-m band, whose use was rapidly expanding. Jansky had a steerable antenna built to work at this wavelength and a receiver as advanced as the state of the art at the time allowed. As his antenna was directive, it enabled him to determine, even though crudely, the direction of arrival of a signal.

By the end of 1932 this first radio astronomer had accumulated enough records of the background-noise level to be able to confirm its extraterrestrial origin. He had observed a maximum of intensity that recurred regularly each day, not with a period of 24 solar hours, but with a period of one *sidereal day*. At the end of a paper published in 1933, he wrote: "In conclusion, data have been presented which show the existence of electromagnetic waves in the earth's atmosphere, which apparently come from a direction that is fixed in space. The data obtained give for the coordinates of this direction a right ascension of 18 hours and a declination of −10 degrees." These coordinates are those of the densest part of the Milky Way.

Well before this discovery, attempts had several times been made to detect extraterrestrial radio waves. Scientists the world over suggested, shortly after Hertz's experiments, that the sun might emit radio waves. Several nations can congratulate themselves on having produced one of these visionaries, who almost all attempted verification using the means available at the time. Unfortunately, the Branly coherer and the galena detector were not sensitive enough. But the strange thing is that, after Jansky's discovery, 10 years had to go by before another American, Grote Reber, applied up-to-date radio techniques to explore the new field opened up in 1932. From 1932 to 1940, there was no astronomer sufficiently in touch with radio publications to be able to foresee the future of this new means of astronomical observation. Truth to tell, Reber's experiments were quite an achievement, even by 1940. Reber was a radio engineer, but it was with his own funds that he built the equipment he used to make the first map of the radio sky at 460 Mc/s. Assuming that the radio emission from the sky was of thermal origin, he deduced that the chances of detecting it would be improved by using shorter waves. This also gave him better directivity. He used a 30-foot parabolic reflector, constructing the framework of wood. His judgment proved to be good; further progress, however, did not take place until after the second world war. It was in fact for military purposes that the short-wave techniques were developed that were to allow radio astronomical observations.

During 1939–1945 meter waves, then decimeter and centimeter waves, were used for radars with greatly improved receivers. While Reber was working on 67 cm, Hey in England discovered that the sun was a powerful and variable radio source, so powerful that it occasionally jammed meter-wave radars. In the United States, Southworth was measuring solar radiation on 3,000 and 10,000 Mc/s (10 and 3 cm). But, as Hey and Southworth were working for the armed forces, their results remained secret until 1945–1946. Reber, on the other hand, was free to publish his results and announced them first.

Since the war, the discoveries of radio astronomy have followed one another in rapid succession. Sources other than the sun have been discovered, and different kinds of emission have been found to be coming from our galaxy and other external galaxies. Finally, and most importantly, there is the 21-cm emission from neutral hydrogen in the ground state, whose study has made it possible, for the first time, to map our own galaxy, the Milky Way.

Recent developments in this new field can be conveyed simply by a few figures. Several fully steerable 80-foot antennas are now in use, one of 250 feet, and a 210-foot precision reflector has been completed in Australia.

The development of a new science does not take place without rather profound changes. Because the problems in the beginning were of a technical nature, the observers were skilled in radio techniques. Today there are still technical problems, but of a different kind. The radiometer, which is a radio receiver specially adapted for this kind of work, has become a well-known instrument and can be purchased from the catalogue; one can even buy radio telescopes to stock designs specially developed for this purpose; but it remains a delicate matter to interpret the observations. Radio astronomy is no longer just a matter for engineers; it is a new branch of astronomy. This stage of evolution is emphasized by the decision to hold no more international symposia devoted purely to radio astronomy, but only meetings devoted to particular astrophysical problems, meetings which will be attended by both optical and radio observers and by theoreticians.

Apart from the purely scientific interest of radio astronomy, a certain number of applications can be pointed to. For example, the temporal and spatial variations of the radiation received at the ground on various wavelengths show that the earth's atmosphere, while not so significant as for optical observations, nevertheless can modify extraterrestrial radio waves. This fact allows valuable data to be obtained on the local inhomogeneities of the ionosphere and troposphere, which perturb the propagation of meter and centimeter waves respectively. It has been possible to develop instruments that automatically track the sun and moon by means of their microwave emission. These instruments, known as radio sextants, can determine positions at sea, even if clouds cover the sky. It is probable that in the future it will be possible to guide on certain radio sources in the same way, and applications to rockets are already contemplated.

Finally, the study of the sun, which is the closest star to us, has led to considerable progress in our knowledge of this body which so strongly influences such terrestrial phenomena as magnetism, the aurora, and radio propagation over long distances by ionospheric reflections. Solar radio observations are already being used to forecast the course of these practically important phenomena with greater reliability.

From the standpoint of astrophysics the contribution of radio astronomy is seen to be fundamental. The astronomer can now see farther, study new physical processes, and take account of the presence of matter that is quite inaccessible to optical observation.

It now seems certain that the radio telescopes of the early sixties, simple as they are, reach as far as the greatest optical telescopes, the most famous of which is situated on Mount Palomar. At least this is the most probable conclusion to be drawn from the present situation where some 70 percent of the numerous radio sources catalogued have not been identified with optically visible objects. The radio spectrums and temperatures of the sources that are too distant to be seen optically can be measured.

Cosmic radio waves are produced by mechanisms very different from those responsible for luminous emission. Light is mostly emitted by atomic or molecular processes, but with the exception of the 21-cm hydrogen line, this is not the case in radio astronomy. The radio emission is due to the interaction of electrons with ions or with magnetic fields. In certain cases, electrons with speeds approaching the speed of light have had to be invoked, i.e., particles with energies comparable with cosmic-ray energies. So, thanks to radio astronomy, the origin of cosmic rays has now come under study.

The hydrogen line, the only radio-frequency line so far observed in the sky, is emitted by masses of neutral hydrogen that are totally invisible optically. How this matter was distributed and how it moved were virtually unknown to us.

Interstellar neutral hydrogen is not the only constituent of the universe which was almost invisible through not emitting light. The solar corona, which is practically transparent to light, was also difficult to study. Now the atmosphere of the sun is opaque in the radio spectrum. Furthermore, it emits, at any given height about the visible surface, a certain limited range of wavelengths. Thus we now have an extremely powerful method of studying these solar regions, and we have already seen that the corona extends much farther than was thought, possibly as far as the earth.

The power of the new tool now available to astrophysicists unfortunately cannot be applied until several difficult problems are first solved. The radiation received is very weak, and receiving techniques must be developed to the maximum sensitivity. Again, the wavelengths of radio astronomy (from a few millimeters to a few decameters) are much larger than the wavelength of light (less than a thousandth of a millimeter). This involves, as we shall see, great difficulty in achieving good resolving power, i.e., in constructing antennas capable of revealing fine detail on the celestial sphere. A radio telescope 3 kilometers long, working on a wavelength of 1 m, would give no more detailed a picture of the sky than the human eye, whose aperture is not much more than a millimeter.

This is saying that the vast horizons opened to astronomers by radio observation will not be easily conquered. But the results obtained in 10 years have certainly repaid the efforts which have been made, and are still being made, to overcome these difficulties.

BIBLIOGRAPHY

Several books on radio astronomy may be consulted, among them the following:

Pawsey, J. L., and R. N. Bracewell: "Radio Astronomy," Clarendon Press, Oxford, 1955. A new edition is in preparation.

Smith, F. G.: "Radio Astronomy," Penguin Books, Inc., Baltimore, 1960.

A special issue of the *Proceedings of the Institute of Radio Engineers,* edited by F. T. Haddock, was devoted to radio astronomy in January 1958. It contains numerous original articles and an extensive bibliography.

A comprehensive account, at specialist level, of current developments with a valuable bibliography will be found in R. N. Bracewell (ed.), "Paris Symposium on Radio Astronomy," Stanford University Press, Stanford, Calif., 1959.

THE ROLE OF
THE ATMOSPHERE

1

Our whole knowledge of the universe is derived by studying those extraterrestrial radiations which can reach our instruments.

Optical astronomy and spectroscopy study all wavelengths of light which can penetrate the optical window, that portion of the optical spectrum in which the atmosphere is more or less transparent (Fig. 1-1). This zone is bounded toward long wavelengths by the near infrared and toward short wavelengths by the ultraviolet. For some years rockets have been lifting instruments which are sensitive in the far ultraviolet above the densest part of our atmosphere, but this type of observation is still exceptional.

Radio astronomy uses the second atmospheric window, the radio window, which extends from millimeter to decameter waves. Around a few millimeters wavelength, the frequency of the waves (of the order of 100,000 Mc/s) is in the neighborhood of the absorption frequencies associated with vibration and rotation of oxygen and water-vapor molecules. Molecular absorption can already be felt at around 3 cm wavelength; in particular,

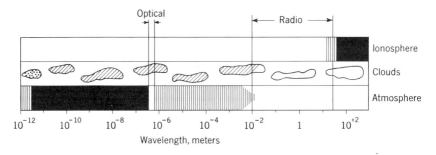

Fig. 1-1   Transparency of the atmosphere to radiation of different wavelengths.

water-laden clouds begin to absorb. At intermediate wavelengths the atmosphere is perfectly transparent, clouds causing no hindrance to radio astronomical observation.

Toward the longest wavelengths (wavelengths of a few tens of meters, as used in radio communication) cosmic radio waves are absorbed or totally reflected by the ionized layers of the upper atmosphere (the ionosphere). In these layers various solar radiations detach electrons from the atoms which compose the atmosphere. The free electrons are set into vibration by the electromagnetic field and lose the energy borrowed from the field through collisions with atoms or *ions* (atoms from which one or more electrons have been detached). The incident wave is thus attenuated in the course of its propagation. Below a certain frequency, known as the critical frequency, the ionized medium becomes totally reflecting and cosmic radio waves can no longer reach us. The value of the critical frequency depends on solar activity, on the time of day, and on the geographic location of the observer. Under favorable circumstances frequencies a little below 9 Mc/s have been usable for astronomical observations (wavelengths of about 35 m).

It should be noticed that the spread of wavelengths available for radio observation is considerably wider than that available optically. But we should not be misled by this frequency spread. No radio wavelength plays a unique role, save that of the hydrogen line at 21 cm. On the other hand, the optical spectrum contains a very large number of special wavelengths, those of the spectral lines emitted by chemical elements in known states. The optical spectrum contains chemical information on the abundance of the different elements, for example, but the radio spectrum is defective in such information except in the case of neutral hydrogen, which, incidentally, does not emit light.

Absorption is not the only atmospheric property. Atmospheric refraction is also observed, which is due to the variation of atmospheric density and refractive index with altitude. The rays are curved toward the regions of increasing refractive index. As the density and refractive index decrease as the altitude increases, the rays are always curved downwards, and thus stars are seen higher than they really are. This phenomenon is well-known in optics and has been rediscovered in radio astronomy. At the shortest wavelengths, the refraction is approximately equal to the optical refraction. On the long wavelengths affected by the ionosphere, the phenomenon depends on variations in the density of free electrons and no longer follows exactly the same laws.

Finally, it has long been known that the properties of the atmosphere do not depend on altitude alone; they are not constant along a circle of equal altitude. There exist local inhomogeneities to which the phenomenon of scintillation is attributed. It is well-known that the lower the stars on the

Fig. 1-2 The 210-foot radio telescope of the Australian National Radio Astronomy Observatory at Parkes, New South Wales. In use since 1962, on wavelengths down to 10 cm, this precision instrument is slaved to a master equatorial to well within a minute of arc. The total cost was approximately 1.8 million dollars.

horizon, the more they twinkle, and their brightness varies from moment to moment in an unpredictable fashion. The structure of the atmosphere can be represented by a stack of blobs of various dimensions, and in the interior of these blobs the density can be greater or less than the average density of the medium. These blobs behave like so many lenses which concentrate or disperse light or radio waves. But these lenses are not sufficiently large, measured in wavelengths, for refraction to dominate; rather, the incident wave is diffracted by these inhomogeneities. By means of difficult experiments one can measure the dimensions of the inhomogeneities from the irregular shadows that they throw on the ground. Moving with the winds, the blobs and their shadows give rise to fluctuations of intensity at the point of observation. The lower the observed object is on the horizon, the larger the number of perturbing blobs, since the thickness of atmosphere traversed by the rays is greater; this explains why the scintillations increase in intensity as the star falls low on the horizon.

This model is valid for light waves and the shortest radio waves. It is valid also for meter waves, but it has been shown that the latter are perturbed in the ionosphere, where the variations of refractive index are caused by local variations in the density of free electrons.

The scintillations observed on different wavelengths are due principally to blobs of different dimensions, a few centimeters for light, a few meters for centimeter waves, a few kilometers for decameter waves. There certainly exists a continuous distribution of dimensions among these inhomogeneities; through the analysis of scintillations this distribution can be studied.

The scintillation of radio sources on centimeter wavelengths contributes to our better comprehension of the propagation of the same waves beyond the horizon by terrestrial transmitters. As a result of diffraction by the inhomogeneous medium, certain rays are deviated from their direction of emission and can reach receivers far beyond the horizon. This would be impossible without the presence of the inhomogeneities. The same phenomena are observed in the ionosphere, and novel procedures of increasing importance for radio communication have been based on these properties of our atmosphere.

BIBLIOGRAPHY

Refraction

Allen, C. W.: "Astrophysical Quantities," Athlone Press, London, 1955.
Danjon, A.: "Astronomie générale," Sennac, Paris, 1952–1953.

Diffusion and diffraction

Kastler, A.: "Diffusion de la lumière par les milieux troubles," Actualités scientifiques, Hermann & Cie, Paris, 1952.

Ionospheric propagation

Budden, K. G.: "Radio Waves in the Ionosphere," Cambridge University Press, New York, 1961.

Dumont, R.: "L'ionosphère," Dunod, Paris, 1958.

Ratcliffe, J. A.: "The Magneto-ionic Theory and Its Applications to the Ionosphere," Cambridge University Press, New York, 1959.

THERMAL
RADIATION

2

All hot bodies emit thermal radiation. This fact is well known; it is customary to gauge the temperature of iron by its color: cherry red, bright red, white. Thermal radiation increases in intensity with the temperature. The changes in color show that the wavelengths emitted with the most intensity move toward shorter wavelengths as the temperature increases.

The thermal radiation of a body transfers energy: a second body can be warmed by exposing it to the radiation of a first body raised to a certain temperature. This energy propagates in the form of electromagnetic waves whose frequencies are principally in the visible region for high industrial temperatures. If the temperature is low (room temperature, for example), the radiation is mainly infrared and therefore invisible. Whatever the temperature, the spectrum of thermal radiation reaches right down to radio frequencies.

The study of thermal radiation by means of the spectrograph shows that there are no lines; the spectrum is said to be continuous. It contains components of all frequencies with different intensities. To describe the variation of intensity with frequency, the geometrical conditions are fixed and the energy emitted in a given frequency interval, for example, between v and $v + dv$, is measured (v is the frequency and dv a small increment of v).

ENERGY TRANSFERRED BY RADIATION

Consider a very small area S emitting radiation into a transparent medium (Fig. 2-1). The amount of energy which crosses a certain area S' per second is called the flux. Since the radiated energy travels in a straight line, the

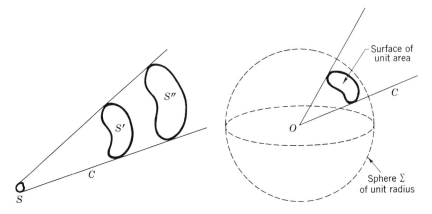

Fig. 2-1 Explaining flux density.   *Fig. 2-2* The unit of solid angle, the steradian.

energy which crosses S' propagates inside a cone C defined by the contours of S and S'. If a second surface S'' defined by this same cone is considered, the flux which crosses S'' is the same as that which crosses S'.

If, instead of S', 1 square meter of S' is considered, we get the amount of energy crossing unit area per second. This is the *flux density*. It is clear that the flux density is equal to the flux which crosses S' divided by the area of S'. Since the flux that crosses S'' is the same as crosses S', the flux density on S'' will be weaker than that on S', in the ratio S'/S''. If the surfaces S' and S'' are approximately plane and perpendicular to the central ray coming from S, the ratio S'/S'' is equal to the square of the ratio of the distances of S' and S'' from S. The flux density therefore varies inversely as the square of the distance from the emitting source.

Thus we see that the flux crossing S' depends only on the properties of the surface S and the interior of the cone C considered above. In the same way as the portion of the plane bounded by two straight lines converging at O is referred to as an angle, the portion of space within the cone C is called a solid angle (Fig. 2-2). Unit solid angle is that solid angle subtended at the center of a sphere of unit radius by unit area of its surface. The unit of solid angle is the steradian, by analogy with the radian measure of angle.

The flux density completely specifies the energy that crosses S' and is received and measured by the observer. It is a measurable quantity, but it gives no information on properties of the emitting surface and their variations from point to point. The flux density is used only for sources on which no detail or variation from point to point can be distinguished. Such sources are said to be *point sources*. A given object can be a point source for a particular instrument, and yet not for some other instrument endowed with better resolving power. The majority of heavenly objects are point sources for our eyes, but details may be seen on them with a telescope.

The flux density is an amount of energy crossing unit area per second, or the power crossing unit area: it is expressed in watts per square meter.

For an extended source (Fig. 2-4) whose various parts emit differently, *brightness* is used. Brightness is the flux density received from a

Fig. 2-3 Eighty-five-foot telescope at the University of Michigan. Commissioned in 1959, this instrument is usable beyond 2 cm wavelength, and possesses particularly fine pointing accuracy. Note the sizable drive gears. *(University of Michigan photo.)*

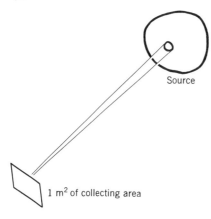

Source

1 m² of collecting area

Fig. 2-4   Explaining brightness.

source element subtending a given solid angle, divided by that solid angle. According to this definition, the unit of brightness is the watt per square meter per steradian. In general, the flux density and the brightness of a body depend on the part of the spectrum chosen for observation. These same quantities can also be measured over a frequency interval dv in the vicinity of the frequency v. If dv is small enough, the flux density and the brightness may be considered constant over the interval dv. Let us refer these quantities to an interval of 1 c/s, obtaining the *monochromatic flux density* in the vicinity of the frequency v, in watts per square meter per cycle-per-second. In the same way, the brightness referred to an interval of 1 c/s will be called the *monochromatic brightness,* expressed in watts per square meter per cycle-per-second per steradian.

BRIGHTNESS OF A BLACK BODY
AND BRIGHTNESS TEMPERATURE

The monochromatic brightness $B(v)$ of a body in the vicinity of the frequency v depends only on its temperature and on its capacity to absorb radiation of frequency v. This law can be deduced from very general considerations of thermodynamics.

A black body is a body that completely absorbs all radiation it receives. It can be shown that, for such a body, the monochromatic brightness $B(v)$ depends only on its temperature T and the frequency. This is the black-body radiation law or Planck's law (Fig. 2-5)

$$B(v) = \frac{2hv^3}{c^2} \frac{1}{e^{hv/kT} - 1}$$

In this formula, h is Planck's constant $(6.62 \times 10^{-34}$ joule-second), c is the velocity of light, k is Boltzmann's constant $(1.38 \times 10^{-23}$ joule per degree), T is the absolute temperature of the body (temperature in degrees centigrade plus 273 degrees), and $e = 2.71828$.

For radio waves, hv becomes much smaller than kT, and Planck's law simplifies to

$$B(v) = \frac{2kT}{c^2} v^2$$

a law found by Rayleigh prior to the formulation of Planck's law.

The monochromatic brightness $B(\nu)$ thus rapidly increases as λ diminishes.

If the total brightness integrated over all frequencies is considered, it is found to be proportional to T^4 and is thus a very rapidly increasing function of temperature.

The *brightness temperature* of any body is the temperature of the black body which would have the same monochromatic brightness at the frequency of observation.

GRAY-BODY RADIATION

A gray body is one which is not perfectly absorbing. If outside energy is incident upon it, it absorbs only a certain fraction $A(\nu)$ in the vicinity of the frequency ν. As it can absorb no more energy than it receives, $A(\nu)$,

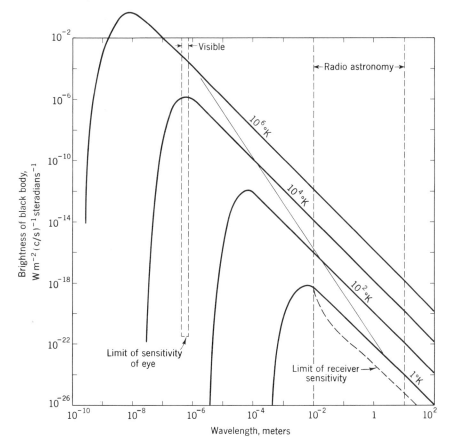

Fig. 2-5 The black-body spectrum for different temperatures (Planck's law). (*After Pawsey and Bracewell.*)

which is referred to as the absorption coefficient or absorbing power, is less than 1. In general it depends on ν and on the direction of arrival of the energy relative to the surface of the body; it depends also on the physical state of the body, in particular on its temperature.

It may be shown that the monochromatic brightness of a gray body is equal to that of the black body of the same temperature at the same frequency, multiplied by $A(\nu)$. This is Kirchhoff's law. As $A(\nu)$ is always less than 1, the brightness of a gray body is always less than that of a black body at the same temperature. For a perfectly reflecting body all the incident energy is reflected, none is absorbed, and $A(\nu)$ is zero; the thermal emission is zero. It is not known how to construct a body possessing this property for all frequencies. The brightness temperature of such a perfectly reflecting body is zero even if its physical temperature is high.

Kirchhoff's law can be expressed in another way: a body cannot emit thermal radiation that it cannot absorb. It emits this radiation in proportion as it absorbs it more strongly. Consequently, a perfectly reflecting medium emits no thermal radiation.

The consequences of Kirchhoff's law are very numerous in radio astronomy; this is the law that allows the calculation and interpretation of all the phenomena of absorption of radiation. Let a celestial body of brightness temperature T_s be seen through a thin absorbing region of temperature T_a. Suppose that in the vicinity of a frequency ν a fraction L of the incident energy is lost in the absorbing region. The flux coming from the source is proportional to T_s (Rayleigh's law); a fraction L is lost in the absorbing region, and a flux proportional to $(1 - L)T_s$ crosses the screen. This screen itself behaves like a gray body of absorbing power L and so radiates a flux proportional to LT_a. The flux finally reaching the ground is that of a black body with apparent temperature T' given by

$$T' = (1 - L)T_s + LT_a$$

| Flux received at the ground | Flux emitted by the source, as diminished by absorption | Radiation from the absorbing screen itself |

These results will be rederived later from microscopic arguments.

ORIGIN OF THERMAL RADIATION

The electromagnetic radiation of hot bodies is a fundamental property of matter. The microscopic concept of temperature is only the external aspect of the agitation of the microscopic particles which constitute matter. The higher the temperature, the more rapid is the agitation of the elementary particles. This agitation can reveal itself in different ways. In the case of a hot solid body, the first theories of black-body radiation postulated the presence of a large number of elementary oscillators radiating on all possible frequencies. This theory leads to Rayleigh's law, which is valid for radio waves but quite inexact for light. The oscillators are the electrons bound to the atoms of the solid body; they emit radiation by oscillating and are excited by absorbing other radiations. The study of this equilibrium leads to the black-body radiation law.

Planck was able to establish theoretically the law which bears his name, and which represents the observed phenomena perfectly, by introducing the notion of a minimum quantity of energy, or quantum. It is assumed that the electrons can radiate energy only in bursts or quanta of amount $h\nu$, where ν is the frequency radiated and h is Planck's constant. When ν becomes small (radio frequencies), the quanta are very small and everything behaves as if the energy were radiated continuously. In Rayleigh's law, Planck's constant disappears. Throughout the radio frequencies $h\nu$ is always much less than kT as long as T is not too close to zero.

Thermal radiation results from a large number of independent elementary processes taking place at random; it is an essentially incoherent radiation whose parameters cannot be computed in detail but only as statistical averages. In this respect, it is distinctly unlike radiation observed in certain electron tubes, where the electrons are artificially bunched in space and sorted as to speed. In this case we have coherent radiation where the electrons radiate in phase.

The purely thermal radiation observed in nature is emitted both by solids (moon and planets) and by gases (clouds of ionized hydrogen), and the thermal radiation from the ground is a very awkward phenomenon for radio astronomical observation. Although the brightness of the ground is low, ground radiation may be received from such a large solid angle, compared with that of the wanted source, that it can mask it completely.

PRACTICAL CONSTRUCTION
OF A BLACK BODY

Black-body radiation is described in full by Planck's law, or, in the radio range, by Rayleigh's law. Both laws have been verified many times by experiment. A standard of brightness is thus available, provided we can make a black body. To do this, it is not at all necessary to have perfectly absorbing material. Consider a closed container C, made of material that absorbs frequencies around ν. Place this container in an enclosure kept at temperature T. Pierce a small hole in the container C and in the enclosure E, and send unit flux through this hole (Fig. 2-6). Let A be the absorption coefficient of the walls, and R the reflection coefficient. After the first re-

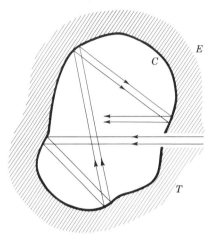

Fig. 2-6 A cavity with absorbing walls behaves like a black body.

flection on the walls of the container C, a flux A is absorbed and R is reflected. Both A and R are less than 1. After two reflections, R^2 remains, and after n reflections, R^n. It is easily seen that after a rather small number of reflections, only negligible energy will remain, even if A is not large. In the case where $A = 0.5$, less than $1/1,000$ of the energy will remain after ten reflections. If the area of the hole is small enough compared with the total area of the enclosure, the ray has no chance of escaping; a black body has been achieved; the hole radiates according to Planck's law. An oven is

Fig. 2-7 Practical application of a black body to calibration. The black body has been placed over the feed of the antenna on the left, while the one on the right has been left uncovered.

a perfect black body for light waves, and black bodies can also be constructed on this principle for radio astronomy (Fig. 2-7). A box is built of absorbing material, shielded on the outside to keep out extraneous radiation, and a big enough hole is left to allow the antenna to be inserted. Calculation shows that the box behaves like a black body provided that its dimensions are sufficiently big with respect to the wavelength (at least five times bigger).

BIBLIOGRAPHY

For a discussion of the foundations of the subject of this chapter, refer to the sections on thermal radiation in the standard texts on thermodynamics.

SIMPLE RADIO
TELESCOPES

3

The radio telescope is the fundamental instrument of observation in radio astronomy. It consists of two essential parts, the antenna and the receiver.

The antenna is an arrangement for transforming the electromagnetic energy which falls on it into a potential difference which can be measured. For a given source, the signal induced in the antenna will be proportional to the surface area of the antenna. A source is characterized by its flux density S, and we shall use the term collecting area, or *effective area*, of the antenna to mean the area A such that the available power P is given by $P = AS$. It is necessary to introduce this idea, for the quantity A can be very different from the physical area of the antenna seen from the direction of the source.

A further essential characteristic of the antenna is its ability to discriminate between signals coming from different directions. If the antenna can give no indication of the direction of arrival of the signal, it is said to be omnidirectional or isotropic and has no interest for radio astronomy. The antennas of radio astronomy are directive; i.e., they furnish a particularly strong output signal when the source is in a certain direction with respect to the antenna. This direction is the axis of the antenna.

The principle of the receiver is in no way different from that of an ordinary radio receiver, which is essentially an amplifier plus detector. Its role is to amplify the signal received by the antenna until it has sufficient power to deflect a measuring instrument, usually a recording voltmeter or ammeter. The receiver is generally constructed so as to amplify only the signals contained in a band of frequencies known as the passband of the receiver. It is said to be selective. The antenna itself is also usually selective, but its passband is almost always wider than that of the receiver, which therefore assumes the essential role of a wave filter.

Finally, the receiver produces an unavoidable noise signal of the same nature as that collected by the antenna; this is known as background noise. It is desirable to keep it at the lowest level possible. The level of this internal noise sets the sensitivity of the receiver.

Broadly speaking, one can say that the antenna chooses the directions of the sources, while the receiver makes the choice of signal frequencies. The antenna corresponds to a telescope. The receiver combines the roles of a spectrograph and a photographic plate. One should not conclude that the properties of the antenna are independent of those of the receiver; and just as one may not use any spectrograph with a given telescope, so a given antenna may not be connected to a receiver chosen at random. The receiver parameters very often modify those of the antenna, as we shall see below.

BACKGROUND NOISE

If one has a sensitive amplifier connected to a loudspeaker, with no signal applied to the input, a noise resembling that of a waterfall will be heard. This noise is the background noise. To hear it or measure it, we need a very high amplification. There has been constant striving to reduce this awkward phenomenon, and an absolute limit has been encountered in the thermal noise of resistances. Consider a resistance of R ohms and a sensitive amplifier working in the vicinity of the frequency v with a passband B cycles per second. This means that the amplifier amplifies only signals lying between $v - B/2$ and $v + B/2$. If the amplifier has been calibrated in advance with a known signal, the voltage across the terminals of R can be measured. It can be calculated also from Nyquist's formula

$$\overline{e^2} = 4kTRB$$

where k is Boltzmann's constant (1.38×10^{-23} joule per degree) and T is the absolute temperature of R. The quantity $\overline{e^2}$ is the mean square of the voltage e existing instantaneously across the terminals of R. This voltage is sometimes positive, sometimes negative. It can be recorded on paper with the aid of a recorder, and it may be ascertained that on the average it is zero. The measured quantity is its mean square value over a certain length of time. If this interval is very long, we measure $\overline{e^2}$, the mean square value. Bars placed over symbols signify mean values. The quantity $\overline{e^2}$ is proportional to R, B, and T. A resistance R is thus equivalent to a source of voltage e (of mean square $\overline{e^2} = 4kTRB$) in series with the resistance R, which is supposed to be noiseless (Fig. 3-1).

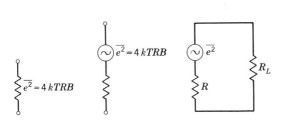

Fig. 3-1 Representation of thermal noise from a resistance R by a noise generator in series with a noiseless resistor. (a) Resistance producing noise; (b) equivalent generator; (c) equivalent generator delivering power to a load.

If such a voltage source is connected to an external load resistance R_L, it will deliver a certain power to it, which will be a maximum if the load resistance is equal to that of the source. The power delivered will then be $\overline{e^2}/4R = kTB$, and will amount to kT in a passband of 1 c/s. At room temperature [1] ($T = 300°K$) a resistance of 500,000 ohms produces, in a 5,000-c/s band, a voltage of 6.4 microvolts, which is perfectly measurable. If the resistance is 50 ohms, the passband staying at 5,000 c/s, the measured voltage is only 6.4 hundredths of a microvolt at room temperature.

Note that, in Nyquist's formula, the frequency on which the passband B is centered does not appear. The thermal noise of resistances does not depend on frequency. The spectrum is said to be white, containing all frequencies with the same strength.

NOISE THERMOMETER AND EFFECTIVE TEMPERATURE

If one measures $\overline{e^2}$ at the terminals of a known resistance R placed in a temperature bath of unknown temperature T, with a measuring instrument of passband B, one can measure T. Such an instrument is a noise thermometer.

Conversely, suppose that a voltage of mean square value $\overline{e^2}$ has been found at the terminals of R. This voltage may be produced by any process whatever; for example, it may be injected by an external circuit. In this case an effective temperature T' of the resistance R may be defined by Nyquist's formula. It is the temperature to which R must be raised to produce across its terminals the voltage $\overline{e^2}$ which results from supposing that e is due entirely to the thermal noise of R.

---

[1] For room temperature ($300°K$) and $B = 1$ c/s, $kTB = 10^{-20.4}$ watt per cycle-per-second.

ORIGIN OF THE THERMAL
NOISE OF RESISTANCES

The origin of the background noise is the same as that of the thermal radiation of hot bodies, mainly the agitation of electrons in the resistance. Nyquist's law can be deduced from a microscopic theory of electrons in conductors. It can also be deduced from purely thermodynamic considerations, without assuming any particular mechanism. It is the electrical aspect of a fundamental property of matter. Boltzmann's constant k, which appears in Nyquist's law, appears also in the Planck black-body radiation law, again in the form of the product kT.

Electrons are in motion in all conductors and also in insulators. Nevertheless, only resistances produce background noise. The collisions of electrons with molecules are responsible for thermal noise. They are the same collisions which heat a resistance when a current, i.e., a stream of electrons, is passed through it. In this case the electrons are subjected to an electric field caused by the voltage applied to the terminals of the resistance, and a certain velocity is thus imparted to them. They acquire a certain energy which they draw from the voltage source. They lose part of it by collisions which heat the molecules and the resistance. The existence of background noise is linked absolutely with the presence of resistance. If the electrons undergo no collisions, nothing opposes their motion under the influence of the external field, the body is perfectly conducting, and no background noise is observed.

Resistance gives rise to two phenomena: a voltage applied to the terminals of the resistance heats it; conversely, heating the resistance produces a voltage.

This voltage is the result of a large number of elementary collisions taking place at random; the voltage which results can be defined only statistically. From a knowledge of its value at time t_1, its value at time t_2 will not be predictable with certainty, its parameters are defined only on the average, and they can be determined only by means of a large number of instantaneous measurements (assuming it is known how to make them). Noise voltages are fluctuating, or random, quantities.

The importance of background noise in radio astronomy is fundamental, because the voltages induced in antennas by celestial electromagnetic waves are of the same nature as background noise. They are random voltages with the same statistical properties as the background noise of resistances. This similarity makes it difficult to separate the wanted signals from the unavoidable-noise voltages generated in receivers. The fundamental reasons for this analogy will become clear later on in connection with antenna theory.

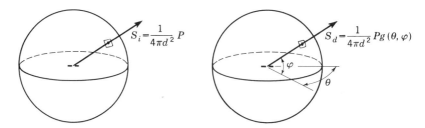

Fig. 3-2 Defining the gain of an antenna. Left, radiation from an isotropic antenna; right, from an antenna of gain g (θ,φ) in the direction θ,φ.

THE ANTENNA

The antenna is, as we have seen, an arrangement intended to intercept a certain flux of radio energy and to transform it into an electric current propagating on a transmission line. If S is the density of the incident flux, the available power at the terminals of the antenna has a value P such that $P = AS$. The quantity A, which has the dimensions of area, is the collecting area.

Conversely, if the antenna receives a power P from its transmission line, the flux density will again be S at the place where the same flux density existed in the case of the receiving antenna. It sends into space a flux S per square meter of collecting area, equal to that which it received previously. With all antennas used in practice, the power P is not radiated equally in all directions (Fig. 3-2). If it were, the flux density S_i at a distance d, in an arbitrary direction with respect to the antenna, would be $P/4\pi d^2$ (this is the flux per square meter of the sphere of radius d). The total flux which crosses the sphere, whose area is $4\pi d^2$, clearly amounts to $4\pi d^2 \times S_i = P$. If, on the other hand, the emitted energy is concentrated in a certain direction, the flux density produced by the antenna varies from one point to another over the sphere of radius d. The antenna is then directive. In general we have

$$S_d = g \frac{P}{4\pi d^2}$$

where g is the gain of the antenna in the direction defined by the angles θ and ϕ. It will be seen that g is the ratio of the flux density produced by the antenna to that produced by an isotropic antenna, at the same distance, in a given direction. It is clear from this definition itself that the gain is greater than unity in certain directions and less in others.

The total flux which crosses the sphere of radius d should still be equal to P, the total power radiated by the antenna. It is thus necessary that the sum over the whole sphere of all the densities S_d, in all the directions, should be equal to P. If this condition is written down, one arrives at the relation

$$\int_{\substack{\text{sphere of} \\ \text{radius } d}} g\,d\omega = 4\pi$$

In this formula, $d\omega$ is a small solid angle about the direction where the gain is g.

In practice, antennas are always built so that their gain is a maximum in a given direction or plane. The antenna concentrates the energy that it radiates into this direction or plane, and it is in this direction or plane also that the sensitivity of the antenna, when used for reception, is a maximum.

The distribution of g in space as a function of θ and ϕ is the *radiation pattern*, or polar diagram, of the antenna (Fig. 3-3). To represent this distribution, it is customary to give two sections in the planes of symmetry which the antenna nearly always possesses.

If the same antenna is used for reception, its properties will be characterized by its collecting area in the direction θ,ϕ of arrival of the wave of flux density S. This collecting area will depend on the direction θ,ϕ if the antenna is directive. The available power at the terminals of the antenna will be given by

$$P = A(\theta,\phi)S$$

We shall show below that for a given direction θ,ϕ, the gain $g(\theta,\phi)$ of the transmitting antenna is related to the collecting area $A(\theta,\phi)$ of the same antenna, used for reception, by the relation

$$g(\theta,\phi) = 4\pi \frac{A(\theta,\phi)}{\lambda^2}$$

where λ is the wavelength. Thus it is seen that the sensitivity of the receiving antenna [given by $A(\theta,\phi)$] and the transmitting gain [$g(\theta,\phi)$] vary with direction in the same way. They are proportional. There is perfect

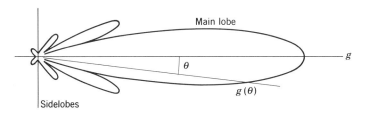

Fig. 3-3 Radiation pattern of an antenna, showing a cross section of the pattern in a plane containing the axis of the antenna.

reciprocity between the properties of an antenna for transmission and reception. The reception pattern coincides with the radiation pattern.

In these patterns, one usually distinguishes the main beam, where almost all the emitted energy is concentrated, from the sidelobes, whose maximum gain is from 10 to 200 times less than that of the main beam, but which occupy a large fraction of the space. Even if the gain of the sidelobes is less than one-hundredth of the on-axis gain, it is not unusual for 30 percent of the emitted energy to be radiated in the sidelobes.

Suppose that the antenna receives energy from identical sources S_1 and S_2, located in different directions, but with the same flux density S. Let α be the angle between the two directions. To find the direction of each source, we try to point the antenna at the first, then at the second, and measure the angle through which the antenna has had to be turned. The less the power received from S_2 when the antenna points at S_1, the easier this will be. The power received from S_1 when it is on axis is SA_0 (A_0 is the maximum collecting area of the antenna), while the power received from S_2 at the same time is $SA(\alpha)$. If $SA(\alpha)$ is too close to SA_0, it will not be possible to separate the two sources, which will appear as one. On the other hand, if $SA(\alpha)$ is much less than SA_0, the separation will be easy. The capacity of the antenna to separate two neighboring sources thus depends on the way in which $A(\alpha)$ or $g(\alpha)$ varies with α. The notion of angular resolution stems from this observation. The angular distance between the two directions in which the gain of the antenna is equal to half the maximum gain is referred to as the angular resolution. This definition is obviously somewhat arbitrary, but it is justified in practice, for two sources of the same flux density which are significantly closer together than the angular resolution are very difficult to separate.

The resolution of an antenna depends essentially on its dimensions reckoned in wavelengths. In a given plane, the angular resolution in radians is given approximately by

$$\frac{\lambda}{L} = \frac{\text{wavelength}}{\text{length of antenna}}$$

In the case of an antenna with rotational symmetry, the angular resolution is practically the same in all planes containing the axis. In other cases, the resolution is not the same in different planes.

The on-axis collecting area of reflector antennas is approximately equal to the physical area of the reflector. The larger the area, the larger the dimensions and the greater the resolving power. Thus we see that an antenna of large area possesses a large on-axis gain, a large collecting area, and a large resolving power.

THE THERMODYNAMIC PROPERTIES
OF THE ANTENNA

The antenna transforms radiant energy into traveling electric energy in a circuit or on a transmission line. Its electrical properties are reciprocal; that is, if energy is injected into a transmission line connected to an antenna, part of this energy will be radiated. In this second arrangement, the

Fig. 3-4 The 84-foot radio telescope of the Naval Research Laboratory, Washington, D.C., whose parabolic reflector is usable to 10 cm. *(United States Navy photo.)*

Fig. 3-4a The 22-meter precision paraboloid of the Lebedev Physical Institute at Serpukhov, U.S.S.R. Completed in 1959, the instrument has been used for a variety of researches at wavelengths down to 8 mm. (*Photo G. W. Swenson, Jr.*)

part of the energy which has been radiated disappears from the transmission line. It is thus as though, from the electrical point of view, it has been absorbed in a fictitious resistance representing the antenna; this is referred to as the radiation resistance (Fig. 3-5).

For some time there was a question whether this radiation resistance produces background noise, and if so, how much. Nyquist's formula is

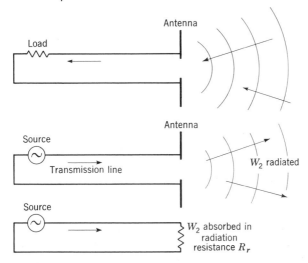

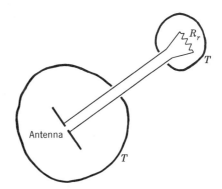

Fig. 3-5 Energy exchanges in an antenna. Above, the radiated energy is received and carried by a transmission line to an absorbing load; center, the energy produced by a generator is radiated by the antenna; below, the energy thus radiated disappears from the line just as it would do if the antenna were replaced by its radiation resistance.

indeed absolutely general and should apply to any type of resistance. Why not to a radiation resistance? An argument due to Dicke allows us to see why background noise is certainly observed and where it comes from (Fig. 3-6). Consider an antenna placed in the interior of a black body raised to an absolute temperature T, whose walls are perfectly absorbing for the frequencies considered. Couple this antenna by a loss-free line to a resistance outside the black body, of value equal to the radiation resistance R_r, also at temperature T. Suppose that the line is so proportioned that all energy incident on the antenna is completely absorbed in the external resistance; this implies that the full available power at the terminals of the resistance is radiated by the antenna. In such a system there is an energy exchange between the black body and the resistance. Of the radiation from the black body, part is intercepted by the antenna, conducted

Fig. 3-6 Apparent temperature of an antenna placed in an enclosure raised to a temperature T.

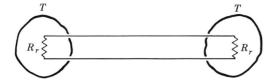

Fig. 3-7 Thermal equilibrium between two resistances raised to the same temperature *T*.

by the transmission line, and absorbed in the resistance. Similarly, the noise power available at the terminals of the resistance propagates toward the antenna, is radiated, and is completely absorbed by the walls of the black body. As the resistance and the black body are at the same temperature, the second law of thermodynamics requires that the net energy exchanged be zero. The energies propagating in opposite directions on the transmission line are equal.

Thermodynamic equilibrium exists. The same reasoning applies to the system formed of two resistances equal to R_r raised to temperature T and connected by a loss-free line (Fig. 3-7). This results in the radiation resistance of the antenna producing a background noise which is equal to that of the external resistance R_r at temperature T, as given by Nyquist's formula.

The apparent temperature of the radiation resistance will thus be referred to as the effective antenna temperature, or simply *antenna temperature*. To sum up, it is the temperature to which the radiation resistance must be raised in order to produce the same noise power as the antenna.

GAIN AND COLLECTING AREA

Let an antenna be placed inside a black body at temperature T (Fig. 3-8). The antenna is connected to a resistance also kept at the temperature T. Inside the black body is a second small black body at the same temperature T. All the elements are thus in thermodynamic equilibrium. Let us consider the radiation exchanges between the antenna and the small black

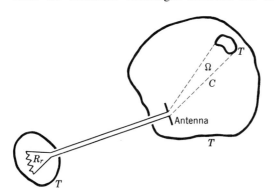

Fig. 3-8 Deducing the relation between gain and collecting area.

body C. The principle of detailed balancing allows us to assert that the net energy exchange between the antenna and the small black body C is zero.[1]

We now calculate the energy exchanged. In the direction of C the antenna gain is g, and its collecting area is A. The body C subtends a solid angle Ω. The brightness of C is given by Rayleigh's formula $2kTB/\lambda^2$, where B is the bandwidth. As the solid angle subtended by the body is Ω, the flux density is $\Omega 2kTB/\lambda^2$, and the power received by a collecting area A is $A\Omega 2kTB/\lambda^2$.

Meanwhile, the resistance produces a thermal noise power kTB which is radiated into the full 4π steradians. By the definition of gain, the power radiated toward C is given by $kTBg\Omega/4\pi$. Equating these two powers, we find

$$kTB\frac{4\pi}{g} = 2kTB\frac{A}{\lambda^2}$$

whence $g = 2 \times 4\pi A/\lambda^2$. The coefficient 2 must be canceled because the antenna cannot receive a power $2kTBA/\lambda^2$ but only half this power. An antenna accepts only electric fields having a certain polarization, as we shall see later. Thus finally we have the relation $g = 4\pi A/\lambda^2$, which allows A to be determined when g has been measured and vice versa.

OBSERVATION OF A LOCALIZED SOURCE

Suppose that we observe a source of uniform brightness temperature T_s which subtends a solid angle ω. If the source is strong, the background emission of the sky may be neglected, at least on centimeter wavelengths. Let us try to calculate the corresponding antenna temperature T_a. The antenna must be specified. We shall suppose that it has a gain which is constant over a solid angle Ω and negligible elsewhere (Fig. 3-9). This amounts to approximating the real polar diagram by a rectangle of width

---

[1] The principle of detailed balancing can be expressed as follows: In any system in thermodynamic equilibrium each elementary process is exactly counterbalanced by the converse process.

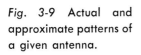

Fig. 3-9 Actual and approximate patterns of a given antenna.

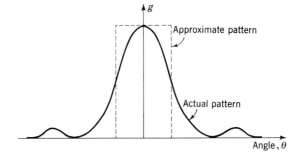

equal to the angular resolution of the antenna. The temperature T_a is by definition the temperature to which the radiation resistance of the antenna must be raised in order to produce the same noise power as the source. It is also the brightness temperature of a black body which, if it completely surrounded the antenna, would induce the same noise power. This black body would be seen only over the solid angle Ω since we have taken the gain to be negligible outside the main lobe. It would therefore radiate a power given by $\frac{1}{2}(2kT_a\Omega/\lambda^2)$. The source radiates a power $\frac{1}{2}(2kT_s\omega/\lambda^2)$. These two powers are equal according to the definition of T_a; thus we have

$$T_s\omega = T_a\Omega \qquad \text{or} \qquad T_a = T_s\frac{\omega}{\Omega}$$

And if $\omega \geqq \Omega$, then $T_a = T_s$. The antenna temperature T_a stops increasing as Ω diminishes, as soon as this solid angle is equal to that subtended by the source. Decreasing Ω is equivalent to increasing the gain g. If Ω becomes smaller than ω, T_a remains equal to T_s. Beyond this value, which corresponds to an angular resolution equal to the apparent diameter of the source in the case of an approximately circular antenna, the increase in gain gives no further increase in T_a, but it would become possible to detect bright, or dark, details of small diameter.

In the case of a point source, brightness and brightness temperature may no longer be used, but only flux density S. The power received is then SA, where A is the collecting area of the antenna. The antenna temperature is then given by

$$T_a = SA/k$$

CASE OF EXTENDED BRIGHTNESS DISTRIBUTION

The case of an antenna in thermodynamic equilibrium with a black body completely surrounding it obviously does not occur in practice. But we must know how to calculate the antenna temperature in the presence of a distribution of sources located in different directions. To do this, divide the celestial field into elementary areas of which the ith has a brightness temperature T_i and subtends a solid angle ω_i at the observer. This element has a brightness kT_iB/λ^2 over the bandwidth B (Rayleigh's law for one polarization only). From this we deduce that it produces a flux density S_i given by $S_i = kT_iB\omega_i/\lambda^2$. If the collecting area of the antenna in the direction of the element i is A_i, a power $B_i = S_iA_i$ will be extracted, which is given by

$$P_i = \frac{kT_iB\omega_i g_i}{4\pi}$$

where we have put $g_i = 4\pi A_i/\lambda^2$. If we sum the powers P_i received from the different elements i, we obtain

$$P = \Sigma P_i = \Sigma \frac{kT_i}{4\pi B\omega_i g_i}$$

and this total power is equal to kT_aB, the available noise power from a resistance at temperature T_a in a bandwidth B, according to the definition of antenna temperature T_a. We can put this relation in the form of an integral,

$$T_a = \frac{1}{4\pi}\int Tg\ d\omega$$

We see that most of the energy comes from regions where T and g are large. But if regions exist that subtend a very large solid angle, even though T and g are small, their contribution may not be negligible.

ROLE OF SIDELOBES

In most radio telescopes the maximum gain in the sidelobes is at least 100 times less than that of the main lobe. But the preceding remark shows that this does not justify their neglect.

For one thing, the sidelobes introduce a fundamental difficulty in the interpretation of records. A source passing through the main lobe cannot easily be distinguished from a source 100 times stronger passing through a sidelobe. If the antenna is small, there are few detectable sources in the sky, and the problem may be disposed of. But if the antenna is very large and can detect a few thousand sources, it is almost impossible to eliminate this ambiguity. Furthermore, if the antenna is big, the strongest sources may cause interfering signals not only in the first sidelobe, but also in far sidelobes whose gain is even less. For this reason the big catalogues have blank areas in the neighborhood of the strongest sources. The only known method of elimination depends on the fact that sources cross sidelobes in half the time it takes to cross the main lobe because they are half the width.

But there is also the back lobe due to diffraction of waves by the edges of the reflector (see Fig. 3-3). The back lobe possesses a very low gain, but it fills the whole hemisphere of 2π steradians. On decimeter and centimeter wavelengths the back lobe receives radiation from the ground, which behaves like a black body of approximately ambient temperature, say 300°K (Fig. 3-10). Experience shows that the antenna temperature due to the ground can reach 100°K; this considerably hinders observations of sources giving signals of a few degrees Kelvin.

The ground contribution is constant as the antenna is pointed in different directions in space, only if the altitude of the antenna axis above the

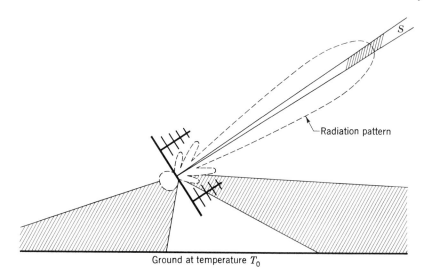

Radiation pattern

Ground at temperature T_0

Fig. 3-10 The antenna receives ground radiation in the shaded zones from directions outside the main beam.

horizon is constant. To measure weak sources, it is often preferable to have the radio telescope mounted with a vertical axis instead of on the equatorial mount which is more convenient in other cases.

The effect of sidelobes can be expressed quantitatively by introducing the idea of beam efficiency of an antenna. Divide the gain integral into two parts,

$$\int g \, d\omega + \int g \, d\omega$$

main lobe   sidelobes

Then let

$$\frac{1}{4\pi} \int g \, d\omega = \rho$$

sidelobes

and let

$$\frac{1}{4\pi} \int g \, d\omega = 1 - \rho$$

main lobe

where $1 - \rho$ is the beam efficiency of the antenna. It rarely exceeds 60 percent; this is the same as saying that if the antenna were placed inside a black body at temperature T, only 60 percent of the available energy would enter through the main lobe. This figure alone shows how necessary it is to know the gain precisely in order to get from antenna temperature to flux density, the sole parameter of a point source.

GAIN MEASUREMENT

Gain measurement is the fundamental difficulty in determining the absolute flux density of a source. Flux density, measured at different frequencies, leads to a knowledge of the spectrum of the source. From the spectrum alone can it be hoped to deduce the mechanism responsible for radio emission, as will be seen later in Table 6-1.

Gain can be measured in the following ways:

1 The radiation pattern may be measured by means of a terrestrial transmitter. This is the most convenient method because the power level can be chosen sufficiently strong to overcome receiver background noise, but its use is limited to antennas whose dimensions are small measured in wavelengths. Indeed, a terrestrial source can never really be at infinity. Assume that the spherical wave from the transmitter should not deviate from the plane wave which would be received from a celestial source by more than one-tenth of a wavelength (Fig. 3-11). Then the minimum distance D from the transmitter to the antenna is related to the radius R of the antenna by

$$\frac{D}{\lambda} \gg 10 \left(\frac{R}{\lambda}\right)^2$$

This shows that for an antenna 50 λ in radius, D must be greater than 25,000 wavelengths. If $\lambda = 3$ cm and the diameter of the antenna is 3 meters, as is common, the distance is 750 meters. If the antenna diameter is increased to 30 meters, as has already been achieved, a transmitter 75 kilo-

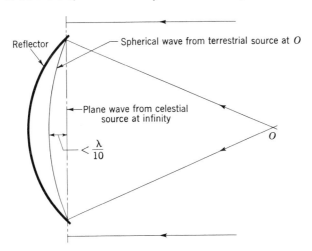

Fig. 3-11 Antenna gain measurement is possible only with a transmitter far enough away for the received wave front to be considered plane. This is not always attainable in practice.

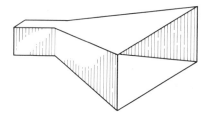

Fig. 3-12 Receiving horn. The gain of this type of antenna can be accurately calculated.

meters away would be needed, but this is impossible because of the earth curvature. Consequently, this method is restricted to small antennas with low resolving power.

2 A suitable celestial source may be used instead of a terrestrial transmitter. The source must be strong and of small apparent diameter relative to the angular resolution of the antenna. If the gain is wanted as a function of direction, but not the absolute gain or the collecting area, it is not necessary to know the flux density of the source.

There are few sources which satisfy these conditions if the gain of a large antenna has to be measured. Furthermore, the signal level received on the sidelobes may be so close to the limit of sensitivity set by receiver noise that they become difficult to measure precisely; as has been seen above, it is vital to know them well.

3 Finally, the antenna may be compared with another whose gain is calculable to good precision. This is the case with horns (Fig. 3-12). This method appears the best insofar as the gain of an actually existing horn is known, rather than of one described by working drawings. The antenna and the horn are pointed at the same source and their signals compared. This gives the maximum gain, but gives no information on ground radiation. This method can be used only in connection with the flux density of the strongest sources, in which case the ground radiation need not be so well known.

Thus we see that the future of absolute flux-density measurement depends on constructing antennas with much lower sidelobe levels. It seems possible to make considerable progress in this direction. Unfortunately, progress may be at the expense of less effective use of the physical area of the antenna: the collecting area for a given physical area will be less.

SIGNAL MEASUREMENT

An amplifier is necessary. The average noise power per unit bandwidth produced by a resistance at ambient temperature is of the order of 10^{-20} watt, and no measuring instrument budges at such low powers. The most sensitive demand 10^{-12} to 10^{-10} watt for an observable deflection.

The necessary amplifier must thus possess these fundamental properties of a measuring instrument: (1) stability: response to a calibrating signal must be constant with time; (2) sensitivity: the least noise possible must be introduced. The necessary amplification, say a power gain of 10^{12}, is relatively easy to obtain.

The behavior of the receiver depends on the character of the signal which it will be used to measure. Here we are dealing with background noise of essentially random character. We must therefore study the response of an amplifier to background noise.

TRANSMISSION OF NOISE
THROUGH AN AMPLIFIER

We have pointed out that resistance noise is the electrical aspect of the thermal agitation of electrons in conductors. It is due to electronic collisions. The higher the temperature, the stronger the thermal agitation and the more numerous the collisions in a given time interval.

All the collisions contributing to the noise produce equal electrical impulses, but the collisions are distributed randomly in time. It can be shown that to observe these collisions of extremely brief duration, an amplifier with a practically infinite bandwidth would be necessary.[1]

Each collision, or each corresponding electrical impulse, as it is applied to the amplifier input, gives an output signal such that the narrower the passband of the amplifier, the longer the signal runs on. The amplifier response to a very short impulse depends only on the shape and width of its passband. The duration of this response is inversely proportional to the bandwidth B.

The resistance noise is composed of a large number of collisions which take place randomly in time. At ordinary temperatures, there are a great number each second, each causing a response of duration $1/B$. The individual responses all superimpose to give a fluctuating voltage which is the observable output noise. It is composed of individual signals each of which corresponds to a collision at the input, each lasting $1/B$ second and distributed randomly in time. The number of collisions per second is proportional to the temperature T.

NOISE MEASUREMENT
AND STATISTICAL FLUCTUATIONS

Noise measurement amounts to counting the average number of electronic collisions per second, or the collision frequency. Assuming this to be possible, we will not always find the same number of collisions in each 1-second interval, because the collisions occur at random. We will find a set of col-

---

[1] As is fairly well known, percussion instruments are the most difficult to reproduce electrically and require the greatest bandwidth.

lision totals n_1, n_2, n_3, . . . , n_j, . . . , whose mean overall 1-second intervals must be taken. Repeating this measurement infinitely many times, we obtain the exact value n_0 of the collision frequency. If we are limited to N measurements, it may be shown that the probable error Δn in the measurement of n_0 is proportional to $1/\sqrt{N}$, thus [1]

$$\frac{\Delta n}{n_0} \propto \frac{1}{\sqrt{N}}$$

But this relation is exact only on condition that all the individual measurements are independent. For example, one cannot use this relation if the same measurements of n are used several times over.

Because the effects of collisions are small, an amplifier must be used to count them. As there is no way of constructing an amplifier of infinitely wide bandwidth, the bandwidth B is limited. Each collision thus gives a response of duration $1/B$ second. At the input of the amplifier there are on the average n_0 collisions per second which are completely independent and occur at random, but at the output of the circuit each lasts $1/B$ second. No more than B per second can therefore be counted which are really independent. The error in n_0 will thus be inversely proportional to $1/\sqrt{B}$. But there is no reason to count the number of collisions in a 1-second interval. Let them be counted over τ seconds. In each interval of τ seconds, there will be on the average τB independent collisions.

Consequently

$$\frac{\Delta n}{n_0} \propto \frac{1}{\sqrt{B\tau}}$$

The quantity Δn is the mean square value of the discrepancy between the value of n found by counting the collisions over τ seconds, with an amplifier of bandwidth B, and the exact value n_0. If one puts the values of n found in different intervals τ on a graph, a curve will be obtained which fluctuates about a mean value n_0. Since n_0 is proportional to T, $\Delta T/T$ is proportional to $1/\sqrt{B\tau}$. If the values n_1, n_2, . . . , n_j, . . . , instead of being read off, are transformed into an electric current actuating a recorder, the record will fluctuate from one side to the other of the value corresponding to n_0. This fluctuation will be proportional to $1/\sqrt{B\tau}$.

These fluctuations of the record are inevitable. They are the microscopic expression of the fundamental fact that the noise voltages are random variables whose behavior is not predictable in detail. Every time such a magnitude has to be measured, these fluctuations will be present and they can be diminished only by increasing the time of measurement τ. The quantity τ is called the *time constant* of the receiver.

---

[1] This law is valid for many random phenomena; in particular it applies to tossing coins.

Unfortunately there is often a limit to what can be done this way. Suppose that the apparent temperature of a resistance R varies with time. If a significant change takes place in a time less than τ, it will not show. If changes of duration θ are to be studied, the time constant τ must be significantly less than θ. This is the situation when a source of small apparent diameter passes through a narrow beam of a fixed radio telescope. If the source transits in 1 minute (antenna beamwidth 15 minutes of arc), it cannot be observed with a time constant much greater than a minute without changing the observed strength and position (Fig. 3-13).

Another method exists to reduce the statistical fluctuations, viz., to increase B as much as is possible. This method has been explored effectively, especially in the United States, where bandwidths of 1,000 Mc/s have been used, whereas most current receivers do not exceed 10 Mc/s. A factor of 10 can thus be gained over the relation $\Delta T/T = 1/\sqrt{B\tau}$. But we are limited by two difficulties. The first is technical: we do not know how to construct electron tubes which amplify over more than a 1,000-Mc/s bandwidth. The second is more serious: by widening the band, we lose all spectral information inside this band. The method is applied only for high frequencies, from 10,000 to 11,000 Mc/s, or, if absolutely necessary, from 3,000 to 4,000 Mc/s, when it is certain that there will be no need to record phenomena whose spectrum might exhibit significant variations over the 1,000-Mc/s band. Such receivers have been used for the measurement of thermal radiation from planets and for the radiation from certain sources with a flat spectrum.

It is nonetheless still true that for stable radiation such as all radio astronomical radiation (except the sun and Jupiter), there is no theoretical limit to the accuracy that can be obtained with stable equipment for the measurement of noise. The longer the observing time, the less the statistical fluctuations. The behavior of an amplifier is significantly different from that of a photographic plate where the blackening ceases beyond a certain exposure time (saturation phenomenon).

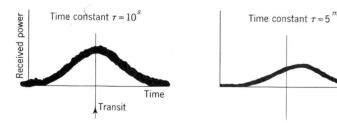

Fig. 3-13 Record of the passage of a source through the beam of a radio telescope. The right-hand sketch shows how the introduction of a long time constant changes the apparent time of transit and reduces the random fluctuations.

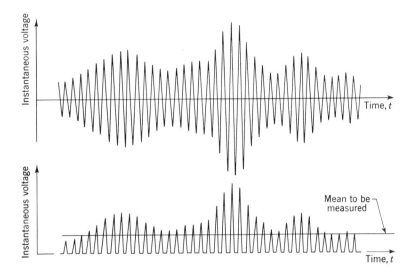

Fig. 3-14 Variation of a noise voltage before (above) and after (below) detection as a function of time. Detection produces a nonzero mean value which can be measured.

THE ROLE OF DETECTION

It is not sufficient to amplify the signal; it must also be detected. From Fig. 3-14 it is seen that the output signal of an amplifier is a fluctuating voltage whose mean value is zero. Now a measuring instrument will not deflect under the influence of a current going randomly positive and negative with zero mean value. Detection consists essentially of decreasing the negative voltages (or the positive) while retaining the voltages of the other polarity at full strength. There are various types of detectors, but it is enough to note that they are essentially equivalent from our point of view.

FREQUENCY CHANGING AND
SUPERHETERODYNE RECEIVERS

It happens that for lack of suitable tubes, signals of too high a frequency cannot be correctly amplified. In any case, we now use only superheterodyne receivers using the same principle as commercial radio receivers. Suppose we wish to amplify a signal of frequency v_s. We change the frequency by means of a mixer allowing it to assume a value of v_{IF} (intermediate frequency), usually lying between 10 and 60 Mc/s, that is then amplified.

The mixer is essentially a nonlinear device which takes a current i in response to a voltage v, such that $i = f(v)$, where $f(v)$ is nonlinear (Fig.

3-15). The operation of this arrangement is easily understood by taking a simple example, e.g., the case where $i = v^2$. One then applies a strong signal of the order of 1 volt to the mixer from a local oscillator of frequency v_{LO} which is superimposed on the signal of frequency v_s. Then at the output of the nonlinear mixer, we have

$$i = (m \sin 2\pi v_s t + \sin 2\pi v_{LO} t)^2 = m^2 \sin^2 2\pi v_s t + \sin^2 2\pi v_{LO} t$$
$$+ 2m \sin 2\pi v_s t \sin 2\pi v_{LO} t$$

The first term has the frequency $2v_s$, the second has the frequency $2v_{LO}$, and they may easily be eliminated by filters. The third term breaks into two, one of frequency $v_s + v_{LO}$ which is eliminated, the other of frequency $v_s - v_{LO}$ which is amplified. One thus has $v_s - v_{LO} = v_{IF}$.

The mixer possesses three important properties:

1 It conserves phase; if the phase of a signal is changed by 180 degrees, the phase of the intermediate-frequency signal also changes by 180 degrees.

2 If the amplitude of a signal is small compared with that of the local oscillator, the mixer behaves like a linear circuit: the intermediate-frequency voltage varies in proportion to the signal voltage and vanishes at the same time.

3 If no precaution is taken to prevent it, a mixer is sensitive to signals of at least two different frequencies: $v_{LO} + v_{IF}$ and $v_{LO} - v_{IF}$. This can be awkward.

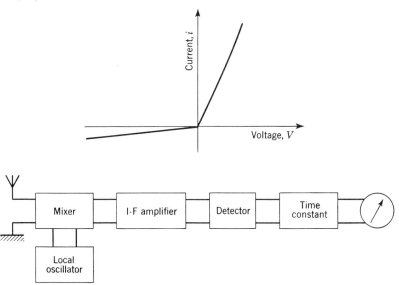

Fig. 3-15 Above, current-voltage characteristic of a semiconductor diode used in mixers; below, block diagram of a superheterodyne receiver.

A mixer requires, as we have seen, a nonlinear circuit element, i.e., a device such that the current through it is not proportional to the applied voltage. For this purpose we use diodes (two-electrode tubes), which allow the current to flow in only one direction. Their resistance is very high in the backward direction when the cathode is positive with respect to the plate; and it is low in the other direction. The diodes may be thermionic diodes (hot cathode and plate in an evacuated envelope) or semiconducting diodes of germanium or silicon.

The local oscillator and nonlinear element combined are equivalent to a time-modulated nonlinear resistance. More recently nonlinear capacities and inductances have been used; they give much better results because nonlinear resistances cannot yield power gain and classical mixers are a strong source of noise. We shall study these solutions later.

RECEIVER SENSITIVITY AND RECEIVER NOISE

We do not know how to amplify a signal without the introduction of additional noise, which originates in the resistances and in the electron tubes. This is referred to as receiver noise. Tube noise is also due to the granular nature of electricity: the electric current which flows through a tube fluctuates by an amount whose mean square value $\overline{i^2}$ is given by Schottky's law

$$\overline{i^2} = 2eIBM^2$$

where e = the charge on the electron = 1.6×10^{19} coulombs

  I = the mean current taken by the tube (amperes)

  B = the bandwidth in which $\overline{i^2}$ is measured (c/s)

  M^2 = a positive coefficient less than or equal to 1

The essential fact is as follows: all noise of whatever microscopic origin has identical statistical properties. It is always equivalent to the thermal noise of a resistance raised to a certain temperature. The radiation resistance of the antenna is usually chosen as the reference resistance. The receiver noise is then expressed by the equivalent noise temperature T_R. It is the temperature to which the radiation resistance of the antenna would have to be raised in order to produce, on its own, the same noise power as the complete receiver.[1]

The value of T_R depends solely on the circuits and amplifying devices incorporated in the receiver. The values given in the following table are typical of the best receivers that can be built in the present state of the art.

---

[1] Radio engineers specify also the noise of a receiver by the noise factor N, defined with respect to a reference temperature T_0 (usually 290°K). The relation between N and T_R is $T_R = (N - 1)T_0$. As the physical meaning of N is much less clear than that of T_R, we shall refrain from using it. If the receiver is assumed perfect and introduces no noise, then $T_R = 0$ and $N = 1$.

Frequency, Mc/s	From 10 to 300	1,000	3,000	10,000
Wavelength	From 30 to 1 m	30 cm	10 cm	3 cm
T_R, °K	600 (at 200 Mc/s)	400	600	600
Remarks	In general T_R is proportional to frequency for a given input tube	Mixers with nonrefrigerated semiconducting elements		

Under these conditions, the overall temperature measured at the output of a receiver breaks down as follows:

T_a *antenna temperature due to external radiation, coming partly from the sky and the rest interference coming mainly from the ground*

T_R *equivalent noise temperature of the receiver*

The receiver may be specified from the standpoint of noise by its equivalent noise temperature T_R. The total noise power available at the input is $k(T_a + T_R)B$ where B is the bandwidth. At the output this power is multiplied by a factor G known as the power gain of the receiver. It does not seem useful to go into details here of the techniques for reducing T_R to a minimum. With present tubes and semiconducting elements used in mixers, the values given above are minima. But there are strong hopes for significantly reducing T_R by means of new techniques which we shall refer to later.

We believe the following remark is fundamental: at 1,000 Mc/s an antenna temperature of 1°K which one may have to measure represents an increase in receiver output noise of only 1/400. The statistical fluctuations observed on the record are given by

$$\frac{\Delta T}{T_a + T_R} \propto \frac{1}{\sqrt{B\tau}}$$

and may be greater than 1°K, but we know that this difficulty can be overcome by increasing τ. It is thus possible to measure 1/400 of T_R on condition that the gain G is rigorously stable, under penalty of confusing accidental variations of output power $G(T_R + T_a)$ with the passage of a source through the antenna. The essential problem is ultimately that of gain stability.

GAIN STABILITY AND SWITCHED RECEIVERS

It is relatively easy to maintain T_R constant over the lifetime of the receiver. If this temperature varies, it does so so slowly that it can easily be taken into account. The output noise power is proportional to $G(T_a + T_R)$, of

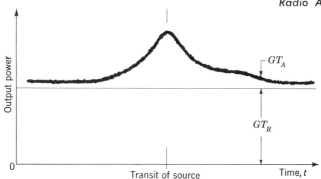

Fig. 3-16 Variation of the output power of a radio telescope as a function of time. The power GT_R is generated by the receiver itself and is constant only if G is stable. The power GT_A coming from the antenna is the quantity to be measured and is, in general, much weaker than GT_R.

which only the part GT_a concerns us (Fig. 3-16). One generally records GT_a alone, and to do this, GT_R is steadily compensated, for example, by means of a very stable battery. Everything would be ideal if the gain G were rigorously constant with time. The stability of G can in fact be assured by means of relatively simple techniques: stabilization of supply voltages to the amplifier and use of special compensating circuits. Experience shows that to keep G constant to about one part in 1,000, the plate voltage of the tubes (about 250 volts) must be stabilized to about one part in 10,000, and the heating power for the same tubes to about one part in 3,000. This is achievable. But other causes of variation in G remain. Some reside in the tubes themselves: variations in the properties of the cathodes which emit the electrons, deterioration of the vacuum, migration of impurities. The radio astronomer is helpless against these disturbances. He has to accept their existence and try to escape their consequences.

In fact, everything depends on the intensity of the signal to be measured, as we shall see. Suppose that the gain G has changed by a small quantity ΔG. The output power which was $G(T_a + T_R)$ before the change in G becomes $(G + \Delta G)(T_a + T_R)$. We have compensated GT_R. Thus in the first case there remained GT_a, and in the second case $GT_a + \Delta G(T_a + T_R)$; now there is no way of discriminating between $\Delta G(T_a + T_R)$ and a variation ΔT_a in T_a due, for example, to the passage of a source through the antenna beam. If such a confusion were made, it would cause the observer to see a variation ΔT_a such that

$$G\Delta T_a = \Delta G(T_a + T_R)$$

or again

$$\frac{\Delta T_a}{T_a} = \frac{\Delta G}{G}\left(1 + \frac{T_R}{T_a}\right)$$

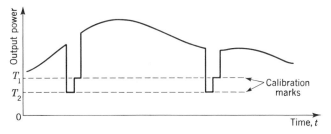

Fig. 3-17 Radio astronomical record with two calibrations at known antenna temperatures T_1 and T_2. If the response to T_1 and T_2 changes, the necessary corrections can be deduced.

We thus see that a variation $\Delta G/G$ can be confused with a change $\Delta T_a/T_a$ which is greater by a factor $1 + T_R/T_a$. So if T_a is much greater than T_R, which is the case for a very good radio telescope observing a particularly strong source, the factor $1 + T_R/T_a$ will be close to unity. But if we try to detect very faint sources, T_R/T_a will be close to 1,000 and a change of $1/1,000$ in G will entail an error of 100 percent in the measurement of T_a.

How then can we ensure that G remains constant to the desired accuracy? The method in widest use is frequent calibration of the radio telescope; the antenna is pointed at regular intervals to the same region of the sky, or it is surrounded by an absorbing box doing duty as a black body of constant temperature, etc. Records similar to that of Fig. 3-17 are thus obtained, where the calibrations are clearly visible. One can even calibrate T_R and G simultaneously by injecting two successive calibrating signals. But between these calibrations the stability of G must be depended upon. What can be hoped for in ultimate stability? Experience shows that keeping

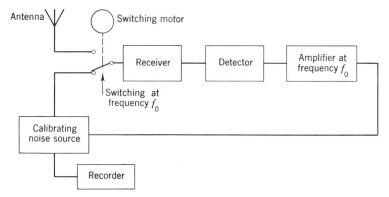

Fig. 3-18 Ryle-Vonberg system. The receiver is used as a null instrument, whose drifts do not influence the observations.

G constant to about 1/1,000 presents no difficulties if the operating temperature of the amplifiers is kept constant to about a degree. Temperature variations cause variations in the resistances, dimensions of coils, spacing between the electrodes of the tubes, and properties of the cathodes. The gain *G* is thus sensitive to temperature, but it can be compensated by the judicious introduction of certain thermosensitive elements into the circuits.

When a stability of 1/1,000 is not enough, what can be done?

A perfect solution is available into which *G* does not enter at all: the receiver is used as a null instrument. Ryle and Vonberg, in Great Britain, were the first to use this technique (Fig. 3-18). They alternately connect the antenna and the calibrating noise generator to the input of the receiver. This switching is done at a low frequency ν_0 of several tens of cycles per second. If the apparent temperatures of the antenna and the noise generator are different, a signal of frequency ν_0 appears at the output of the receiver. It is amplified and used to control the noise produced by the generator in order to make it equal to that of the antenna. When the instrument is in equilibrium, this condition is always achieved. It is necessary only to record a voltage connected with the apparent temperature of the noise generator.

In such an equipment, the gain *G* no longer enters. But several other inconveniences appear: it is not known how to vary the noise power of calibrating generators rapidly, and the equipment cannot follow rapid variations of T_a with great accuracy. But, above all, the antenna delivers

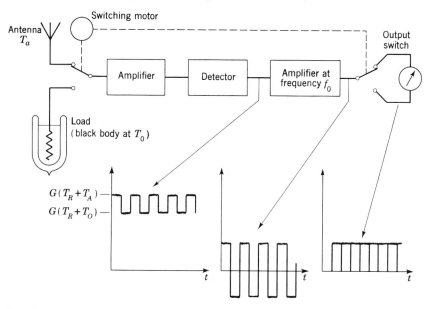

Fig. 3-19 Dicke switching system. The receiver is calibrated many times per second.

power to the measuring instrument for only half the time; this amounts to dividing τ by two. Few instruments of this type are at present in service.

To overcome the difficulties due to the adjustable noise generator, we use the Dicke method (Fig. 3-19), which amounts to very frequent calibration of G. The input to the receiver is switched ν_0 times per second between the antenna and a constant noise source, for example, a resistance kept at a constant temperature T_0. If there is a difference between T_a and T_0, there appears after detection a signal of frequency ν_0 which is proportional to $T_a - T_0$.

This procedure amounts to canceling the receiver noise by imposing a known modulation on the wanted signal. It can easily be shown that a change ΔG in the gain G produces an error ΔT_a in T_a given by

$$\frac{\Delta T_a}{T_a} = \frac{\Delta G}{G}$$

The relative error in T_a is equal to the relative change in G, whereas in simple compensation systems it is $1 + T_R/T_a$ times higher.

It seems that in recent years direct receivers with simple compensation have been used more and more. This is largely due to the development of new circuits, the use of better tubes, the improvement of regulated power supplies, and the construction of larger antennas giving higher antenna temperatures on a larger number of sources. Nevertheless, most observers think that when T_a is less than about 1°K, switching or other methods leading to the same results are required. It is clear that if T_R can be significantly decreased, the 1°K limit will be pushed back. Progress may occur in the direction of maser amplifiers and parametric amplifiers.

MASER AMPLIFIERS

In the classical receivers it is essential to change the frequency of the signal before amplifying it and to use for this purpose a crystal mixer, which inevitably introduces noise. Recent research nevertheless offers some ways around this impasse.

A new very-high-frequency amplifier was constructed in 1954 by Gordon, Zeiger, and Townes and christened a maser, a name coined from the initials of *Microwave Amplification by Stimulated Emission of Radiation*. The first application of the maser to radio astronomy was as recent as April 1958.

Completely abandoning electronic methods, the inventors of the maser tackled the properties of matter itself. It has been known since 1934 that molecules and atoms can emit and absorb radio waves. As in optics, an atom gains energy if it absorbs a radio photon, or loses energy by emitting a photon. Suppose, for simplicity, that the energy of the atom can take

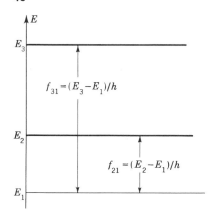

Fig. 3-20 Quantum transitions in a three-level maser.

only two values E_1 and E_2. If the atom is in the lower energy state E_1, it will be able to absorb a radio photon by passing to energy state E_2, providing that the energy of the photon is equal to $E_2 - E_1$. This means that the wave to which the photon belongs must have a frequency ν such that $h\nu = E_2 - E_1$ (where h is Planck's constant). Conversely, an atom with energy E_2 can fall back to the state E_1 by emitting a photon with energy $E_2 - E_1$. This emission can take place either spontaneously (*spontaneous emission*) or by the action of a photon whose energy is just equal to $E_2 - E_1$ (*induced,* or *stimulated, emission*). In this case, the photon emitted by the atom combines with the one that triggered the emission. It is seen that the induced emission may produce an amplification, which is the more favorable if the process takes place many times in succession in the medium containing enough active atoms.

In such a medium subjected to the action of a wave of frequency $\nu = (E_2 - E_1)/h,$ the absorption and the two types of emission occur simultaneously. Depending on circumstances, the wave may be partially absorbed or, on the other hand, reinforced, if the induced emission outweighs the absorption. We shall see in Chap. 6 that amplification will take place if, among the numerous atoms present in the medium, there are a greater number in the upper energy state E_2 than in the state E_1. In normal conditions the reverse is always the case. It is therefore possible to amplify the wave of frequency ν directly only if the upper energy level can be populated artificially more than the lower level.

There now exist several methods of doing this. We shall describe, by way of example, the one used in the first radio astronomical maser developed for the Naval Research Laboratory, Washington, by Alsop, Giordmaine, Mayer, and Townes. The principle of this type of maser is due to Bloembergen. It utilizes a ruby crystal in which chromium ions Cr^{3+} are present as impurities and play the part of active atoms. Placed in a magnetic field, they can assume several energy levels, three of which are used (Fig. 3-20). A strong auxiliary electromagnetic wave of frequency ν_{31} such that $E_3 - E_1 = h\nu_{31}$ is absorbed by the medium and depopulates the energy level E_1 at the expense of the level E_3, whence the name *pump* given to this wave. The level E_1 comes to be less populated than the intermediate level E_2, and conditions for amplification of a wave of frequency

Fig. 3-21 The 50-foot radio telescope of the Naval Research Laboratory, Washington, D.C. The reflector of this instrument was machined to tolerances of less than a millimeter, allowing it to be used at millimeter wavelengths. The 3-cm receiver incorporating the Columbia University maser is at the focus. *(United States Navy photo.)*

$\nu_{21} = (E_2 - E_1)/h$ are realized. If the antenna is coupled to the cavity in which the ruby crystal is situated, the signal frequency ν_{21} will be amplified, the energy needed for amplification being drawn from the wave of pump frequency ν_{31}.

In the example cited, the amplified frequency is 9,400 Mc/s, which corresponds to the wavelength of 3.2 cm, and the pump frequency provided by a separate oscillator is 23,100 Mc/s. In fact, amplification will not take place at a single frequency but over a band of 5 Mc/s, because the energy levels E_1 and E_2 have a certain width. Unfortunately one cannot greatly increase this bandwidth without reducing the gain of the maser: the bandwidth B and the gain G are, in fact, connected by a relation $B\sqrt{G} =$ const. This is a serious drawback of the maser. Furthermore, it is necessary to immerse the cavity containing the ruby crystal in liquid helium at 1.4°K. The performance achieved with this equipment, however, has been quite remarkable. Figure 3-22 shows two recordings of the passage of the radio source Cygnus A through the beam of the 50-foot radio telescope, obtained under identical conditions, the lower with a standard receiver, the other with the same receiver preceded by a maser before the mixer. The

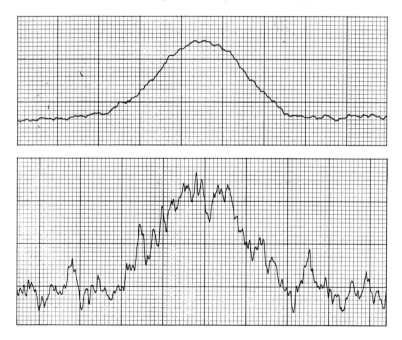

Fig. 3-22 Records of the radio source Cygnus A at 3 cm. Below, with an ordinary receiver; above, under the same conditions with a maser, showing the great reduction in receiver-noise fluctuations. *(Alsop, Giordmaine, Mayer, and Townes.)*

maser allows the relative noise to be reduced by a factor of approximately 16. The noise temperature of the receiver, T_R, is estimated as low as about 60°K. Notice that only a small part of this noise originates in the maser itself.[1] The larger part is due to loss in the transmission lines between the antenna and the maser, and to ground radiation. This situation is very different from that encountered with standard receivers, where the noise due to losses in the line and the antenna is usually small compared with that of the mixer. If the use of masers or other types of low-noise receivers becomes more general, this will always have to be taken into account.

In spite of its remarkable performance, the maser does not seem for the moment to be in widespread use. Apart from unusual difficulty of adjustment, it has the inconvenience of working in liquid helium. Therefore we turn rather for the immediate future to other types of low-noise receivers about which we shall say a few words.

PARAMETRIC AMPLIFIERS

Parametric amplifiers constitute a new category of amplifying devices based on principles whose importance has been fully understood only since 1950. The first attempts where not unlike the mixer circuits which have been described above, with the nonlinear resistive element replaced by a nonlinear capacity or inductance.

We know that a mixer in the form of a nonlinear resistance, or resistive mixer, cannot give power gain. It is important to see why: in order for there to be power gain, it is necessary for power to be supplied to the main circuit. In a tube amplifier, the energy comes essentially from the source of plate voltage. In the case of the mixer, the power can be provided only by the local oscillator. If the mixer is resistive, the modulation of the nonlinear element usually absorbs a certain fraction of the local-oscillator power, but this fraction cannot be delivered to the main circuit acting on a frequency ν_{IF}; it is lost in the resistance and dissipated in the form of heat.

The fact of modulating a resistance placed in a circuit cannot bring external energy into the circuit. If this were not so, it would not be possible to vary a resistance, for example, a rheostat, without using a certain amount of energy. Now to do this, it is necessary only to overcome the friction, and there is no fundamental reason preventing the energy lost as friction from being reduced to a negligible value with respect to the energy controlled by the rheostat.

---

[1] Maser noise is essentially due to spontaneous emission of excited atoms and is completely random, whereas induced emission is in phase coherence with the signal. Fortunately, induced emission is usually much stronger than spontaneous emission in the radio-frequency range.

The situation is quite different in the case of a capacity. Suppose that we wish to modulate a capacity mechanically, for example, by varying the spacing between its plates. The capacity has an initial value C, and it is charged to a potential V. The charge on each plate is given by $Q = CV$ and the stored energy is $CV^2/2$. Let us increase the capacity by bringing the plates together. Since C increases and Q remains the same, it follows that V decreases as $1/C$. The energy $CV^2/2$ decreases, the lost energy going to the mechanical system which moved the plates together. Of course the plates are attracted to each other as soon as the capacitor is charged. If C is to be decreased by separating the plates, a certain amount of work must be furnished and energy will be given to the capacity which thus behaves as an energy reservoir. There is nothing like this in a resistance.

We now see why a modulated nonlinear capacity is capable of transferring part of the local-oscillator energy into the circuit; thus it is a mixer which can furnish power gain. The theory of these devices shows that the power gain is equal to the ratio of the output frequency to the input frequency. To make use of this property, we choose an intermediate frequency much greater than the signal frequency (Fig. 3-23).

To understand the importance of the power gain obtained in this mixer, consider two circuits producing the same output noise power P_o, one with unity gain, the other having a gain G greater than unity. Apply the same signal to the input of both circuits. In the first case, the signal power P_s will be found at the output superimposed on a noise power P_o. In the second case, we find $GP_s + P_o$. The second circuit thus improves the signal/noise ratio, while the first only maintains it. If instead of taking $G = 1$ in the first case, we had taken G less than 1, which is the case of an actual resistive mixer, the signal/noise ratio would have been degraded.

Furthermore only resistances produce thermal noise, capacities produce none. The parametric amplifier is theoretically devoid of internal noise. The nonlinear capacities in use are semiconducting diodes whose capacity is sufficiently variable for their purpose, but which are not entirely devoid of internal resistance. Consequently they produce some noise.

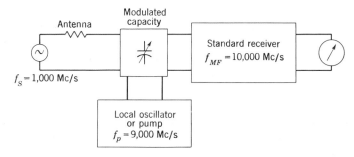

Fig. 3-23   Block diagram of a parametric-amplifier receiver.

Nevertheless, after only a few years of development, it seems that these amplifiers will permit a gain of a factor of 10 in receiver noise between 1,000 and 10,000 Mc/s. A new electron tube depending on the parametric principle (Adler tube) may even allow this result to be achieved over a wider band.

POLARIZATION AND ITS MEASUREMENT

An electromagnetic wave can be represented by the propagation of alternating electric and magnetic fields. Each of these fields is, at each instant, in an isotropic medium, perpendicular to the direction of propagation. They vary sinusoidally in time. The plane in which the electric field vibrates is called the plane of polarization of the wave. It contains the direction of propagation and plays a quite special role. If we try to measure the electromagnetic field, it is necessary to sample it through an antenna in which it will induce a measurable current. The antenna may be a dipole coupled electrically to the field. The dipole will have to be parallel to the electric field of the wave in order for the current to flow in it. If the dipole is perpendicular to the electric field, and thus to the plane of polarization, no current will be induced.

The simple electromagnetic wave so described may be emitted by another dipole fed by the high-frequency voltage from a transmitter. It is easy to see that the electric field of the wave will be parallel to the transmitting dipole. The elementary electromagnetic wave of which we speak is said to be linearly polarized: its electric field always remains in the same fixed plane with respect to the transmitter. We always try to resolve more complicated waves into a smaller number of elementary waves which we know better how to deal with.

In the case of thermal radiation *in vacuo,* we have seen that the emission comes from incoherent vibrations of electrons contained in the emitting medium. These electrons behave like so many small dipoles emitting linearly polarized waves. In the absence of significant external fields, these dipoles are oriented at random in the medium and radiate waves whose planes of polarization can assume all possible orientations with respect to the direction of propagation. If we try to receive such a wave on a dipole, we get a practically constant signal as we rotate the plane of the antenna about the direction of propagation. There are in effect at each instant as many elementary dipoles vibrating in a given plane as in any other possible direction. The wave is said to be unpolarized or *randomly polarized.* It has become statistically symmetrical with respect to the direction of propagation. If this wave is received simultaneously on two mutually perpendicular crossed dipoles, the voltages induced in the two antennas are unrelated to each other, because they do not come from the same vibrating electrons, and are said to be uncorrelated or statistically independent.

The symmetry properties of the received wave depend on the state of the emitting regions. A perfectly isotropic medium can emit only unpolarized thermal radiation. Conversely, if partially polarized radiation is observed, it is because the emitting medium or the media intervening between the emission and the earth have become anisotropic, usually as the result of the permanent magnetic field in these regions. Later we shall see in detail how the presence of a magnetic field modifies the medium by orienting the electron trajectories.

Under certain conditions, the electric field of the received wave rotates steadily about the direction of propagation. Such a wave can be decomposed into two perpendicular components at the same frequency. If the two components have the same amplitude and are a quarter cycle out of phase, we are dealing with a circularly polarized wave which has the same symmetry as a randomly polarized wave, but the two components are no longer statistically independent. A medium immersed in a uniform magnetic field, parallel to the direction of observation, in certain cases emits polarized waves in this manner. According to the sense of rotation of the plane of polarization, we shall say that the wave has left-handed or right-handed circular polarization. This sense depends on that of the magnetic field with respect to the direction of observation.

ANTENNAS FOR POLARIZATION MEASUREMENT

Most antennas (dipoles, loops) are sensitive only to linearly polarized waves. In the field of an unpolarized wave, they respond to only one component of the wave. It can be shown that with such an antenna only half the power carried by an unpolarized wave can be received. This is the origin of the factor ½ introduced in the calculation of thermal radiation received from a black body by an antenna (see p. 31). We can also construct antennas which are sensitive to right-handed or left-handed polarization, but never to both senses at once. Two antennas of this kind (helices or dipoles connected with a phase difference of $\lambda/4$), polarized in opposite senses, give a signal of the same intensity when the same unpolarized wave falls on them. But in the presence of a circularly polarized wave, one will absorb the full power of the wave, and the other nothing.

An unpolarized wave may be resolved into two linear components whose intensities are equal and which are uncorrelated. It can be resolved also into two circularly polarized components with the same properties.

On the other hand, a fully polarized wave resolves into two perpendicular linear components, in general with different intensities and having a certain correlation which shows up through a phase relation between the two components. Such a wave resolves equally well into two circularly polarized waves with opposite senses of rotation having the same properties.

Knowledge of the state of polarization of a wave of cosmic origin requires the measurement of four parameters:

1 The intensity of the unpolarized component
2 The intensity of one linear or right-handed circular component
3 The intensity of the other linear component perpendicular to the first, or the left-handed circular component
4 The relative phase of these two components

In the case of strongly polarized radiation, as in the case of the sun, the problem is relatively easy to solve. It becomes very difficult for galactic and extragalactic sources, which are faint and weakly polarized. Ground radiation may be partially polarized, and so may sky radiation after reflection from the ground or certain parts of the antenna. These phenomena introduce instrumental polarization, which is especially awkward because it varies with the pointing of the antenna. We now tackle the separation of the polarized component from the received radiation. A linearly polarized antenna may be rotated about the direction of pointing. In the presence of a certain percentage of polarization, a variation in the energy received will be observed in the course of this rotation. But any asymmetry of the reflector or its supports will produce a similar result even if the observed source is completely unpolarized. Nevertheless, this is how the polarization of the Crab nebula was measured on 10 and 3 cm. Two differently polarized antennas may also be employed. If one is separated from the other, an interferometric polarimeter results (see Chap. 4) and the record exhibits interference fringes whose measurement allows the parameters 2, 3, and 4 to be calculated. If they are placed at the same point, at the focus of a reflector, for example, the interconnection is varied and measurement of the signal received in the different cases allows the state of polarization to be determined.

Finally, by calculating the product of the signals received by the two differently polarized antennas, it is possible to measure the correlation of the two components.

These three types of arrangement can be used in such a way that the output signal is zero in the absence of a polarized component, which is thus more easily placed in evidence. Unfortunately there exist several instrumental factors which are difficult to control; these may introduce a certain percentage of polarization, for example, ground reflection or reflection from certain parts of the reflector. The determination of the state of polarization of the radiation from radio sources is not yet possible with satisfying precision except in the case of the sun. Demonstration of a polarized component down to 1 percent of the flux of the strongest sources is the limit of present possibilities; any reduction of this threshold will be of great astrophysical importance.

CALIBRATION EQUIPMENT FOR RECEIVERS

We have seen that an arrangement giving a calibrating noise power is always necessary in the long run to calibrate a receiver. One could use sinusoidal waves, but this method is inaccurate and it is always delicate to compare two signals of different nature, a noise signal and a sinusoid.

The most commonly used noise generator is called a saturated diode. It depends on Schottky's law

$$\overline{i^2} = 2eIBM^2$$

which we have quoted earlier. If a diode is saturated—i.e., if all the electrons emitted by its cathode are collected by the plate—the coefficient M^2 is equal to unity. Under these conditions, the fluctuating current $\overline{i^2}$, if passed through a resistance R, will produce across its terminals a fluctuating voltage given by

$$\overline{v^2} = R^2 i^2 = 2eIR^2B$$

and an available power equal to

$$\frac{\overline{v^2}}{4R} = \frac{eIB}{2}$$

It is sufficient to measure I, the mean current of the diode, to know the available noise power. The receiver which is to be calibrated determines B completely.

This method is valid up to frequencies around 250 Mc/s. Beyond that, the corrections to be applied to Schottky's law become too large and uncertain.

For centimeter and decimeter waves, rare-gas discharge tubes are available; these radiate thermal energy just as other gases do on a cosmic scale. The brightness temperature can be measured, but it cannot be calculated with the necessary precision. These are secondary standards, but

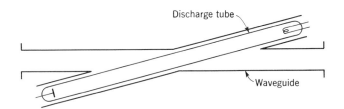

Fig. 3-24   Calibrating noise source for centimeter wavelengths.

their time stability can attain 1/1,000 or even 1/10,000 over a wide range of operating conditions. The brightness temperature of these tubes is always greater than 10,000°K (Fig. 3-24).

But the use of the hot load remains the favorite method, i.e., a known resistance heated or cooled to a known temperature. This gives us a primary standard provided we know how to build a resistance that is constant with temperature and if possible over a rather wide frequency range. Nyquist's formula provides a calibrating procedure of very high precision. Practical methods exist for temperature measurement of a resistance between 4°K and several hundred degrees centigrade. The possibility of having a temperature standard equal to that of the antenna, no matter how low, is also an important advantage over the two other methods.

BIBLIOGRAPHY

Background noise and antenna noise

Burgess, R.: *Proc. Phys. Soc. (London),* **53:** 293 (1941).

Grivet, P., and A. Blaquière: "Le Bruit de Fond," Masson et Cie, Paris, 1958.

Signal measurement

Bracewell, R. N.: Radio Astronomy Techniques, "Handbuch der Physik," vol. 54, Springer-Verlag, Berlin, 1962.

Delannoy, J., J. F. Denisse, E. Le Roux, and B. Morlet: *Ann Astrophys.,* **20:** 222 (1957).

Masers

Wittke, J. P.: *Proc. IRE,* **45:** 291 (1957).

Polarization

Born, M., and E. Wolf: "Principles of Optics," Pergamon Press, New York, 1958.

Brouw, W. N., C. A. Muller, and J. Tinbergen: *Bull. Astron. Inst. Neth.,* **16:** 213 (1962).

Cohen, M.: *Proc. IRE,* **46:** 172 (1958).

Westerhout, G., C. L. Seeger, W. N. Brouw, and J. Tinbergen: *Bull. Astron. Inst. Neth.,* **16:** 187 (1962).

INTERFEROMETERS AND APERTURE SYNTHESIS

4

We have seen that the resolving power of an antenna depends only on its dimensions referred to the wavelength of observation. For meter waves this law leads to considerable dimensions, since 3,000 wavelengths of aperture are required to obtain the resolving power of 1 minute of arc comparable to that of the eye.

To achieve a resolving power of 1 minute, it is not necessary to construct a continuous antenna 3,000 wavelengths long: two antennas, spaced 3,000 wavelengths, give the same result. A continuous antenna can be even more closely approximated by distributing a certain number of antennas (working on a wavelength of 1 meter) over 3 kilometers, provided that the separation of the extreme antennas is 3,000 meters. The principle of such *interferometers* is that of Michelson's stellar interferometer.

One immediately realizes the considerable simplification which this result represents for the construction of antennas of high resolving power: an interferometer with two or more antennas is simpler and cheaper to construct than a continuous antenna of the same resolution.

We have seen above that the gain and the resolving power of an ordinary antenna increase with its dimensions. The greater the physical area of such an antenna, the greater its collecting area and the narrower the main beam of its radiation pattern. This is strictly correct only for an approximately circular antenna; but it is not the same with an interferometer, which is superior to the more usual antenna in *resolving power*. It may be composed of two small antennas connected together and widely spaced one from the other. The resolving power of the combination is increased by an increase of the spacing, but that does not change the total collecting area, which remains equal to the sum of the collecting areas of the two elementary antennas. The interferometer is an arrangement whose resolving power greatly exceeds that of the elementary antennas which comprise it, but its capacity to collect energy, its area, equals only the sum of the separate areas. For the detection of faint sources, where a large area is indispensable for collecting the maximum possible energy, interferometers are not always suitable.

The simplest interferometer, that used since 1946 by Ryle and the Cambridge group in England, is the two-antenna interferometer, a literal translation of Michelson's apparatus into the radio-frequency domain.

THE TWO-ANTENNA INTERFEROMETER

Let two fixed antennas be mounted on an east-west base line, at a distance $D = n\lambda$ apart, λ being the wavelength of observation (Fig. 4-1). We suppose provisionally that the source is a point source and that the two antennas are not directive; i.e., that their gain is the same in all directions. The two antennas are connected by transmission lines of the same length to a single receiver situated in the center of the system. A wave arriving in phase at the two antennas induces voltages which propagate toward the receiver and arrive there in phase. This is the case if one points at a source situated in the meridian plane. But if, at the beginning of the experiment, the source is in this plane, the rotation of the earth will move it gradually away; a wave originating in the source then no longer arrives in phase at the east and west antennas; it is retarded in the east with respect to the west (Fig. 4-1). The two waves which propagate along the lines thus get

Fig. 4-1 Diagram of a two-element interferometer. Above, perspective view; below, view in the plane containing the source and the antennas.

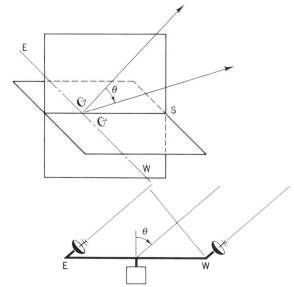

out of phase, and the total power reaching the receiver falls to zero when the two waves are in phase opposition. The path difference d is then equal to ½ wavelength, and one may easily calculate the angle through which the source has moved when the power falls to zero. The path difference d is given by

$$d = D \sin \theta = n\lambda \sin \theta$$

and we have

$$d = \frac{\lambda}{2} = n\lambda \sin \theta$$

More generally, zeros will occur wherever $d = \lambda/2 + p\lambda$ (p integral) or $\lambda/2 + p\lambda = n\lambda \sin \theta$, and successive angles $\theta_1, \theta_2, \ldots, \theta_j, \ldots$ will be found as solutions of this equation.

Similarly there will be maxima of received energy when $q\lambda = n\lambda \sin \theta$ (with q integral).

If we are interested only in angles sufficiently small that $\sin \theta$ is approximately equal to θ, then we have

$$\text{Minima} \quad \theta_m = \frac{(p + \frac{1}{2})}{n} \text{ radians}$$

$$\text{Maxima} \quad \theta_M = \frac{q}{n} \qquad \text{radians}$$

The maxima and minima are equally spaced in the vicinity of the meridian; the reception diagram of the interferometer is then given by Fig. 4-2. It consists of equal lobes, and it is easy to show that the maxima are separated by an angle n^{-1} radian. In the course of its diurnal motion, the source will move with constant velocity through successive lobes, and the record will exhibit interference fringes as in Fig. 4-3.

If there are several point sources in the same region of the sky, an interferometer with a large number of distinct lobes will give records in which it will be difficult to separate the signals coming from different sources. This difficulty may be overcome in different ways by complicating the simple equipment we have just described. In its simple form, the interferometer is used essentially to measure the position of bright sources.

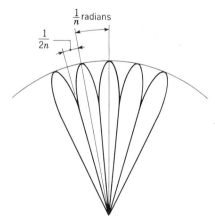

Fig. 4-2 Reception pattern of a two-element interferometer spaced n wavelengths.

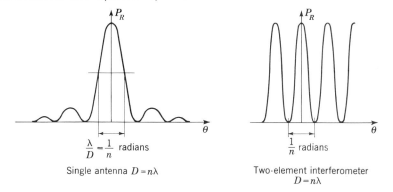

Fig. 4-3 Comparison between reception patterns of a single antenna and an interferometer of the same total width.

MEASUREMENT OF POSITION OF SOURCES

Because of the earth's rotation, sources observed at fixed points on the sky appear to rotate about the earth's axis. Their position on the celestial sphere is given by their hour angle (equivalent to terrestrial longitude) and by their declination (analogous to latitude). As time elapses (Fig. 4-4), only the hour angle varies, and the source moves through the successive lobes of the interferometer. One need know only the precise position of the lobes with respect to the earth to obtain the hour angle of the source.

This requires a knowledge of the exact position of the east-west base line joining the antennas and of whether there are phase changes intro-

Fig. 4-4 Angular coordinates of a source A on the celestial sphere; H = hour angle, δ = declination.

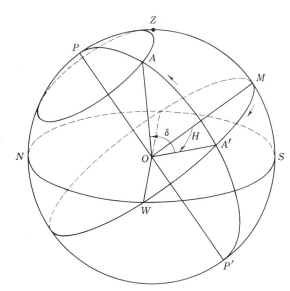

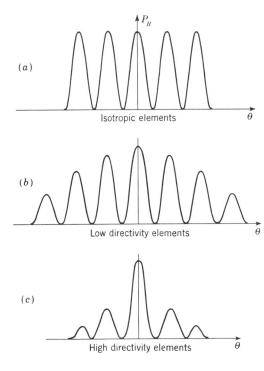

(a)

Isotropic elements θ

(b)

Low directivity elements θ

(c)

High directivity elements θ

Fig. 4-5 Interference fringes obtained with interferometers with the same resolving power but having elements of different widths.

duced by the antenna itself or by the transmission lines. The best method at present available to do this is to observe a source whose position is known absolutely from independent observations. The one most used is the Crab nebula, whose position is precisely known from observations of its occultation by the moon.

The declination of a source is determined by measuring the time which elapses between its passage through the central lobe and one other lobe. It is easily seen that a source near the celestial pole takes a long time to pass from one lobe to the other. In fact, this duration is proportional to sec δ, where δ is the declination. Evidently one must know the angle between neighboring lobes and hence the distance between the two antennas. One may measure this directly over the ground or use an observation of the Crab nebula.

Position measurements in recent years have attained considerable precision, in some cases permitting the identification of the radio source with an optical object. This precision, of the order of some tens of seconds of arc, nevertheless remains far from that of optical measurements (of the order of tenths of a second of arc).

VARIOUS TYPES OF TWO-ANTENNA INTERFEROMETER

In practice, fixed isotropic antennas are never used as we have supposed above, for their gain would be too low; directional antennas are used instead. In this case the interference fringes do not have a constant amplitude as the source crosses the radiation diagram; they vary in amplitude in proportion to the gain of each fixed antenna. The diagram of the interferometer is the product of the diagram of a simple antenna using isotropic antennas with that of one elementary antenna. With fixed elementary antennas of high gain, we see (Fig. 4-5) that the number of observable fringes is low. We may overcome this difficulty by tracking the source with both antennas, which would then have to be suitably mounted. In this case, the source is always on the main axis of each of the elementary antennas, and advantage can thus be taken of the maximum gain of these antennas for as long as is desired.

Of course, the interference fringes are always superimposed on the

Fig. 4-6 Two-element, variable-spacing interferometer of the California Institute of Technology. The 90-foot reflectors are on mounts that can be moved along a special railway. *(Cal Tech photo.)*

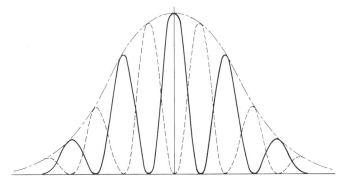

Fig. 4-7 Reception pattern of a phase-switching interferometer. Heavy line, no phase shift; broken line, with a 180-degree phase shift, or ½ wavelength delay, inserted in one transmission line. In the second configuration, the sensitivity maxima are replaced by zeros and vice versa.

receiver noise, on the ground radiation, and on the continuous sky background from which the bright sources stand out. For the detection of faint localized sources, it is worth using a switching method to eliminate the effect of slowly variable noise that may often be much stronger than the fringes themselves.

To obtain this result, Ryle artificially accelerates the interference fringes. For antennas 2,000 wavelengths apart (1.5 minutes resolution), the period of the recorded fringes is about 7 seconds, which is too long to be separated by present techniques from a slowly varying component. One may shorten this period in the following manner. Into one of the transmission lines connecting the antennas to the receiver, introduce a supplementary length of cable ½ wavelength long. It is easily seen (Fig. 4-7) that the interference pattern is modified; the maxima of received energy are replaced by zeros and vice versa. If the length of one of the lines is periodically varied by ½ wavelength at a frequency ν_0, the whole diagram will be displaced on the sky, causing a localized source to give a signal at the frequency ν_0. This frequency can be quite high (some hundreds of cycles per second), and this signal is easily separated from the slowly varying noise which is to be eliminated. The modulation of phase can equally well be done continuously (phase-swept interferometer). In all cases, the signal recorded at the modulation frequency ν_0 is out of phase, with respect to the impressed phase modulation, by an angle which depends on the position of the source with respect to the interference diagram. This relation can be used to measure the position of the source at a given instant.

We have seen that the period of the interference fringes (without phase modulation) depends on the angular velocity of the source. In the case of localized solar sources, this angular velocity is composed of the apparent velocity of the sun and the proper motion of the sources, if they are in movement with respect to the sun. These movements are generally rapid but do not last long enough (some seconds) to be recorded without accelerating the fringes of phase modulation. This latter technique, which is due to Little and Payne-Scott, allows the number of fringes recorded per second to be increased artificially so that a sufficient number of them can be seen to measure the proper motion of solar sources during their short existence (Fig. 4-8).

CONSTRUCTION OF TWO-ANTENNA INTERFEROMETERS

To obtain a high resolving power, we have to increase the distance $D = n\lambda$. In so doing, we run into a difficulty: we have to bring the signal received on each antenna through a long length of transmission line to the receiver with consequent heavy signal loss.

Several methods have been adopted to solve this problem:

1 The signal may be amplified in the vicinity of each antenna before being fed into the line. The amplifiers must have constant gain and stable phase shift. The problem is difficult but can be solved. The solution which has been adopted in the large 32-antenna interferometer at Nançay is good over the range of frequencies which can be amplified directly, i.e., below 300 Mc/s at the present time.

2 The signal frequency can also be changed in a mixer before amplification at the intermediate frequency. This frequency, which is much

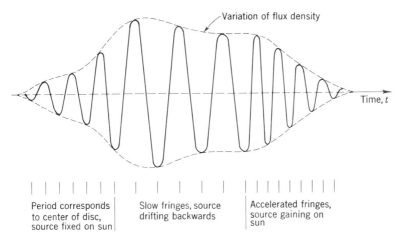

Fig. 4-8 Interferogram made with a phase-swept interferometer showing the motion of a source over the solar disk.

Fig. 4-9 Two-element interferometer working on 3 cm at Nançay, France.

lower than that of the signal, is the one that is transmitted over the line. Since line losses in general decrease with frequency, less total amplification is needed to compensate the losses, and cheaper lines may also be used. To drive the mixers, a local oscillator which is common to the two antennas is needed. The local-oscillator signal must be transmitted by another line; but the losses in this case are unimportant, for it is easy to construct a sufficiently powerful local oscillator. In certain cases such an arrangement can be economical. Since mixers preserve the phase of the signal, as we have seen above, using them in interferometers involves no difficulty.

When the cost of cables becomes too high, or if for some reason or other they cannot be laid, a radio link is used between the receiver and the antennas. This solution has been adopted in Great Britain, in Australia, and at the Saint-Michel Observatory in France. The local-oscillator signal is radiated from the center of the arrangement, and the intermediate frequency is radiated back from each antenna. In most cases, the radiating link introduces losses as large as those of cables. Phase instability of propagation can also be expected. Nevertheless, over base lines of several kilometers (now up to 50 kilometers), radio links remain the only possibility, especially if the base line of the instrument is to be easily varied.

Finally, one last method is available, viz., the use of mirrors to reflect the received signal from an antenna to the receiver. This technique was demonstrated at the very beginning of radio astronomy by McCready, Payne-Scott, and Pawsey in Australia, the mirror being constituted by the surface of the sea. In this case, if H is the height of the antenna above sea level, it is as if an image antenna existed. The base line of the instrument

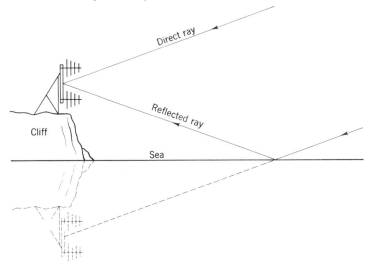

Fig. 4-10   Sea interferometer (Lloyd's mirror).

is given by $D = 2H$. The interference fringes are perpendicular to the line joining the two antennas and so are horizontal (Fig. 4-10).[1]

Another technique, suggested by the Soviet group in Leningrad, but not yet put into practice, consists in reflecting the signal toward the receiver by two steerable mirrors (or radio coelostats) (Fig. 4-11).

[1] This is the radio equivalent of Lloyd's mirror in optics.

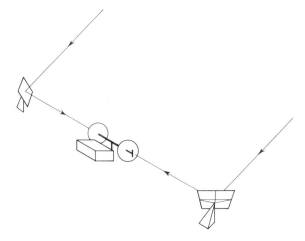

Fig. 4-11   Interferometer involving two radio coelostats proposed by the Pulkovo group in the U.S.S.R.

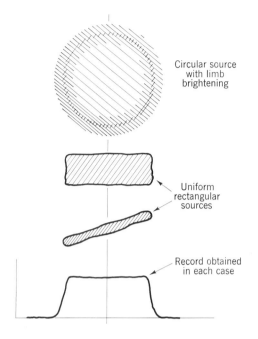

Circular source
with limb
brightening

Uniform
rectangular
sources

Record obtained
in each case

Fig. 4-12 Scanning the three
source distributions with a fan
beam would give the same record (shown below) in each case.

EXTENDED SOURCES,
APERTURE SYNTHESIS

The case of extended sources is more complex, but interferometry permits
numerous observations of their structure. Let us note to begin with that an
east-west interferometer allows details to be distinguished only in the plane
containing the source and the east-west line. The east-west resolving power
is that of the interferometer, but the north-south resolution is that of a
single antenna alone. Furthermore, this is true for all antennas or interferometers having large east-west dimensions but small vertical dimensions;
as Fig. 4-12 shows, the antenna delivers, at each instant, a power proportional to the total power received in the receiving beam and makes no distinction between what it receives from different points in the vertical plane.
The brightness of the source is thus integrated along a north-south line.
From the recording obtained, one cannot reconstruct the original two-
dimensional distribution without making risky assumptions about the symmetry of the source.

An interferometer integrates also along the north-south line, just like
a rectangular antenna with a single beam, as shown in Fig. 4-13. It is as
though it saw a linear source whose longitudinal brightness distribution was
given by Fig. 4-13c.

In such a case, what will be the response of the interferometer? As its
radiation pattern consists of equidistant lobes, there will be a periodic re-

sponse as the rotation of the earth carries the lobes across the source. The period T of the record depends on the angle between successive lobes (and thus on the base line) and on the angular velocity of the source. The sky appears to rotate once in 24 hours, or 1 degree in 4 minutes of time. But a source near the pole rotates only slowly. The angular velocity of a source depends on its declination; it is 15 minutes of arc per minute of time, multiplied by cos δ, where δ is the declination of the source.

As the gain of the interferometer varies sinusoidally with hour angle, the power received varies sinusoidally with time. It can be shown that the amplitude of the fringes is equal to the amplitude of the component of period T obtained by analyzing the record into elementary sinusoids as in Fourier analysis. Thus the interferometer with base line $D = n\lambda$ allows measurement of the sinusoidal component of the source distribution whose spatial period is n^{-1} radian.

When one tries to analyze a brightness distribution into elementary sinusoids (Fig. 4-14), it is generally found that an infinite number of sinusoids would be required to reproduce it perfectly. The curve which represents the amplitude of these elementary sinusoids as a function of their period is the spatial spectrum of the distribution under study.[1] From this spectrum, the interferometer selects the harmonic whose spatial, or angular, period is n^{-1} radian. A spatial frequency, which is the reciprocal of the

[1] This is the Fourier transform of the brightness distribution of the source.

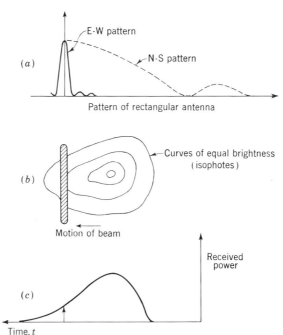

Fig. 4-13 Scanning an extended source with a fan beam. (a) Antenna patterns in the east-west and north-south planes; (b) the antenna beam and the source seen on the celestial sphere; (c) record obtained as the antenna sweeps over the source as a result of the earth's rotation.

(a)

E-W pattern

N-S pattern

Pattern of rectangular antenna

(b)

Curves of equal brightness (isophotes)

Motion of beam

(c)

Received power

Time, t

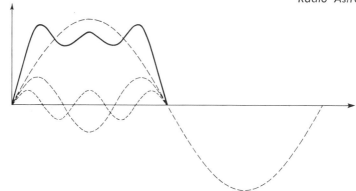

Fig. 4-14 Resolution of a brightness distribution (heavy line) into elementary sinusoids (broken lines).

spatial period, may also be defined. An interferometer of spacing $D = n\lambda$ is thus sensitive only to the spatial frequency n. It is apparent that if we change n or the length of the base line, we change the spatial frequency to which the instrument responds; we measure a different spatial harmonic of the brightness distribution under study. Hence it is easy to see that by making several observations with different base lines, we may measure the intensity of these different harmonics and synthesize the brightness distribution over the source by summation.

The concepts of angular, or spatial, spectrum and spatial frequency were first introduced into optics by the work of Duffieux and of the Institut d'Optique in Paris under the leadership of A. Maréchal. They have permitted quantitative study of the quality of an optical instrument. The resolving power of such an instrument may be characterized by the maximum spatial frequency that it can transmit, i.e., by the angular diameter of the finest detail that it can distinguish. Bracewell and Roberts, and Arsac, are responsible for the application of this theory to radio telescopes. We shall see later how useful this approach is for the study of aperture synthesis.

Suppose that the brightness distribution over the sun is to be measured at 3 cm. For simplicity we suppose that we are working at noon in the vicinity of the equinox. The sun's declination is close to zero and its angular velocity is 360 degrees per 24 hours, or 1 degree in 4 minutes. We shall use an east-west base line and two antennas that can be moved along it. We begin by placing them close enough together so that the sun appears to them as a point source. The angular diameter of the sun is about 0.5 degree, and so it is necessary for the angle between two successive lobes of the interferometer, n^{-1} radian, to be large compared with 0.5 degree. The number of wavelengths n_0, such that $D_0 = n_0\lambda$, will be taken equal to 10 or 20 at the most. The situation is represented in Fig. 4-16a. It is seen that in the neighborhood of the zeros of the interference pattern, a very weak signal will be obtained. It will be close to zero because each point of the sun will be close to the zero of the pattern. If each antenna receives a power P_0, the two antennas taken together receive $2P_0$. But near the maxima, the received power reaches $4P_0$ because of the phase relations existing between the two waves reaching the receiver from the two antennas.

If now we wish to measure the brightness distribution, we must separate the antennas and place them at a distance $D_1 = n_1\lambda$ that is greater than D_0; for example, let n_1 equal 50. The angle between two successive maxima is then $1/50$ of a radian, or 1.1 degrees. The width of a fringe to half power is 0.55 degree, and the angular diameter of the sun is 0.5 degree. When the center of the sun falls on a null of the interferometer pattern, it is evident that not all points of the solar disk can do so, and so the signal received from the whole sun is not zero. The mean power received is still $2P_0$. The power received at the maxima is less than $4P_0$ because not all the points of the sun are seen with the maximum gain of the interferometer. We then measure the amplitude of the fringes (Fig. 4-16b).

Fig. 4-15 The 21-cm interferometer with two moving reflectors at Nançay, France. The mounts are carried on trucks moving on a railway with east-west and north-south branches.

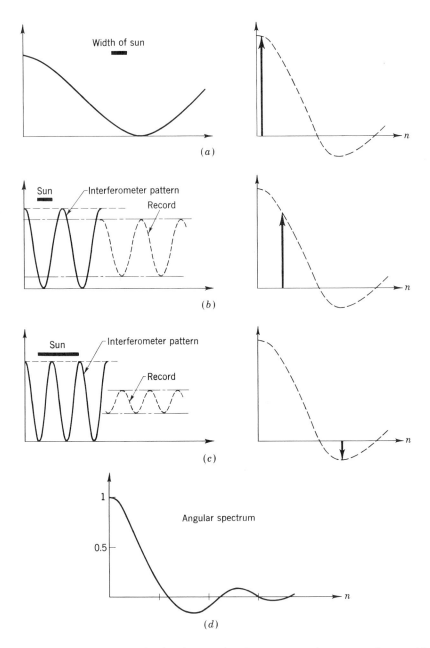

Fig. 4-16 Investigating the brightness distribution over the sun at 3 cm with a variable-spacing interferometer. Parts *a, b,* and *c* correspond to different distances between the antennas. On the left are shown the interference pattern and the recording obtained. At *c* the scale has been extended for convenience. On the right is shown the spatial frequency *n* of the Fourier component observed. At *d* is shown the spectrum (curve of fringe visibility) resulting from a large number of observations such as *a, b,* and *c.*

When further measurements are obtained at increasing spacings, it will be noticed that the amplitude of the fringes diminishes. In the case of the sun observed at 3 cm the amplitude goes through zero for $D = 125\lambda$ approximately. If the distance is increased beyond this value, the fringes again increase in amplitude, but their phase changes (Fig. 4-16c). The sun is then seen in more than one lobe of the interferometer at a time.

The brightness distribution over the equivalent linear source (at 3 cm wavelength) may be obtained from several records of this kind. The results are usually plotted on curves such as that of Fig. 4-16d. This curve represents, as a function of n, the amplitude of the harmonic component of order n in the brightness distribution over the sun. Hence the distribution may be calculated.[1] This done, the brightness distribution over the sun in two dimensions must be found. This is not fully possible from observations made only with an east-west interferometer. A further assumption is necessary. It is usually supposed that the sun has rotational symmetry. In this case, the distribution along a solar diameter, as in Fig. 4-17b, can be deduced by numerical calculation from the distribution of Fig. 4-17a.

The foregoing description shows that this result is not obtained very directly. Measurements made with different base lines at very different

[1] The brightness distribution over the source is the Fourier transform of the curve showing the amplitude of the fringes as a function of spacing between the antennas.

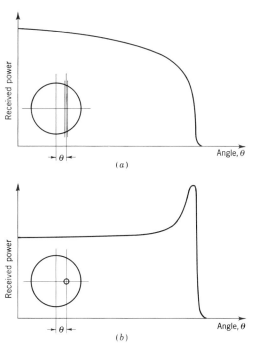

Fig. 4-17 (a) Brightness distribution over the sun as given by a fan beam; this curve comes from transforming the spectrum of Fig. 4-16d by the Fourier transformation. (b) Curve deduced on the assumption that the sun's brightness distribution possesses circular symmetry, a curve that would be directly observable with a narrow pencil beam.

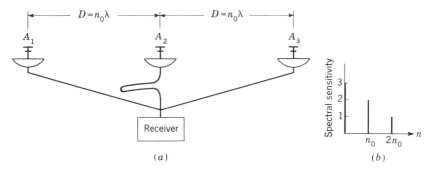

Fig. 4-18 *(a)* Three-element array; the lengths of cable connecting each antenna to the receiver must be equal. *(b)* The spectral-sensitivity function of the arrangement.

dates, and combined by the methods described, furnish a result which would be obtained in one scan with a continuous antenna having a length equal to the maximum interferometer base line.

When the maximum length of the base line is limited to 400 wavelengths, there is an error because the curve of Fig. 4-16d certainly continues beyond that value of n. The high-frequency sinusoidal components which would allow a better description of fine details of the curve in Fig. 4-17b are thus neglected. We shall see below that it would be exactly the same for a continuous antenna with the same total length $L = 400\lambda$.

It is thus seen that the response of an interferometer of length $D = n\lambda$ is a sinusoid whose amplitude is that of the component of angular frequency n in the brightness distribution under study. On the other hand, a continuous antenna responds to a greater number of these spatial frequencies. Between the two-antenna interferometer and the continuous antenna, there exists an intermediate type of antenna, the grating antenna, or multi-element interferometer.

MULTIELEMENT INTERFEROMETERS, GRATINGS

Consider, instead of two identical antennas, three which are mounted at equal distances on an east-west base line. Let us call them A_1, A_2, and A_3, and suppose them connected to the same receiver by equal lengths of transmission line. A_1 and A_2 (Fig. 4-18a) constitute an interferometer of base line $n_0\lambda$. It is sensitive to the spatial frequency n_0. The combination formed by A_2 and A_3 has the same spectral sensitivity. The responses of A_1A_2 and A_2A_3 to the same brightness distribution add. In addition, A_1 and A_3 form an interferometer of base line $2n_0\lambda$ which responds to the spatial frequency $2n_0$. The total spectral sensitivity of the instrument is given in Fig. 4-18b. It

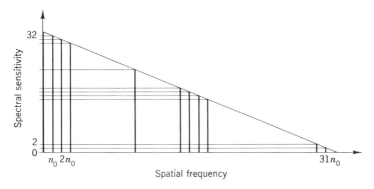

Fig. 4-19   Spectral-sensitivity function of a 32-element array.

is seen that it contains more information than a two-antenna interferometer alone. This arrangement with three antennas has not been used, but instruments based on this principle and using 8, 16, or 32 equidistant elements have been constructed. If $n_0\lambda$ is the distance between two neighboring antennas, it is easy to see that an instrument comprising 32 antennas gives 31 times the response of an elementary pair at spatial frequency n_0, 30 times at spatial frequency $2n_0$, 29 times at frequency $3n_0$, and so on. The total spectral-sensitivity function of such an instrument is given in Fig. 4-19. It contains lines whose amplitudes decrease from 31 at spatial frequency n_0 to unity for frequency 31 n_0. Note that $31n_0$ is the total length of the instrument expressed in wavelengths; it is also the highest spatial frequency to which the antenna is sensitive.

RECEPTION PATTERN OF GRATINGS

To calculate the reception pattern, it suffices to sum the responses given by the different pairs of antennas when a point source is scanned by the antenna. The response of A_1A_2 is given by Fig. 4-20a, and that of A_2A_3 is the same. The response of these two pairs taken

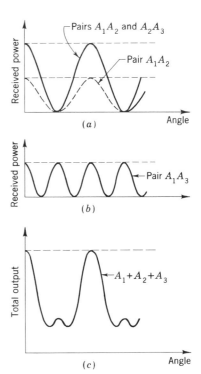

Fig. 4-20   Radiation pattern of a three-element array.

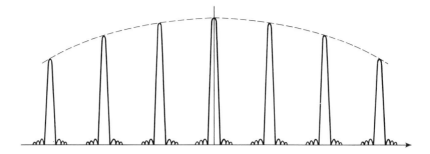

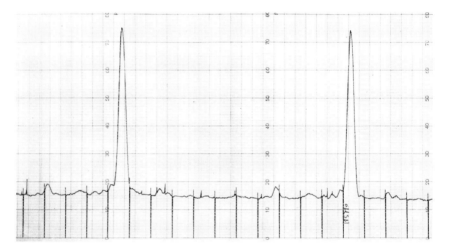

Fig. 4-21 *(a)* Calculated reception pattern of a 32-element array; *(b)* recording of Cygnus A made at 169 Mc/s with the Nançay interferometer showing side-lobes that differ slightly from the theoretical, owing to phasing errors of the elements.

together is simply twice that of one of the pairs considered alone. The response A_1A_3 is that of an interferometer of base line $2n_0\lambda$ and is thus a sinusoid of angular period $1/2n_0$ (Fig. 4-20b). The total response is the sum of the responses, twice A_1A_2 plus once A_1A_3, and is thus a succession of lobes narrower than in Fig. 4-20a. The region of low gain between maxima has widened (Fig. 4-20c).

The case of 16 or 32 antennas can be treated in the same way, but the calculations are longer. The radiation pattern for 32 antennas is given in Fig. 4-21.

If, keeping the total length of the instrument the same, we double the total number of elements, the number of lobes is halved. The width of each lobe, which depends only on the total length of the antenna, does not

Fig. 4-22 General view of the 32-element array at Nançay, France. This instrument, commissioned in 1956, is the largest in the world. It comprises 32 five-meter reflectors working on 169 Mc/s (1.77 m) and provides a resolution of 4 minutes of arc. The signal received on each pair of antennas is amplified before entering underground cables. There are 16 preamplifiers in all, an important original feature of this instrument. Total length 1.55 kilometers.

Fig. 4-23 A 16-element array at Nançay working on 3 cm. This instrument has a resolution similar to that of Fig. 4-22. Total length 23 meters.

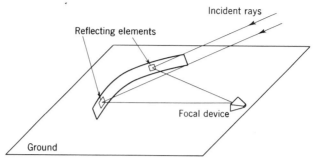

Fig. 4-24 The properties of reflecting antennas are calculated by combining rays reflected by the different elements composing the collecting area. The calculation is like that for an array composed of a very large number of elements.

change. The lines of the angular spectrum of the instrument crowd together and are doubled in number.

In the limit, a continuous antenna of the same total length is sensitive not to a finite number of discrete spatial frequencies alone, but to a continuous spectrum of spatial frequencies whose upper limit is set by the frequency N, corresponding to the total length of the instrument ($L = N\lambda$). A very long parabolic mirror such as that of Fig. 4-24 can indeed be considered as a grating composed of an infinite number of elements. These are just the elements of the reflecting surface, each of which reflects toward the focus the rays which reach it from the source. At the focus all these rays reinforce as they interfere constructively with each other. Of course, this is how the radiation pattern of any antenna is calculated; in this sense any antenna can be considered an interferometer.

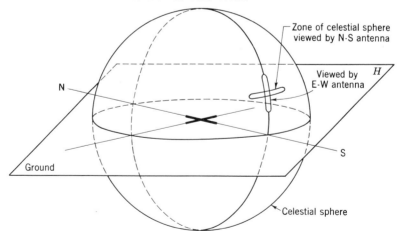

Fig. 4-25 Zones of the celestial sphere from which radiation is received by the arms of a Mills cross.

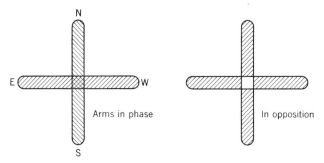

N

E)W

Arms in phase   In opposition

S

Fig. 4-26   Illustrating the geometry of the Mills cross.

SYNTHESIS OF ARBITRARY ANTENNAS

By distributing elementary antennas of various gains in well-chosen positions along an east-west base line, we can achieve any arbitrary radiation pattern determined in advance. However, its resolving power cannot be greater than L/λ, where L is the total length of the instrument. This possibility has been widely used. In particular, composite antennas have been built, formed of

Fig. 4-27   Aerial view of the Mills cross at Fleurs, Australia. *(CSIRO Radio-physics Division photo.)*

Fig. 4-28 Partial view of a cross antenna working at 21 cm at Fleurs, Australia. Each arm is composed of an array of 32 reflectors each 19 feet in diameter. Below the mounts can be seen the five sets of lines interconnecting the antennas. The antennas of the east-west arm are in the background. *(CSIRO Radiophysics Division photo.)*

one large continuous antenna in association with one or several other smaller antennas. The resolving power of the large antenna can thus be increased without prohibitive expense.

The synthesis of an antenna possessing high resolving power in all directions is also possible. An antenna that is greatly extended in the east-west direction does not have a high resolving power in the plane containing the source and the north-south direction. This is often unsatisfactory, for two sources of different declinations, but which transmit at the same time, can be confused. It occurred to the Australian radio astronomer Mills to use two very extended antennas, one in the east-west line, the other in the north-south line, forming a cross on the ground. Several Mills crosses exist in Australia, one is at Stanford, Calif. (Fig. 7-9), and one is in the U.S.S.R. (Fig. 4-29). The radiation pattern of a combination of the two lines would have a cross-shaped outline on the celestial sphere (Fig. 4-25), and the sources situated in this region would all be received by the antenna.

The ideal would be to receive only those which are in the part common to the two patterns. This is achieved by the following procedure (Fig. 4-26). Each of the two antennas is connected to a different cable. If these two cables are connected in phase, the radiation coming from the cross-shaped region will be received, and thus what comes from the central intersection is received twice. Now connect the two antennas in phase opposition; again

Fig. 4-29 An arm of the giant kilometer-long Mills cross at Serpukhov, U.S.S.R., to be used at meter wavelengths. The ribs carrying the reflecting screen are 40 meters across and are tilted by motors. *(Photo G. W. Swenson, Jr.)*

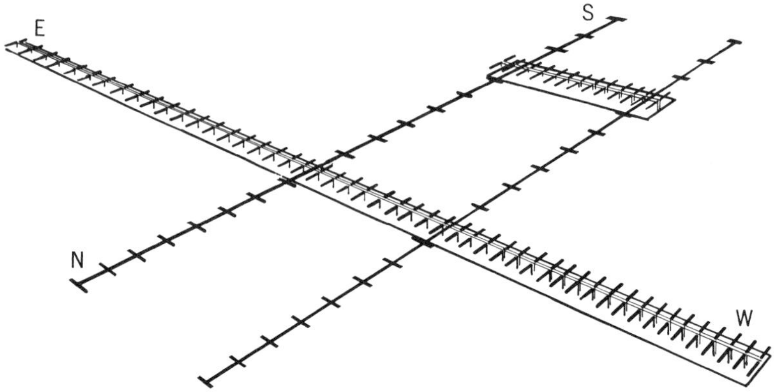

Fig. 4-30   Principle of Ryle's antenna for aperture synthesis.

everything contained within the two patterns will be received, but what comes from the intersection is not received at all. To sum up, (1) with antennas connected in phase, energy comes from the four arms and in double strength from the intersection; (2) with antennas connected in opposition, energy comes from the four arms but nothing comes from the intersection. By a simple electrical procedure, which amounts to subtraction, we can record only that part of the energy coming from the central intersection of the cross-shaped region. The radiation pattern of the Mills cross is the same as that of a square antenna on the ground, of side L, where L is the length of each branch. The interest of this arrangement is now clear. The two antennas are generally formed by dipoles suitably connected together (Fig. 4-27), and by modifying the relative phases of the signals from these different elements, it is possible to point the beam of the Mills cross where desired.

One further step in this promising direction has recently been made by the group in Cambridge. The east-west line of the Mills cross is retained. The north-south section is replaced by a movable antenna on a north-south railway. By observing the same source with several positions of the movable antenna, the equivalent of a Mills cross is achieved, but at less expense. This arrangement is even simpler than the former and theoretically gives the same results. But observations require many records, and the long and tedious calculations necessary to plot a map of the sky with this instrument can be carried out only by an electronic computer (Figs. 4-30 and 4-31).

CORRELATION SYSTEMS

In all the interferometric systems that we have seen, the signals received from the different antennas are always added or subtracted after being transmitted to the receiver by cables. Another class of antennas makes use of the product of the signals received from the antennas. These recently introduced instruments have considerable advantages over those just described.

Consider a randomly fluctuating noise current $i(t)$, whose mean square value will be written $\overline{i^2}$. Let the current pass through a resistance R. According to Joule's law, an instantaneous power $R[i(t)]^2$ will be dissipated, whose mean value with respect to time will be $R\overline{i^2}$.

Now suppose that we have two noise currents $i_1(t)$ and $i_2(t)$ of the same mean square value, coming from two independent sources. Let us pass them together through the same resistance R. The instantaneous power dissipated will be

$$R[i_1(t) + i_2(t)]^2$$

and the mean power which appears in the form of heat will be the mean of this expression, i.e., the mean of $R[i_1(t)]^2 + R[i_2(t)]^2 + 2Ri_1(t)i_2(t)$. The mean of $[i_1(t)]^2$ is $\overline{i^2}$, as is that of $[i_2(t)]^2$. What happens to the term representing the mean of $i_1(t)i_2(t)$? Experience shows this term is zero if the two currents i_2 and i_1 are statistically independent, that is, in practice, if they come from different sources. The mean noise power dissipated in R is exactly doubled.

Fig. 4-31 The movable element of the aperture-synthesis system constructed in Cambridge, England. (*Mullard Observatory photo.*)

The result is different for two currents i_1 and i_2 which are equal to each other at each moment; i_1 and i_2 are then not independent. The mean power dissipated in the resistance is given by

$$R[i_1(t)^2 + i_2(t)^2 + 2i_1(t)i_2(t)] = 4R\overline{i^2}$$

by virtue of Joule's law, since in the end the current in the resistance R is $2i(t)$. It follows that in this case the mean value of $i_1(t)i_2(t)$, or $\overline{i_1(t)i_2(t)}$, is equal to $\overline{i^2}$

Thus we see from this simple calculation that $\overline{i_1(t)i_2(t)}$ is equal to i^2 since i_1 and i_2 are equal at each moment, but it is zero if i_1 and i_2 are independent. We now introduce the quantity

$$\frac{\overline{i_1(t)i_2(t)}}{\overline{i^2}} = \rho$$

which can assume all values between -1 and $+1$ and which we shall call the correlation coefficient between i_1 and i_2. This coefficient characterizes the degree of dependence between i_1 and i_2. If it is zero, i_1 and i_2 are independent; i.e., the probability of having i_1 equal to i_2 at a given instant is zero. On the other hand, if $\rho = 1$, the probability, given i_1, of having $i_2 = i_1$ at some moment t is unity; it is virtually certain that i_1 will be equal to i_2. If $\rho = -1$, we shall have $i_1 = -i_2$ practically everywhere.

If we return to the microscopic description of noise currents as a succession of infinitely short pulses, the coefficient represents the probability of observing an elementary impulse i_1 at the same instant as another i_2. It is clear that if i_1 and i_2 are equal at each instant, all the elementary pulses will coincide in time and the probability of having $i_1(t)$ and $i_2(t)$ equal is always unity, i.e., a virtual certainty.

These concepts may be directly applied to an interferometer consisting of two antennas followed by two amplifiers (Fig. 4-32). The source under observation induces in each antenna noise currents which are fully correlated because they come from the one source. On the other hand, the noise

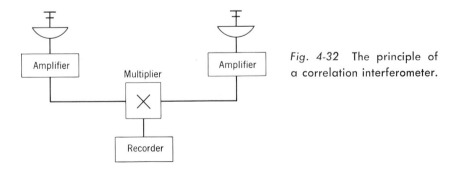

Fig. 4-32 The principle of a correlation interferometer.

introduced by the two amplifiers can be represented by totally independent currents, whose product, formed by a multiplying circuit, has zero mean value. The measuring equipment thus does not receive from the amplifiers any continuous noise power which would have to be eliminated from the measurements. The system is equivalent to a switching radiometer, because its response to zero external signal is always zero in the mean, whatever the gains of the two amplifiers. This new arrangement does not involve any switching, however, and there is thus no loss of useful signal.

It may be shown that the waves received from a single source give rise to interference fringes at the output of the multiplying circuit just as with an ordinary interferometer.

These remarkable properties of correlation receivers were demonstrated in France by E. J. Blum.

INTERFEROMETRY AND INTEGRATORS

Interferometry is a particularly convenient arrangement because it always provides sinusoidal records, whatever source is observed. The period depends only on the position of the source and the spacing of the interferometer; it does not depend on the gain of the receivers or the radiation pattern of the antennas.

The full value of this property appears in observations of a very faint source whose fringes are practically lost in the statistical fluctuations of the record. If this source is being looked for in a particular part of the sky, it is known in advance that if the source exists, it will show up as a sinusoid whose period is known in advance. The source response may be distinguished, no matter how faint, from the statistical fluctuations; being sinusoidal with a known period, it is foreseeable, while the details of the statistical fluctuations are not.

The fact that one cannot predict the statistical fluctuations in detail means in practice that the erratic movements they cause in the recorder are independent from one fringe period to the next. On the other hand, the sinusoid which represents the fringes is exactly the same in one period as in any other.

Special integrators enable us to take advantage of these remarks. As we have seen above, the sensitivity of a given radio telescope can be increased only by extending the time of observation and diminishing the relative strength of statistical fluctuations by signal integration. In the case of an interferometer, we are searching the noise for a signal of known period. By means of suitable electronic circuits we record several instantaneous values of signal plus noise, say 10. The samples are spaced at equal intervals over one period. The 10 values n_1, n_2, n_3, . . . , n_{10} are stored in 10 memory circuits. In the next period, 10 new readings are made and added to the corresponding readings obtained during the first period, and so on. All these operations are carried out automatically, and the cycle is determined by the fringe period, which is known in advance. At the end of, say, 100 periods, we are left with the quantities n'_1, n'_2, . . . , n'_{10}. From what we have said above, the sinusoidal segments add up in phase, so that that part of the content of a particular channel which is due to the sinusoids will be 100 times greater at the end of 100 periods. On the other hand, the fluctuating parts of the readings, being independent from one period to the next, are multiplied only by $\sqrt{100}$, i.e., by 10. The signal/noise ratio, which in the present case means the ratio of the fringe amplitude to the statistical fluctuations, is improved 10 times, the price paid being a large number of readings. Such an instrument has been built in France by M. Vinokur, and it bears out the expectations raised by the foregoing reasoning. This type of *data processing* can be used with any type of radio telescope. When a source drifts across the beam of a fixed antenna, the observer knows beforehand the shape of the response to be expected; it depends on the reception pattern of the antenna he is using. The radio astronomer wants to know the peak deviation obtained from the source and also the time of transit. This time is the same from day to day for a given source if the antenna is fixed and if sidereal time used. It is therefore possible to add up daily records, adjusted to the same time, to increase the signal with respect to noise fluctuations. Most recent radio telescopes are fitted with data-processing equipment which store the observations on tape or cards in digital form to speed up this integrating process.

NUMBER OF SOURCES OBSERVABLE
BY A GIVEN RADIO TELESCOPE

Suppose that we are using a reflecting radio telescope which can work over a wide range of frequencies. Let it also be equipped to receive low frequencies, for which, as we have seen, excellent receivers can be built. But the resolving power of the instrument at low frequencies will be poor because D/λ will be small. The radiation pattern will cover a large area of the celestial sphere within which the different sources that are present will not be distinguishable. The radio telescope will be very sensitive, but the number of distinct sources that it can resolve is limited by its resolving power, or what is called "confusion" between neighboring sources.

Let the operating frequency of our instrument now be increased. The receiver noise (expressed by its noise temperature T_R) increases, but only slowly. The area of the celestial sphere observed in a given position of the antenna diminishes as $(\lambda/D)^2$. In each of these positions only one source can be observed for certain.[1] The number of observable sources therefore increases as the frequency increases.

As the frequency is increased still further, the number of observable sources continues to increase because the resolving power of the instrument gets better and better. On the other hand, as a result of the mean spectrum of the sources, the flux density received goes down, and at the same time receivers become worse. In the end, the radio telescope is limited by its ability to detect sources against the background noise of the receiver. This situation gets worse and worse as shorter and shorter wavelengths are used.

The number of sources that can be studied with a given instrument depends on the frequency of observation (Fig. 4-33). There is an optimum

[1] It is now admitted that it is impossible to detect even one source for certain under these conditions, as confusion between two neighboring sources is too likely. It seems that one cannot count on reliable detection of more than one source in a region of the celestial sphere whose area is less than 20 to 80 times the solid angle of the radiation pattern.

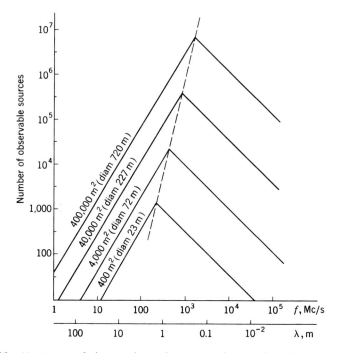

Fig. 4-33 Variation of the number of sources observable with a given radio telescope as a function of wavelength of observation for different collecting areas. This graph, which depends on a number of plausible hypotheses, brings out clearly the existence of an optimum wavelength. *(Kraus.)*

frequency which depends on several hypotheses about the mean spectrum of sources and their distribution in space and also on the characteristics of available receivers. The optimum wavelength will get shorter and shorter in years to come, as great improvements are in sight in receiver technique for very high frequencies. It will be possible to detect and localize an increasing number of sources.

BIBLIOGRAPHY

Interferometers with two antennas

Bracewell, R. N.: *Proc. IRE,* **46:** 97 (1958).
Bracewell, R. N.: *IRE, Trans. Antennas Propagation,* **9:** 59 (1961).
Pawsey, J. L., and R. N. Bracewell: "Radio Astronomy," Clarendon Press, Oxford, 1955. A new edition is in preparation.
Ryle, M.: *Proc. Roy. Soc. (London), Ser. A,* **211:** 351 (1952).

Aperture synthesis

Arsac, J.: *Rev. d'Optique,* **34:** 65 (1955) and **35:** 396 (1956).
Ryle, M.: *Nature,* **180:** 110 (1957).

The Nançay 32-element array

Blum, E. J., A. Boischot, and M. Ginat: *Ann. Astrophys.,* **20:** 155 (1957).

Correlation receivers

Blum, E. J.: *Ann Astrophys.,* **22:** 140 (1959).

Number of detectable sources

Kraus, J. D.: *Proc. IRE,* **46:** 92 (1958).
von Hoerner, S.: *Pubs. Natl. Radio Astron. Obs.,* **2:** 19 (1961).

SPECTRAL
OBSERVATIONS

5

THE 21-CM LINE

The radiations studied by radio astronomy at present contain only one singular wavelength, the 21-cm line (1,420 Mc/s) emitted by hydrogen in the neutral state. We have seen that interstellar neutral hydrogen has become an object of study only since the discovery of the 21-cm line.

Position and intensity measurements in this line are of fundamental importance for astrophysics. They alone can tell us about the speed and density of the masses of hydrogen which emit it. It has been possible in the laboratory to measure the exact frequency of the 21-cm absorption line of the hydrogen atom with a precision of a few hundredths of a cycle per second. If the interstellar hydrogen under observation is moving away from the earth, the position of the emitted or absorbed line is shifted toward long wavelengths, according to the well-known Doppler effect for spectral lines. If the hydrogen is coming toward us, the frequency of the line exceeds its value for gas at rest.

The experimental problem is thus to trace the profile of the line, that is, the intensity of the radiation as a function of frequency. We have seen before that the spectrum of a radio source could be measured by accumulating numerous independent absolute measurements of the flux received on different frequencies. Since absolute measurements are very difficult and a large number of line profiles are needed to work out, for example, the distribution of neutral hydrogen in a galaxy, other techniques have been developed. These techniques, which are peculiar to 21-cm observations, are adapted to the exploration of narrow frequency bands, as the line profile barely covers a few megacycles around 1,420 Mc/s. The passband of

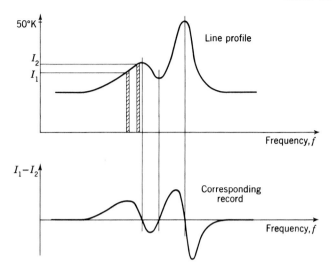

Fig. 5-1 Principle of operation of a swept-frequency radiospectrograph for observation of the 21-cm line.

the antenna itself does not enter into these measurements. The problem is all the more difficult because the apparent brightness temperature of the masses of neutral hydrogen only rarely exceeds $100°K$. Thus, improvements in the antenna cannot lead to antenna temperatures greater than $100°K$; in fact, antenna temperatures of $0.5°K$ are becoming common.

There are two principal methods of observing the 21-cm line. In one, the profile is explored by varying the frequency to which the receiver is tuned. In the other, a large number of amplifiers whose frequencies are suitably distributed over the spectrum are simultaneously brought to bear.

SWEPT-FREQUENCY RECEIVERS
FOR 21 CM

To trace out the profile of the line, it is sufficient to tune a good receiver through it. A slice of the spectrum equal in width to the bandwidth of the intermediate frequency amplifier could be shifted as required by changing the frequency of the local oscillator. Unfortunately this method is not directly applicable to the hydrogen line. When the local-oscillator frequency changes, its power output changes and so do the characteristics of the mixer, with the overall result that the receiver gain changes, and it would be necessary to calibrate for each frequency. In other words, the difficult problem of absolute measurement would have to be faced all the time.

As the line profile and its position in the frequency spectrum are of more interest than its absolute intensity, a differential method is used (Fig.

5-1). The energies received in two frequency bands of the same width centered on two frequencies whose spacing is constant are compared. Let ν_1 and ν_2 be two frequencies such that $\nu_1 - \nu_2$ is constant and very small compared with ν_1 and ν_2. Let I_1 be the energy received in the band centered on ν_1 and let I_2 be that received in the band ν_2. First I_1 is received and then I_2, and simple electronic circuits are used to switch periodically n times per second so that $I_1 - I_2$ can be recorded. Since $\nu_1 - \nu_2$ is constant, the quantity $I_1 - I_2$ is proportional to the slope of the line profile, $(I_1 - I_2)/(\nu_1 - \nu_2)$. The frequency ν_1 is varied while keeping $\nu_1 - \nu_2$ constant and the variation of the slope of the profile is traced out as a function of frequency. The curve obtained is then integrated to get the real spectrum.[1] It is easy to see that this method has all the advantages of switching, in particular, virtual independence of gain changes.

[1] The two reception channels are more commonly widely separated, one being on the line profile and the other well outside. In this case, $I_1 - I_2$ varies with frequency in accordance with the line profile and not the derivative.

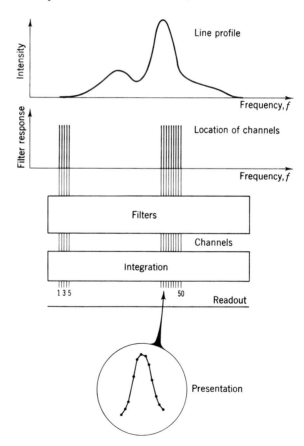

Fig. 5-2 Principle of a multichannel spectrograph for observation of the 21-cm line. The instruments of this type in use at present involve as many as 50 channels and thus furnish intensities at 50 points on the line profile.

Fig. 5-3 The 25-meter reflector of Leiden Observatory at Dwingeloo, Netherlands. This instrument was the first of its size to be put into use for investigations
of the 21-cm line (1955). It has been used for many important observations.

To reproduce the profile correctly, the passband must be much narrower than the width of the line. Instruments in use have passbands of 20,
10, and even 5 kc/s. The fluctuations in the record are given by
$\Delta T/T = 1/(B\tau)^{1/2}$. Since the bandwidth B of the instrument is very small,
the time constant τ must be increased in order to reduce the relative strength
of random fluctuations. The Dutch instrument at Dwingeloo uses an integrating time of 15 minutes. It takes more than 2 hours to trace out the line
profile in a given part of the sky. During this time it is obvious that the
antenna must remain constantly pointed toward the region under study.

There is no other way of improving the sensitivity than by perfecting the receiver and increasing the integration time, which extends the duration of the measurements still further. This difficulty can be avoided by using several identical channels simultaneously. The new Dwingeloo receiver contains eight pairs of channels.

MULTICHANNEL RECEIVERS FOR 21 CM

A multichannel receiver simultaneously gives the intensity of the line at N points of the spectrum. A receiver is built with a 0.6-Mc/s bandwidth, and by means of suitable electrical filters the passband is divided into 50 channels, each, say, 10 kc/s wide. This is equivalent to building 50 receivers with frequencies so staggered as to cover the 0.6-Mc/s interval. If most of the gain occurs in just one amplifier with a 0.6-Mc/s bandwidth, the gain variations will affect all the channels identically, and the profile will thus be represented correctly.

At the output of each filter an amplifier and detector must unfortunately be connected. The energy received in each channel is thus measured and integrated independently of the others, a device reads the output indication of each channel in turn, and the line profile can thus be made available immediately on an oscillograph or recorder, point by point (Fig. 5-2). Reading off the output indication from one channel will not interfere with the operation of the others. In swept-frequency devices, on the other hand, only one or two frequency bands are received at a time, all the energy outside these bands being lost. It is easy to see that for a given spectral definition a 50-channel receiver gives 50 times more information in the same time than a single swept-frequency receiver.

The first multichannel instrument was built in 1950 by Kerr in Australia. Others have been built since, notably in the United States. Considerable technical difficulties are encountered, but the gain in sensitivity obtained, as compared with swept-frequency instruments, justifies the effort.

New methods of profile measurement using correlation techniques have been proposed recently. There is no doubt that in the future the technique employed will depend essentially on the astrophysical problem under study according as the line is wide or narrow, strong or weak, and more or less Doppler-shifted.

SOLAR RADIOSPECTROGRAPHS

As we shall see later, the sun gives out strong radiation whose spectrum can change very rapidly with time, as, for example, when solar flares occur. Hydrogen-line techniques, which furnish high precision for the determination of spectra and are very sensitive, are abandoned in favor of other

Fig. 5-4. The three rhombic antennas of Wild's solar radiospectrograph at Dapto, Australia. Each mount carries two rhombics constructed of copper wire in perpendicular planes to allow polarization observations. Each antenna operates over a frequency band of about an octave. *(CSIRO Radiophysics Division photo.)*

arrangements permitting faster scanning of a much wider band with a lower sensitivity that is satisfactory for the much stronger solar emission. Whereas 1 Mc/s of the hydrogen-line spectrum is scanned in 1 hour, the solar spectrum is scanned from 40 to 240 Mc/s in about a second.

It is relatively easy to sweep through one octave with a receiver whose tuning is controlled mechanically by motor-driven variable capacitors. More recently electron tubes have been constructed to permit sweeping in the centimeter band. Antennas which operate over a full octave are a problem in themselves (Fig. 5-4). To sweep three octaves, one has to use three swept-frequency (panoramic) receivers and three antennas which are switched in automatically.

The first instrument of this kind was built in Australia by J. P. Wild and his colleagues in 1950. Other similar instruments, operating on higher frequencies, are in use in the United States at the University of Michigan (F. T. Haddock) and in Texas (A. Maxwell).[1] Typical examples of spectra obtained with these instruments, and their importance for the study of movements in the corona, will be dealt with in Chap. 7.

BIBLIOGRAPHY

The 21-cm line

van de Hulst, H. C., C. A. Muller, and J. H. Oort: *Bull. Astron. Inst. Neth.,* **12:** 117 (1954).

Panoramic receivers

Goodman, J., and M. Lebenbaum: *Proc. IRE,* **46:** 132 (1958).
Wild, J. P., and L. L. McCready: *Australian J. Sci. Res.,* Series A, **3:** 387 (1950).

[1] The radio spectrum of the sun can thus be studied from 20 to 4,000 Mc/s.

MECHANISMS OF EMISSION OF RADIO WAVES

6

No sooner was the existence of radio waves from the heavens demonstrated, than the first radio astronomers found that the new sky they were exploring presented a very different aspect from the one to which our eyes have become accustomed. None of the constellations and stars which are familiar to us can be recognized, and the sun itself hardly resembles the visible sun because its radio emission varies enormously in the course of time. New stars appear in the radio astronomical firmament, some of them of remarkable intensity, yet not associated with objects visible to the naked eye. The Milky Way emits very intense radiation; it also presents a different aspect from that of the visible galaxy.

All these discoveries together indicate that the causes of the radio emission from the sky are fundamentally different from those of the optical radiation. The spectra of the radio sources are almost always continuous, while optical spectra always contain very numerous emission or absorption lines, which occasionally are much more intense than the continuous spectrum. In most cases where a radio source has been identified with an optical object, it is found that its radio spectrum is in no way a continuation of the luminous spectrum. We can see that in many cases the mechanism of production of radio waves is not a simple thermal phenomenon and requires the emitting regions to be subject to very special conditions which are generally very difficult, if not impossible, to reproduce in the laboratory.

We should not, therefore, be surprised that radio astronomers have experienced great difficulties in interpreting the radiation picked up by their antennas and that in many cases its origin remains obscure. Of the several emission mechanisms that are possible, we shall study the main ones. Doing so, we shall touch on many points which are unclear or unexplored and on others which are still in the domain of speculation; nevertheless we wish to present to the reader some phenomena of considerable importance in the universe. Among the possible emission processes, the following main ones may be mentioned:

1 Emission of the neutral-hydrogen line on 21 cm, which until now is is the only one to have been detected in the radio spectrum
2 Thermal emission from solid objects radiating as classical black bodies
3 Thermal emission from ionized gases
4 Oscillations of ionized gases
5 Gyromagnetic emission by electrons
6 Emission by high-energy electrons in a magnetic field (synchrotron effect)
7 Čerenkov radiation

The second type of emission was studied sufficiently in an earlier chapter and need not be returned to, save only to say that it is rather faint. So far, the thermal radiations of the moon, Venus, Mars, Jupiter, Saturn, and Mercury have been detected.

We shall take up the study of radiation mechanisms by recalling a few ideas relating to the general laws of emission and absorption of electromagnetic waves.

GENERAL LAWS OF EMISSION
AND ABSORPTION

Einstein has the credit for having established, by purely phenomenological reasoning, laws of emission and absorption of radiation which are valid, whatever the physical mechanism producing the emission or absorption.

We know that any electromagnetic wave of frequency v consists of basic entities known as photons, whose energy W is connected with the frequency by Planck's fundamental relation

$$W = hv$$

where h is a universal constant known as Planck's constant.

The emission of a photon is thus accompanied by the loss of an energy W from the system, for example, from the atom which emitted it. Conversely, a system which absorbs a photon has its energy increased by an amount hv. These energy transfers between material systems and electromagnetic radiation are called transitions.

For example, consider an atom of hydrogen, consisting of a single electron rotating about a nucleus, which is just a proton. Quantum mechanics tells us that the electron can occupy only a certain number of possible orbits, each corresponding to a definite energy. The closer the electron is to the nucleus, the lower the energy. It is obvious that the electron can jump from one orbit to another, and if its energy diminishes by ΔE, it will emit a photon of frequency v such that v equals $\Delta E/h$.

Conversely, it may capture a photon of suitable energy coming from an external luminous source and jump to an orbit of higher energy.

It is seen that the spectrum of the light given out by hydrogen atoms is composed of discrete lines, each corresponding to one of the possible values of the energy jump ΔE. According to the physical conditions in which the hydrogen and the electromagnetic radiation incident on it are situated, these lines will appear in emission or in absorption on the continuous spectrum of the background.

Transitions can also occur, in other cases, between arbitrary energy levels. In the optical region, this is the case with ionization, where the electron is torn from the atom and acquires a kinetic energy which can assume any value. We shall see that this is almost usual as regards emission and absorption in the radio region, which thus exhibits a continuous spectrum in which no singular frequency, or any particular energy jump, appears. Nevertheless the general laws of absorption and emission take into account only the transitions that take place between two of the energy levels that the system can occupy.

Denoting these levels by subscripts 1 and 2, and so writing E_1 and E_2 respectively for the energy levels (Fig. 6-1), we have the following three laws:

1 The phenomenon of absorption corresponds, as we have said, to a transition from the lower energy state 1 to the upper state 2. The energy is delivered to the system on the arrival of a photon of energy $E_2 - E_1$.

2 Likewise a system in energy state 2 can emit a photon of energy hv spontaneously and fall back into state 1. This process is called *spontaneous emission*.

3 Finally, suppose that a system of energy E_2 encounters a photon whose frequency v corresponds to the transition. (This photon could come from neighboring systems or external sources.) Stimulated by this photon, the system can fall back into state 1 by emitting a new photon which combines with the incident one, which may be regarded as a sort of catalyst for the emission. This process is called *stimu-*

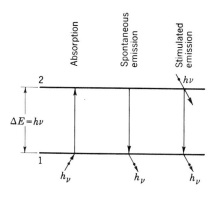

Fig. 6-1 Absorption and emission of radiation by an atom.

lated emission. The photon is emitted in the same direction as the incident photon, and emission is thus anisotropic.

Einstein established the relations connecting the respective probabilities of occurrence of these three processes. As regards spontaneous emission, a system in state 2 has a probability A_{21} of relapsing spontaneously into state 1 in the course of 1 second. This probability of spontaneous emission depends only on the nature of the system and the transition in question.

Stimulated emission, on the other hand, clearly depends on the number of photons $h\nu$ contained in the medium, a number which is expressed by the monochromatic flux density $\rho_\nu = 4\pi B(\nu)$ expressed in watts per square meter per cycle-per-second. This is the flux of energy traversing unit volume per second per cycle-per-second in all directions, and $B(\nu)$ is the brightness which we defined in Chap. 2.

The probability that a system initially in state 2 passes into state 1 by stimulated emission in the course of 1 second is expressed by the product $B_{21}\rho_\nu$, where B_{21} is a constant depending on the system under study.

The character of absorption is rather similar to that of spontaneous emission since its probability also depends on the radiation flux density at frequency ν. It is expressed by the product $B_{12}\rho_\nu$.

Starting from Planck's radiation law (Chap. 2), Einstein established the following relations between the three quantities A_{21}, B_{21}, and B_{12}.

1 The probability of spontaneous emission is connected with the absorption probability, for the same flux density, by the very simple relation

$$g_1 B_{12} = g_2 B_{21}$$

where g_1 and g_2 are small whole numbers known as the statistical weights of levels 1 and 2.

2 The probability of spontaneous emission is related to the probabilities of absorption and stimulated emission by the relation

$$g_2 A_{21} = \frac{8\pi h \nu^3}{c^3} g_2 B_{21} = \frac{8\pi h \nu^3}{c^3} g_1 B_{12}$$

where h is Planck's constant, ν is the frequency, and c the speed of light.

In the optical region, the factor $8\pi h\nu^3/c^3$ is large, and spontaneous emission is generally more important than stimulated emission. The reverse is the case for radio waves, whose frequency ν is much smaller, provided, of course, that the radiation density ρ_ν is sufficient. But the radiation density can be very low in interstellar space, so that spontaneous emission can predominate. This is why the 21-cm line of neutral hydrogen can appear in emission.

For a full calculation of the absorption and emission of a medium at frequency ν, we now have to know the number of systems in states 1 and 2 respectively. Let N_1 be the number of systems per unit volume with energy E_1, and similarly for N_2. Then the energy emitted per second in unit volume in the form of photons of energy $h\nu$ can be written:

Spontaneous emission $\quad W_s = N_2 A_{21} h\nu$

Stimulated emission $\quad W_i = N_2 B_{21} \rho_\nu h\nu$

Absorption $\quad W_a = -N_1 B_{12} \rho_\nu h\nu = -N_1 \dfrac{g_2}{g_1} B_{21} \rho_\nu h\nu$

The total power emitted per unit volume may be written:

$$W = h\nu \left[N_2 A_{21} - \left(\frac{g_2}{g_1} N_1 - N_2 \right) B_{21} \rho_\nu \right]$$

The first factor expresses spontaneous emission, and the second combines stimulated emission and absorption. If N_1 is greater than $g_1 N_2 / g_2$, absorption outweighs spontaneous emission and this factor amounts to a net absorption. It is seen that there will be no emission in the case where $N_2 A_{21} - (g_2 N_1 / g_1 - N_2) B_{21} \rho_\nu$ is positive, i.e., if the flux density is sufficiently small.

It may be shown that in thermodynamic equilibrium the ratio N_2 / N_1 is given by

$$\frac{N_2}{N_1} = \frac{g_2}{g_1} e^{-(E_2 - E_1)/kT_0}$$

where k is Boltzmann's constant and T_0 is the absolute temperature of the medium.

If the medium is not in equilibrium for some reason or other, the ratio N_2 / N_1 may no longer have the value given above. But it may always be written in the form

$$\frac{N_2}{N_1} = \frac{g_2}{g_1} e^{-(E_2 - E_1)/kT_e}$$

where T_e is called the *excitation temperature*. This is just a convenient quantity which has no physical significance. The emission is said to be nonthermal whenever the temperature T_e is different from the true temperature T_0 of the medium.

In some cases a population $N_2 > N_1$ can be produced artificially, which corresponds to a negative excitation temperature. In this case stimulated emission outweighs absorption; far from absorbing the electromagnetic waves which reach it, such a medium is capable of amplifying them. This is the principle used to construct the masers we have already referred to. According to Gabor and Twiss, this process could occur also in certain active regions of the sun, and in this connection we shall have occasion to return to it.

RADIATION TRANSFER IN A GAS

We are now sufficiently well-prepared to see what will take place when a distant region of radio emission is observed through a gas which is itself capable of emitting and absorbing photons at the operating frequency ν (Fig. 6-2).

In radio astronomy it is convenient to deal with the brightness temperature we have defined in an earlier chapter. We need only recall that the energy radiated at a frequency ν by any emitting object may be expressed in terms of the temperature T to which a black body of the same shape would have to be raised in order to radiate the same energy at the frequency in question. This temperature is the brightness temperature.

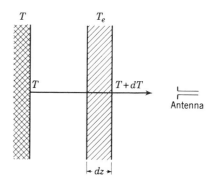

Suppose we were observing an emitting region of brightness temperature T through a thin layer of gas of thickness dz. The whole would appear at a brightness temperature $T + dT$, the increment dT due to the influence of the gas being either positive or negative. It is then easy to show, by use of the fundamental equation previously established, that

Fig. 6-2 Transfer of radiation in a thin layer of gas.

$$dT = \left[\frac{c^2}{8\pi k\nu^2} A_{21} N_2 h\nu - \frac{c^2}{8\pi h\nu^3} A_{21} \left(\frac{g_2}{g_1} N_1 - N_2 \right) h\nu T \right] dz$$

where all the symbols have the meaning given to them above.[1] This expression can be considerably simplified by introducing the excitation temperature T_e of the gas.

In the expression $N_2/N_1 = (g_2/g_1)\exp(-h\nu/kT_e)$ the factor $h\nu/kT_e$ is always very small, and in this case we may write

$$\frac{N_2}{N_1} = \frac{g_2}{g_1}\left(1 - \frac{h\nu}{kT_e} \right)$$

Thus N_2 is seen to be very close in value to $g_2 N_1/g_1$ and we have, to a good approximation,

$$\frac{g_2}{g_1} N_1 - N_2 = \frac{g_2}{g_1} N_1 \frac{h\nu}{kT_e}$$

[1] To get this expression, the monochromatic flux density ρ_ν is evaluated as a function of the brightness temperature T, according to the Rayleigh-Jeans law.

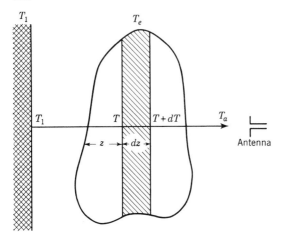

Fig. 6-3 Transfer of radiation in a thick gas cloud.

The equation of transfer becomes

$$\frac{dT}{dz} = \frac{c^2 A_{21}}{8\pi\nu^2} \frac{g_2}{g_1} N_1 \frac{h\nu}{k} \left(1 - \frac{T}{T_e} \right)$$

The absorption coefficient $K(\nu)$ is defined by

$$K(\nu) = \frac{c^2 A_{21}}{8\pi\nu^2} \frac{g_2}{g_1} N_1 \frac{h\nu}{kT_e}$$

The equation of transfer then takes the extremely simple form

$$\frac{dT}{dz} = K(\nu)(T_e - T)$$

A simple examination of this equation reveals properties that are fundamental to radio astronomy.

1 If a region of brightness temperature T is observed through a layer of gas whose excitation temperature T_e is greater than T, the radio emission of the distant region is enhanced by that of the gas. The gas is said to appear *in emission*.

2 Conversely, if the excitation temperature T_e of the gas is lower than the brightness temperature T of the distant region, the gas appears less bright; it is said to appear *in absorption*.

3 Finally, if $T_e = T$, it is as though the gas did not exist.

Thus the propensity which a gaseous mass possesses for absorbing or reinforcing the radiation from an emitting region situated behind it does not depend on its composition or on the radio-emission mechanism itself, but only on the difference between the brightness temperature of the distant emitting region and the excitation temperature of the intervening gas.

What happens in a thick cloud of gas now remains to be studied. It is convenient here to introduce, following the example of astrophysicists, the optical thickness $d\tau$ of an elementary slab of medium of thickness dz. It is the product of the absorption coefficient and the thickness of the slab of gas, i.e.,

$$d\tau = K(\nu)dz$$

The equation of transfer then becomes

$$dT = (T_e - T)d\tau$$

For a thick cloud of gas, where the excitation temperature T_e is taken to be the same throughout, it is easy to integrate this differential equation and we obtain

$$T_a = T_1 e^{-\tau} + T_e(1 - e^{-\tau})$$

where T_a is the observed effective temperature (antenna temperature) and T_1 is the brightness temperature of a distant region lying beyond a cloud of gas with excitation temperature T_e and optical depth τ (Fig. 6-3). The optical depth is simply the sum of the optical thicknesses of the various layers of the gas,

$$\tau = \int_{\text{thickness}} d\tau$$

If the optical depth of the gas is large, it will absorb or emit the radiation strongly. If it is extremely large, we shall have simply $T_e = T_a$. The gas, being quite opaque, will appear as a black body at temperature T_e. If the optical depth is small, as is frequently the case in radio astronomy, we have simply

$$T_2 = T_1(1 - \tau) + T_e\tau$$

From these formulas which we have just established, we can recover the properties we deduced earlier in the simple case of a very thin layer of gas. Fig. 6-4 shows that the apparent temperature T_a is greater or less than T_1 according as the excitation temperature itself is greater or less than the brightness temperature of the distant regions. Similarly, Fig. 6-5 shows how

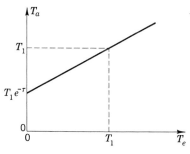

Fig. 6-4 Variation of apparent temperature with excitation temperature of the intervening layers.

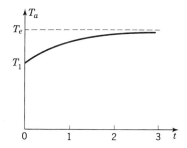

Fig. 6-5 Variation of apparent temperature with optical depth of the intervening layers.

the apparent temperature varies with the optical depth in the case of the gas appearing in emission.

In concluding this topic, we should mention that we have taken account of only the case where the absorption or emission of a wave of frequency ν corresponds to a single possible transition of the system. In fact, however, the energy of the system may assume any value at all (this, as we have said, is often the case in radio astronomy). The one frequency ν can correspond to transitions between all sorts of pairs of energy levels, provided the energy jump is always equal to the product $h\nu$ (Fig. 6-6). In this case, the expression we have given for the absorption coefficient $K(\nu)$ is no longer valid; nevertheless, the general properties of absorption and emission in a gas are still completely correct and the form of the equation of transfer remains the same.

THE 21-CM LINE
OF NEUTRAL HYDROGEN

The simplest emission phenomenon we have to deal with in radio astronomy is quite certainly the 21-cm line from interstellar hydrogen.

Indeed, this line, which so far is the only one to have been detected in the radio emission of the sky, corresponds to a transition between two energy levels of the hydrogen atom. It is fully comparable with an optical line except that its wavelength is much greater. Originally predicted by van de Hulst in 1945 and then by Shklovsky in 1947, it was first observed in 1951 by American, Dutch, and Australian radio astronomers working independently.

It comes from interstellar hydrogen, which, being very rarefied and cold, exists in the form of isolated atoms and perhaps also molecules. As there is no source of optical excitation in regions that are far away from any star, all the hydrogen atoms exist in their ground state, and the single electron rotates about the nucleus on the orbit which is closest in. There can be no emission of light, for no atom is in a higher energy state. But the ground state is itself split into two substates, with very slightly different energies, which correspond to two possible orientations of the spin (or magnetic moment) of the electron and the nucleus. The energy of the atom is a little greater when the spins are parallel than when their directions are opposed. A transition between these two substates is possible, which physicists refer

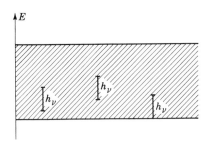

Fig. 6-6 Transitions in a medium with an energy-level continuum.

to as a *hyperfine transition*. The energy jump corresponds to the absorption or emission of a photon whose frequency ν is equal to 1,420 Mc/s, which is equivalent to a wavelength of 21.1 cm.

The general radiation laws established above apply to this line exactly. The probability of spontaneous emission is very low. An atom in the higher energy substate remains there for 11 million years on the average before relapsing into the lower energy state with the emission of a 21-cm photon, if it has to depend on spontaneous emission. The probability of spontaneous emission is only 2.84×10^{-15} per second.

Purcell and Field were able to calculate the excitation temperature in interstellar space. According to these authors, it is essentially determined by collisions between atoms, which are very effective, as long as the excitation temperature T_e is approximately equal to the kinetic temperature of the gas (i.e., the temperature in the usual sense). It is of the order of 100 to 125°K, but seems to fall as low as 50°K in particularly cold regions.

The absorption coefficient $K(\nu)$ can be calculated for the hydrogen line by the formula quoted in the earlier discussion of transfer of radiation. Nevertheless, Doppler broadening of the line must be taken into account. As each atom moves with a radial velocity V with respect to the observer as a result of its thermal agitation, instead of the theoretical frequency ν_0 it emits a frequency

$$\nu = \nu_0 + \nu_0 \frac{V}{c}$$

The absorption coefficient is given by

$$K(\nu) = \frac{g_2}{g_1} \frac{c^2 A_{21}}{8\pi\nu^2} \frac{h\nu}{kT_e} \frac{c}{\nu} N_1(V)$$

where $N_1(V)\, dV$ is the number of atoms per unit volume in state 1 whose radial velocity lies between V and $V + dV$. The statistical weight of the upper level is three times that of the lower; this means that it has roughly three times the population. Thus $g_2/g_1 = 3$, and with $A_{21} = 2.84 \times 10^{-15}$ per second, we have

$$K(\nu) = 5.51 \times 10^{-14} \frac{N_H(V)}{T_e}$$

where this time we have introduced $N_H(\nu)$, the total number of all hydrogen atoms per cubic centimeter with radial velocity V:

$$N_H(V) = 4N_1(V)$$

The optical depth may be written

$$\tau(\nu) = 5.51 \times 10^{-14} \frac{N_H(V)}{T_e}$$

where $N_H(V)$ is the total number of hydrogen atoms with radial velocity V in a column of a unit cross-section area in the direction of the line of sight.

Thus, even when coming from a stationary cloud of hydrogen, the 21-cm line has a certain width due to thermal motion of the atoms. The width of the line is related to the temperature of the cloud by the relation

$$\Delta \nu = \frac{2\nu}{c} \left(\frac{3kT}{m} \right)^{\frac{1}{2}}$$

where m is the mass of the proton and k is Boltzmann's constant. As the observer almost always receives the emission of several clouds situated one behind the other with different radial velocities, the line takes on a complex structure. Each peak corresponds in general to a particular emitting cloud on the line of sight. As we shall see in a later chapter, the study of the profile of the 21-cm line at different positions in the galaxy has allowed astrophysicists to trace out a detailed map for the first time.

In most cases, the 21-cm line appears in emission, because the brightness temperature of the continuous spectrum in the vicinity of the line rarely exceeds $30°K$, which is distinctly less than the excitation temperature of the neutral hydrogen. Nevertheless, the radio emission from point sources can be high enough for the foreground neutral hydrogen to exhibit absorption lines on 21 cm.

THERMAL EMISSION OF RADIO WAVES BY IONIZED GASES

With the exception of neutral-hydrogen emission, which we have just been studying, and thermal emission from solid bodies, radio emission always comes from free electrons. As an electron detached from its atom has no definite energy levels, the energy jumps which it can make by absorbing or emitting a photon are arbitrary, and we are dealing with a continuous spectrum. The spectra of radio sources and the extended regions of emission in the Milky Way are indeed continuous and are punctuated only by the lone 21-cm line, whose origin is quite different. Furthermore, the energy of the photons which compose the radio waves is very small compared with that of X-ray, ultraviolet, or visible photons. It may be shown that in this case it is possible to obtain correct results by calculating the energy radiated or absorbed by an electron, using classical procedures without invoking quantum mechanics.

In the classical theory, the emission of electromagnetic energy by a free electron depends on the accelerations that it undergoes. From the quantum point of view this corresponds to transitions made by the electron between different kinetic energies or different velocities. The total power radiated over the whole range of frequencies by an electron of charge e undergoing an acceleration γ is given by the formula

$$S = \frac{e^2 \gamma^2}{6\pi\epsilon_0 c^3}$$

in the rationalized meter-kilogram-second system of units. The permittivity of free space ϵ_0 is equal to $10^{-9}/36\pi$ in this system of units, which we shall employ throughout.

This formula applies, whatever the acceleration mechanism of the electron, always on condition that its velocity remains small enough with respect to the velocity of light so that relativistic corrections will not have to be introduced.

Free electrons are found in space only where they have been detached from atoms. This detachment of the electron, or ionization, can take place through collision between atoms at very high temperatures, or through the action of ultraviolet or X radiation. This explains the ionization of the solar atmosphere as well as of the interstellar gas clouds surrounding stars that emit strongly in the ultraviolet. In each case radio-frequency emission has been detected from these ionized media. The study of these media is simplified by the fact that they are almost totally composed of hydrogen and that they are almost fully ionized. They can thus be imagined as gases composed of equal numbers of free electrons and hydrogen nuclei, i.e., positively charged protons, whose mass is much greater than that of the electron.

In this apparently simple medium the physical phenomena are very complex and far from being completely understood at the present time, although very advanced studies on the physics of ionized gases are under way in many countries. Their theoretical and practical importance is very great, because it is connected with the problem of future development of controlled nuclear fusion, which will have to take place in an ionized gas.

Radio emission by ionized media is still imperfectly understood; it seems to comprise several types.

The simplest occurs in an unperturbed ionized gas. The free electrons of this gas are in perpetual thermal motion among the protons, which are practically stationary because of their relatively large mass. Consider an electron with velocity v approaching a proton. At each instant, the force exerted on the electron is just the electrostatic attraction $e^2/4\pi\epsilon_0 r^2$, where e is the charge on the electron (coulombs), r is the distance from the proton (meters), and ϵ_0 is the permittivity of free space. Under the effect of this force, the electron undergoes an acceleration γ which is equal to the ratio of the attractive force to the mass m. It describes a trajectory in the form of a hyperbola with the proton at one focus (Fig. 6-7). At each instant the acceleration γ is given by

$$\gamma = \frac{e^2}{4\pi\epsilon_0 mr^2}$$

and at each instant the electron radiates a power

$$S = \frac{e^2}{6\pi\epsilon_0 c^3}\gamma^2$$

The total energy radiated on all possible frequencies amounts to

$$W = \frac{e^2}{6\pi\epsilon_0 c^3}\int_{-\infty}^{+\infty}\gamma^2\,dt$$

This energy can be easily evaluated as a function of the initial velocity of the electron, and then the emission of a volume of ionized gas can be calculated which is sufficiently big to enclose a large number of electrons with a Maxwell distribution of velocities. This distribution, which also applies to the molecules of an ordinary gas, permits the definition of an electron temperature T_e in exactly the same way as one defines the absolute molecular temperature of a classical gas.

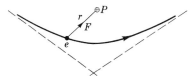

Fig. 6-7 Trajectory of an electron *e* passing near a proton *P*. The electrostatic attraction is F.

For example, one may use the relation $\overline{v^2} = 3kT_e/m$ to define T_e, where $\overline{v^2}$ is the mean square velocity of the electrons, m is their mass, and k is Boltzmann's constant.

The electron temperature is just the excitation temperature discussed above, because the electrons of the ionized gas are in thermodynamic equilibrium.[1] The radiating process is thus thermal, and the excitation temperature is independent of the frequency. We now have only to give the value of the absorption coefficient $K(\nu)$ of the ionized medium to define the emission and absorption completely. Calculation shows that this coefficient depends on the frequency and is essentially given by

$$K(\nu) = 0.133 \times 10^{-12}\,T_e^{-3/2}\,\nu^{-2}\,N_e^2$$

where N_e is the number of free electrons per cubic meter, ν is the frequency in cycles per second, and T_e is the electron temperature in degrees Kelvin.

In interstellar ionized media, N_e is very small and the absorption co-

---

[1] Equilibrium is said to exist when the particle velocities have a Maxwell distribution. The protons may quite well not be in equilibrium with the electrons, but they hardly enter the matter.

efficient is minute. In these conditions it is easy to ascertain from the formulas given above that the brightness temperature of an ionized hydrogen cloud of thickness z, which is given essentially by $T_b = K(\nu)zT_e$, varies inversely as the square of the operating frequency. This property is characteristic of thermal emission in interstellar space and allows it to be distinguished from other types of emission.

In the solar atmosphere, things are far from being as simple. Optical depths can be very large, and, furthermore, radio waves are subject to refraction which can completely change their direction. We shall return to these phenomena at greater length when we come to study the radio emission of the sun.

PLASMA OSCILLATIONS

The emission of which we have been speaking applies to an ionized gas whose electrons are in equilibrium; i.e., they obey Maxwell's distribution law. But if for one reason or another some perturbation upsets this equilibrium, very varied and very complex phenomena are observed which give rise to radio emission during the course of the perturbation. There is no reason for departures from equilibrium to occur in interstellar space, but they are quite possible in the sun's atmosphere. Most of the strong bursts, which are the most outstanding manifestations of solar activity, must necesarily be of nonthermal origin, since brightness temperatures as high as 10^{10} or 10^{11} °K are sometimes observed, whereas the electron temperature rarely exceeds 10^7 °K in the corona.

Very little is yet known about this nonthermal emission. However, an ionized gas is capable of oscillating in various ways. The simplest type of oscillation, which is relatively well known, is called a *plasma oscillation*. (The term "plasma" is roughly synonymous with ionized medium.) It consists of organized oscillations of electric charges originating in a local departure from electrical neutrality. It is quite easy to calculate their approximate frequency. Suppose that in an ionized medium bounded by two plane surfaces all the electrons are displaced together by an amount dx with respect to the ions, which will be taken to be stationary (Fig. 6-8). Two surface charges, one positive and one negative, then develop on the surface of the medium. The electrons are subjected to a restoring force which may easily be calcu-

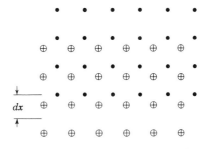

Fig. 6-8 Plasma oscillations. The protons are represented by circles containing a plus sign, and the electrons by dots.

lated by noting that it is analogous to the force on a charged particle placed between the plates of a capacitor, viz.,

$$F = - \frac{N_e e^2 \, dx}{\epsilon_0} \qquad \text{(mks units)}$$

where N_e is the electron density.

The electrons will tend to return to the neutral zone, will overshoot their equilibrium position, and in short will execute sinusoidal oscillations at a frequency

$$\nu_0 = \frac{e}{2\pi} \left(\frac{N_e}{\epsilon_0 m} \right)^{1/2}$$

This frequency, which is known as the *plasma frequency,* is given numerically by $\nu_0 = 9(N_e)^{\frac{1}{2}}$, where ν_0 is expressed in cycles per second and N_e in electrons per cubic meter. In spite of the rather crude way in which this result has been obtained, it is quite general as long as the thermal agitation is not too strong and provided the oscillations remain of low amplitude.

The emission of radio waves by an oscillating plasma raises important theoretical difficulties which we do not wish to emphasize here. Emission could take place only if the plasma were immersed in a magnetic field, if it possessed turbulent motions, or if it contained inhomogeneities. In any case, emission will take place in a very limited range of frequencies centered on the plasma frequency and may exhibit a second harmonic if the oscillations are not linear; this happens when their amplitude is very large.

The mode of excitation of plasma oscillations is still obscure. Two hypotheses seem nevertheless sufficiently well-supported and agree fairly well with radio astronomical observations. On the one hand, Shklovsky supposed as early as 1946 that oscillations can be produced by the passage of charged particles through the ionized medium. The sun ejects plenty of such particles during flares which are accompanied by strong radio emission. On the other hand, Martyn suggested in 1947 that powerful oscillations could be excited by the arrival of a supersonic perturbation. (Plasmas are capable of propagating waves that are essentially equivalent to acoustic waves.) As we shall see, this is the phenomenon which appears to be at the bottom of the very intense bursts from the radio sun.

Of course, electromagnetic waves generated by these nonthermal processes propagate through the solar atmosphere in the same way as the thermal radiation. In particular, they may exhibit more or less circular polarization, which shows that they originate in a region under the control of a magnetic field.

GYROMAGNETIC EMISSION

Another type of nonthermal emission can occur in the solar atmosphere when fast electrons penetrate a zone where there is a magnetic field. We know that electrons having an initial velocity perpendicular to the magnetic field describe circular trajectories around the field lines. It is easy to calculate their frequency of rotation $v_H = eB/2\pi m_0$, which is independent of their velocity as long as this is small. In this equation B is the magnetic induction, and e and m_0 are the charge and mass of the electron. At each instant the electron is subject to a central acceleration equal to Bev/m_0, where v is its velocity, and it radiates a power proportional to the square of this acceleration in the form of radio waves. This emission takes place at a unique frequency, namely, the rotation frequency v_H. In order for the radiation so generated to be able to reach our radio telescopes, it will still be necessary for it to be able to escape from the medium. This it cannot do, for propagation conditions in the presence of the magnetic field are always such that there is no hope of receiving the gyromagnetic radiation of the electrons from the ionized medium. Nevertheless, Twiss and Roberts in Australia have shown that part of the gyromagnetic radiation generated by much-faster-than-average electrons can escape. For such emission to take place, the fast electrons have to be produced, for example, in an active region of the sun, and get into a zone containing a magnetic field. Gyromagnetic emission is of course nonthermal, since the plasma includes foreign electrons and is thus not in a state of equilibrium.

Twiss and Roberts have calculated the rather complex character of this radiation in some simple cases. As we are now dealing with electrons whose energy is of the order of 100,000 electron volts and whose speed is not negligible compared to that of light, relativity corrections must be introduced. The rotation frequency of the electron then becomes

$$v = \frac{eB_0}{2\pi m_0}\left(1 - \frac{v^2}{c^2}\right)^{1/2}$$

where m_0 is the rest mass of the electron, v is its velocity, and c is the velocity of light. Emission will take place simultaneously at the rotation frequency and on harmonics, which can transport a large fraction of the energy. Although the fundamental cannot escape from the ionized medium, certain higher harmonics can, and their emission will be received by radio telescopes in the form of one or more narrow frequency bands. The radio wave will always have strong circular or elliptical polarization.

SYNCHROTRON RADIATION

The gyromagnetic emission that we have just described would be generated in the sun by electrons with speeds of the order of a few tenths of the velocity of light. Electrons certainly exist with much higher speeds still, speeds approaching that of light. Indeed, we know that nuclear particles (protons and nuclei of various elements), the primary cosmic rays themselves, are traveling through the universe with very high speeds. They are certainly accompanied by electrons with energies of the same order of magnitude, and, thanks to space probes, they have recently been detected. When in a magnetic field, very fast electrons emit a type of radiation which was noticed for the first time in the General Electric synchrotron, shortly after the second world war. The American physicists, who were accelerating a circular beam of extremely fast electrons in the strong magnetic field of this machine, observed the emission of intense linearly polarized light. This new effect, called *synchrotron emission,* can just as easily yield radio waves if the electron velocity is a little lower or the magnetic field a little weaker.

The principle behind this phenomenon is roughly analogous to that of the gyromagnetic emission which we have just mentioned; the electron executes a circular motion, is subjected at each instant to a central acceleration, and radiates an energy proportional to the square of this acceleration. But this time we are dealing with electrons whose speed is very close to that of light, and relativity corrections are absolutely fundamental. Furthermore, as we shall see in a moment, the character of the emission is quite different from that of the gyromagnetic radiation.

We know that the total energy of a particle whose rest mass is m_0 is related to its velocity v by Einstein's formula

$$E = \frac{m_0 c^2}{(1 - v^2/c^2)^{1/2}}$$

A relativistic calculation based on this fact enables us to evaluate the acceleration experienced by the electron and the power that it radiates in the form of electromagnetic waves. Schwinger succeeded in 1949 in deducing the properties of the radiation of a relativistic electron rotating in a magnetic field. In this case it does not radiate at all on its gyrofrequency $(eB_0/2\pi m_0)(1 - v^2/c^2)^{1/2}$ but on very high harmonics. As the harmonics are very close together, they give the impression of a continuous band of emission. The radiation may be characterized by a characteristic frequency ν_c given by

$$\nu_c = 1.6 \times 10^{13} BE^2$$

where B is the magnetic induction in gauss, and E is the energy of the electron in Gev (1 Gev $= 10^9$ electron volts). The radiation is a maximum at a frequency equal to $0.30\nu_c$. Furthermore, the radiation is linearly polarized, the plane of the electric field being parallel to the osculating plane of the electron trajectory. Finally, the emission takes place at each instant within a cone whose axis is tangent to the trajectory and whose semivertical angle $\alpha = m_0 c^2/E$ is inversely proportional to the electron energy. Figure 6-9 summarizes these characteristics.

In practice there are always a large number of electrons participating in the radiation; and their energies, and so their frequencies of maximum emission, are rather spread out. If it is assumed that the number of electrons is inversely proportional to a certain power β of their energy, it may be shown that the flux emitted by all the electrons varies according to a law of the form

$$J(\nu) \sim \nu^{-(\beta-1)/2} B^{(\beta+1)/2}$$

Taking a value 2.4 for β, which corresponds to cosmic rays, we find that the flux emitted should vary according to the -0.7 power of the frequency and that the brightness temperature of a region of synchrotron emission is proportional to $\nu^{-2.7}$. The brightness temperature thus increases more rapidly with wavelength than in the case of thermal emission of an ionized medium. This gives a good method for distinguishing these two types of emission. Synchrotron radiation is thought to be very common, as the spectra of most of the radio sources and of much of the galaxy vary with frequency according to the law we have just stated. Polarization measurements in principle provide a means of verifying the existence of synchrotron radiation. Unfortunately changes can set in between the source and ourselves. The Faraday effect, which is the most important, consists of a rotation of the plane of polarization of the wave when it traverses a plasma containing a magnetic field with a longitudinal component. As the rate of rotation varies with frequency, the initial polarization may disappear when the emitting region is observed with a receiver whose passband is too wide. This rather complicates polarization observations. Polarization was first detected with certainty in the Crab nebula, where Faraday effect is very weak. This was the only case in which we were quite sure of dealing with synchrotron radiation. But according to recent measurements at the U.S. Naval Research Laboratory and with the 210-ft radio telescope at Parkes (Australia), many radio sources exhibit linear polarization. Apart from the Crab nebula, whose polarization has long been known, the southern galactic source Vela X is rather strongly polarized (8 percent at 20 cm), and polarization has been detected in several extragalactic sources, the most notable being Cygnus A and Centaurus A. Finally, the galactic background continuum is itself polarized in several regions. These remarkable observations reveal the importance of synchrotron emission in nature and will perhaps permit the magnetic fields of galaxies to be measured.

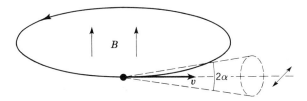

Fig. 6-9 Synchrotron radiation. The electron veering in the magnetic field *B* with a speed *v* close to that of light emits electromagnetic waves in a cone of vertical angle 2α. These waves are linearly polarized in the direction indicated by the arrow.

In certain cases, the polarization of synchrotron radiation can also be circular. This is the case if the emitting region is situated so that the radio waves must traverse plasma containing a magnetic field after they have been emitted. This is often what happens during the emission of the large solar bursts of type IV, which are also attributed to emission by relativistic electrons.

ČERENKOV RADIATION

The discovery of a new type of radiation by Čerenkov in 1934, and its theoretical study by Tamm and Frank, gained the Nobel prize for physics for these three Soviet scientists in 1958. Luminous emission is observed when very-high-energy particles penetrate a medium in which the velocity of light is smaller than their own velocity. The speed of light in a medium of refractive index n is only c/n. When particles with speeds above c/n (but necessarily less than c according to the theory of relativity) penetrate this medium, they are strongly braked with a loss of energy in the form of emission of electromagnetic waves radiated along a conical surface centered about the trajectory of the particle (Fig. 6-10). The light emitted can be used to detect very-high-energy particles, and for this purpose the Čerenkov effect is much used in nuclear physics. There is no theoretical reason why the Čerenkov effect should not occur when very fast particles enter a particularly dense plasma, with the emission of radio waves. According to Cohen the emission falls in a very narrow frequency band in the neighborhood of the plasma frequency. This mechanism could be responsible for some of the radio emission of the sun.

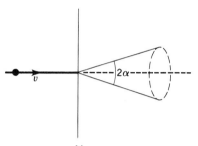

Fig. 6-10 Čerenkov radiation. When the high-energy particle penetrates a dense medium, it emits electromagnetic waves over the surface of a cone of vertical angle 2α whose axis is tangent to the trajectory.

CONCLUSION

The different possibilities of radio emission that we have been studying in turn present extremely diverse characteristics. It is misleading to attempt to classify them; at the most we can distinguish thermal processes (blackbody radiation, plasma equilibrium radiation) from nonthermal processes. The essential characteristics of each are summarized in Table 6-1.

TABLE 6-1

Summary of various mechanisms of radio emission

Type of radiation	Origin	Excitation temperature	Optical depth	Spectrum	Polarization
21-cm line	interstellar neutral hydrogen	$\leq$ absolute temperature (100 to 130 °K)	small	narrow line shifted or widened by Doppler effect	unpolarized
Black-body emission	moon, planets	= absolute temperature	∞	continuous spectrum	unpolarized
Thermal emission from ionized gases	interstellar ionized hydrogen	= electron temperature (10^4 °K)	small	continuous spectrum with absorption coefficient varying as ν^{-2} and N_e^2	unpolarized
	solar corona	= electron temperature (10^6 to 10^7 °K)	may be very large		
Plasma oscillations	sun	may reach 10^{10} to 10^{11} °K	large	fundamental (frequency varying as $N_e^{\frac{1}{2}}$) + harmonics	usually unpolarized
Gyromagnetic emission	sun	very high	?	fundamental (frequency varying as B) + harmonics	circularly polarized
Synchrotron emission	sun	$> 10^{11}$ °K	large	very wide spectral band	linear or circular polarization
	radio sources	always very high	large	continuous spectrum	linear in some cases
	interstellar space	very high	small	continuous spectrum; brightness temperature varying as $\nu^{-2.7}$	linear in some cases
Čerenkov radiation	sun ?	very high	?	narrow band	

BIBLIOGRAPHY

Emission, equation of transfer

Aller, L. H.: "Astrophysics," vol. 1, The Ronald Press Company, New York, 1953.

Ambartsumian, V. A.: "Theoretical Astrophysics," Pergamon Press, New York, 1958.

Condon, E. V., and G. H. Shortley: "The Theory of Atomic Spectra," Cambridge University Press, New York, 1935.

The 21-cm line

Purcell, E. M., and G. B. Field: *Astrophys. J.*, **124:** 542 (1956).

Wild, J. P.: *Astrophys. J.*, **115:** 206 (1952).

Electron radiation, thermal radiation from ionized gases

Denisse, J. F.: *J. de Phys.*, **11:** 164 (1950).

Sommerfeld, A.: "Electrodynamics," Academic Press, Inc., New York, 1956.

Ionized media

Delcroix, J. L.: "Introduction à la physique des gaz complètement ionisés," Dunod, Paris, 1961.

Delcroix, J. L., and J. F. Denisse: "Théorie des ondes dans les plasmas," Dunod, Paris, 1961.

Ratcliffe, J. A.: "The Magneto-ionic Theory and Its Applications to the Ionosphere," Cambridge University Press, New York, 1959.

Gyromagnetic emission

Twiss, R. Q., and J. A. Roberts: *Australian J. Phys.*, **11:** 424 (1958).

Synchrotron radiation

Le Roux, E.: *Ann. Astrophys.*, **24:** 71 (1961).

Oort, J. H., and T. Walraven: *Bull. Astron. Inst. Neth.*, **75:** 285 (1956).

Schwinger, J.: *Phys. Rev.*, **11:** 1912 (1949).

Čerenkov radiation

Jelley, J. V.: "Čerenkov Radiation," Pergamon Press, New York, 1959.

Amplification by stimulated emission

Twiss, R. Q.: *Australian J. Phys.*, **12:** 564 (1958).

RADIO EMISSION FROM THE SUN

7

Up to the beginning of the nineteenth century, man's knowledge about the sun was no more than his eyes allowed him to see. The great astronomer Herschel then got the idea of putting a thermometer in different parts of the sun's spectrum as projected onto a screen by means of a lens and prism, and found out that it warmed up not only where the visible light shone on it but also in the dark beyond the red. He thus discovered the solar radiation in the near infrared, which carries a large part of the heat energy. Later it was discovered that the solar spectrum extends also beyond the violet. But it was only starting from 1947 that observations made at high altitudes from rockets freed us from the earth's atmosphere, which blocks most of the ultraviolet radiation of the sun. Then the existence of solar X rays could also be observed.

At the other end of the spectrum, almost all radiation with wavelengths greater than 5μ is stopped by atmospheric water vapor and carbon dioxide. Observations in the very far infrared are still rare and very incomplete. Beginning with millimeter waves, the atmosphere again becomes transparent; this is where the domain of radio astronomy starts and it carries right on to the decameter waves.

It is very interesting to compare the various wavelength ranges of the solar spectrum. In the visible, where the sun emits most of its energy, the overall emission varies but little in the course of time; variations in the luminous flux do not exceed a few percent. By contrast, the radio emission is essentially variable. On top of a weak and relatively constant quiet component, slow enhancements are superimposed together with sharp bursts

TABLE 7-1

Different types of solar radio emission

Type	Duration	Diameter	Apparent temperature	Spectrum	Polarization	Origin	Remarks
Quiet sun	11-year cycle ?	$\geq 32'$, increasing with wavelength	$< 10^6$ °K	m, dm, cm	unpolarized	thermal	
Slowly varying component	days to months	as for spots and faculae	$< 2 \times 10^6$ °K	dm, cm; m ?	unpolarized	thermal	complex behavior on cm wavelengths with circular polarization
Type III bursts	seconds; often in groups	up to 10' ? increasing with wavelength	$> 10^{11}$ °K	m, dm; 5 mc/s bandwidth; fast drift	usually unpolarized	plasma oscillations ? synchrotron ? Čerenkov ?	caused by fast-escaping particles ? flare-associated
Type V bursts	minutes	large	$\sim 10^{11}$ °K	m; wide bandwidth	sometimes elliptically polarized	synchrotron	following type III
Type II bursts	minutes; complex	?	$< 10^{11}$ °K	m, dm; 50 Mc/s bandwidth; slow drift	usually unpolarized	plasma oscillations	due to shock wave; follows start of flare
Type IV bursts	minutes to hours	up to 10'; increasing with wavelength	$\sim 10^{11}$ °K	m, dm, cm	often circularly polarized	synchrotron	often 10 to 20 min after flare; upward motion; cosmic ray association
Noise storms	hours to days	small (minutes of arc)	$\sim 10^9$ °K	m	circularly polarized	Čerenkov ?	simultaneous continuum and short bursts (type I)

whose intensity can reach several million times that of the quiet component. Table 7-1 gives a summary of the characteristics of these emissions. At the opposite end of the spectrum, solar X rays exhibit somewhat similar variability.

The bursts and slow variations are very remarkable manifestations of solar activity. Solar activity likewise shows up in the optical region, but less spectacularly. We know that the sun's surface (the photosphere) exhibits dark spots surrounded by bright faculae (Fig. 7-1), whose number and dimensions vary in the course of time with the 11-year period that we know as the solar cycle. At the time of maximum activity, flares occur in the neighborhood of the spots. They are accompanied by ejections of matter and coincide with the strongest radio bursts. It is unfortunately difficult to observe them optically without special instruments, and astronomers are always at the mercy of clouds or fog. But as radio astronomers are free from such inconveniences, radio observations constitute a reliable means for detecting and studying flares. Our knowledge of solar activity has made considerable progress in recent years, thanks to the simultaneous development and coordination of optical and radio observations. We wish especially to report on this progress in the following pages, and we shall begin with a few words about the quiet component of the radio sun.

THE RADIO EMISSION
OF THE QUIET SUN

The sun usually appears as a bright disk with perfectly sharp limbs and does not seem to possess an atmosphere. Nevertheless, when the solar disk is completely hidden by the moon during an eclipse, or by an opaque disk, as in the Lyot coronagraph, a luminous corona appears which extends well beyond the disk (Fig. 7-2). As its brightness is about a million times fainter than that of the photosphere, which is the visible surface of the sun, it is not surprising that the corona goes unnoticed under ordinary conditions.

Careful observation of the solar disk reveals the presence of a rather thin layer, brighter than the corona, but less bright than the photosphere, which is known as the chromosphere. Photographs of the sun, taken in light of the H or K line of calcium, or in the Hα line of hydrogen, give an idea of the structure of the chromosphere (see Fig. 7-8).

Although the temperature of the photosphere is no greater than 5000°K, the chromosphere and corona are much hotter. The corona, in particular, appears to have a temperature of the order of a million degrees. The origin of such high temperatures raises problems which are far from being solved. Whatever the cause, the hydrogen, which is the principal constituent of the solar atmosphere, is virtually fully ionized in the high

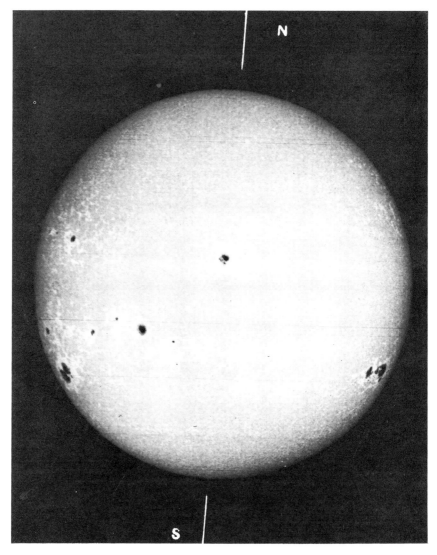

Fig. 7-1 Photograph of the sun in the K_1 line of calcium taken on 30 June 1957 with the spectroheliograph at Meudon Observatory. The dark spots are surrounded by bright facular plages, which are much more visible in the K_1 line than in white light. Note the limb darkening due to the solar atmosphere. *(Meudon Observatory photo.)*

Fig. 7-2 The solar corona. Photograph taken during the total eclipse of 9 May 1929, showing the almost circular symmetry characteristic of maximum solar activity.

chromosphere and in the corona. Figure 7-3 gives values of the temperature and the density of detached electrons at different altitudes in the solar atmosphere. Note that the electron density falls away with height in the corona as a result of the thinning out of the atmosphere itself.

One might expect the solar atmosphere to produce radio emission by the thermal process studied in the preceding chapter. This is indeed observed, but it is found that the dimensions and shape of the radio sun vary with the frequency of observation. On centimeter wavelengths, which correspond to frequencies above 3,000 Mc/s, it appears hardly larger than the optical sun. On meter wavelengths, on the other hand, its dimensions are much greater and its appearance resembles that of the high corona.

These observations lead us to think that the emission comes from lower layers of the solar atmosphere as the wavelengths become shorter. This surmise is easily explained by seeing how radio waves propagate in the ionized medium constituting the solar atmosphere. This medium has a refractive index different from unity for radio waves, and refraction phenomena can be very important. To calculate the refractive index, each free electron of the ionized gas is assumed to move sinusoidally under the influence of the alternating electric field of the incident radio waves. It then emits a wave of the same frequency, as a consequence of its acceleration, and this wave adds algebraically to the initial wave.

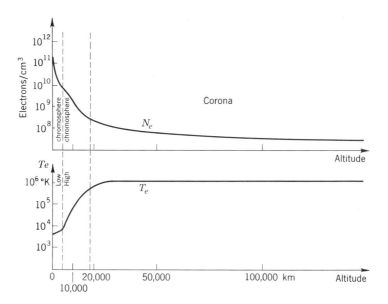

Fig. 7-3 Electron density and electron temperature in the solar atmosphere according to van de Hulst's model.

The calculation, which is not at all difficult, leads to the conclusion that the refractive index n of the medium is given by

$$n = \left(1 - \frac{\nu_c^2}{\nu^2}\right)^{1/2}$$

where ν is the frequency of the radio wave, and ν_c is a certain critical frequency given by

$$\nu_c = \left(\frac{N_e e^2}{4\pi^2 \epsilon_0 m}\right)^{1/2}$$

In these equations, N_e is the number of electrons per unit volume, e is their electric charge, m the mass, and ϵ_0 the permittivity of free space.

Note that the refractive index is less than unity; this means that radio waves are refracted in the opposite sense to light waves when they penetrate a denser medium.[1] Propagation becomes impossible when the quantity $(1 - \nu_c^2/\nu^2)$ becomes negative, i.e., when the wave frequency is less than the critical frequency of the medium, as happens when the density of the ionized gas becomes great enough.

This property is of major importance. In particular it governs the propagation of radio waves to great distances over the surface of the earth. The atmosphere of our globe consists, above a height of 60 kilometers, of partially ionized air layers which block the passage of radio waves of frequency less than the critical frequency (of the order of 10 Mc/s). Lower-frequency waves coming from a terrestrial station are then reflected by the ionosphere and can reach very distant points. Similarly, radio waves from the sky do not penetrate the ionosphere if their frequency is less than 10 Mc/s, i.e., if their wavelength is more than about 30 m. This accounts for the long wavelength limit of the radio window in the atmosphere.

Returning to the solar atmosphere, we find that at each point radio waves of all frequencies are emitted, but at each frequency there exists a critical layer that the waves cannot penetrate (Fig. 7-4). So, with radio telescopes which receive only a narrow frequency band, we detect radiation only from regions of the solar atmosphere which are situated at greater heights than the corresponding critical layer. The less the frequency of observation, the higher the critical layer above the photosphere. In fact, as we have seen, the electron density decreases with altitude, and so does the critical frequency, which varies in the same sense.

Figure 7-5 shows the appearance of the sun on several wavelengths.

---

[1] This seems at first sight to raise another difficulty. The velocity of propagation of the wave should be c/n, which is greater than the velocity of light c, and appears to contradict the theory of relativity. In fact, it may be shown that it is a matter only of the velocity with which the wave form is propagated (or its phase; hence the name "phase velocity"). But the energy transported by the wave travels only at a velocity nc, which is less than c, and the energy is the only thing that counts.

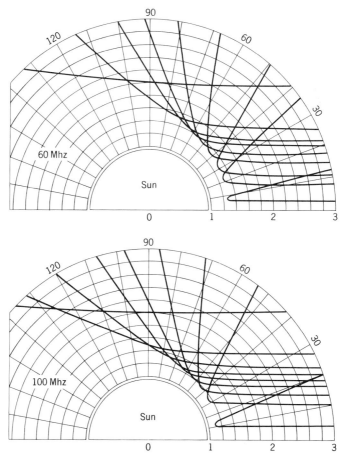

Fig. 7-4 Radio-frequency ray paths in the solar corona at two frequencies. It is seen that the rays undergo total reflection at an altitude which increases as the frequency decreases. *(Jaeger and Westfold.)*

It varies considerably between centimeter wavelengths and meter wavelengths. The overall emission, which also comes out of the calculation, is given in Fig. 7-6 superimposed on the black-body radiation for comparison.

The essential point of the theoretical study of the quiet-sun radiation is that most of the radiation at a given frequency comes from a rather thin layer of the solar atmosphere situated immediately above the critical layer for that frequency. In practice this allows any particular layer of the solar atmosphere to be studied by observing its radio emission at a carefully chosen frequency. The observation can be made in front of the solar disk itself, with no fear of the dazzling phenomena which prevent optical observations of the corona in front of the disk. We shall see that this important property is often valid for the active sun also. In general, the radiation on a given frequency is produced in a particular layer of the solar atmosphere.

What we have just said is strictly applicable only to the central parts of the radio sun. On the limbs the radio-frequency rays stay well above the critical layer, as Fig. 7-4 shows, at least at low frequencies, making the study of these regions particularly difficult.

Furthermore, it is generally very hard to observe the distribution of radio brightness temperature over the sun, i.e., to make up maps with detailed isophotes. This is a result of the small angular diameter of the sun, which subtends an angle of only 32 minutes in the visible, and few radio telescopes or interferometers at the present time have sufficient resolving power to give clear results. Among these we may mention Christiansen's interferometer in Australia, with resolving power of 3 minutes at 21 cm, that of the Carnegie Institution of Washington (4.8 minutes at 88 cm), and those of Covington in Canada (1.2′ × 2° at 10 cm) and Bracewell and Swarup in California (3.1′ × 3.1′ at 9.1 cm). The Nançay interferometer has a resolving power of 3.8 minutes on 1.77 m in the east-west direction and, like Christiansen's, has also a north-south line which permits emitting regions to be localized in that direction.

Eclipses also yield valuable information about the appearance of the radio sun. During an eclipse the moon successively covers up different parts of the sun, and only the radiation from the rest can be received.

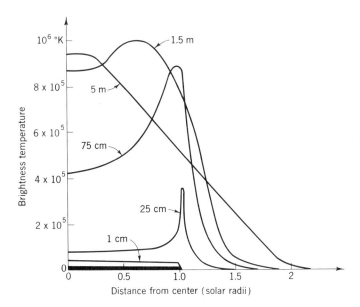

Fig. 7-5 Appearance of the radio sun on different wavelengths of observation. The visible sun is indicated by the heavy line.

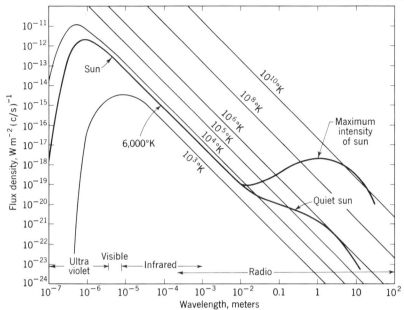

Fig. 7-6 The optical and radio-frequency continuum spectrum of the sun. On this figure the flux-density spectrum that would be received from a black body with the dimensions of the solar disk has been graphed for different temperatures. It is seen that in the optical region the sun radiates approximately like a black body at 6000°K; but it radiates at a much higher temperature on radio wavelengths, where its apparent diameter is larger and the emission originates in much hotter layers. Some radio bursts correspond to much higher equivalent temperatures still, but in such cases the emission is not thermal. *(Kraus and Ko.)*

Roughly speaking, interferometric observations and eclipses have confirmed the theoretical results obtained by Denisse and Smerd: uniform disk at 1 cm, limb brightening from 3 cm to some decimeters, limb darkening on meter wavelengths. The dimensions of the radio sun increase rapidly with wavelength. Whereas the visible disk is perfectly circular, the radio object is flattened, especially on meter wavelengths at the time of solar minimum. Its appearance then recalls that of the optical corona; this is not surprising because we know that the radio emission on long wavelengths comes from there.

The solar atmosphere extends far into space. Though it may not be possible to detect its radio and optical emission at an altitude more than 2 or 3 solar radii above the photosphere, nevertheless it exerts a strong influence on radio waves passing through it, even at much greater altitudes. This fact has been brought out by numerous observations of the Crab nebula, the intense radio source which passes in the neighborhood of the sun each year around 14 June. It appears greatly enlarged when it gets behind the outer corona, and the effect is appreciable as soon as the radio source is within an angular distance of 20 solar radii from the sun. The apparent magnification of the source is accompanied by a change in flux density, although the agreement between different measurements is not very good. Among others, Hewish in England and Vitkevich in the Soviet Union seem to observe a decrease in the flux density on longer wavelengths, while in France Boischot, on the shorter wavelength of 1.77 m, finds an increase in intensity which could be explained by some lens effect due to refraction in the outer corona. However this may be, radio observations demonstrate the considerable extension of the corona beyond its visible limits.

THE SLOWLY VARYING COMPONENT

It is very rare for the radio sun to be perfectly quiet. On centimeter and decimeter wavelengths bright localized regions can be observed almost all the time simultaneously with the steady radiation of the quiet sun; in fact, they interfere with its observation. To overcome their effect, it is necessary to superimpose large numbers of recordings obtained at different times as, for example, Pick-Gutmann has done on 3 cm (Fig. 7-7).

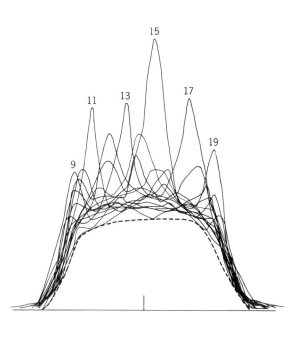

Fig. 7-7 Superposition of 15 solar interferograms taken on 3 cm in July 1959 with the 16-element interferometer at Nançay with a resolution of about 4 minutes of arc. The lower envelope of these curves in principle represents the contribution of the quiet sun, but the number of records is here insufficient and a slight asymmetry without physical significance remains. Note the rotation and evolution of the intense active center as followed at 2-day intervals.

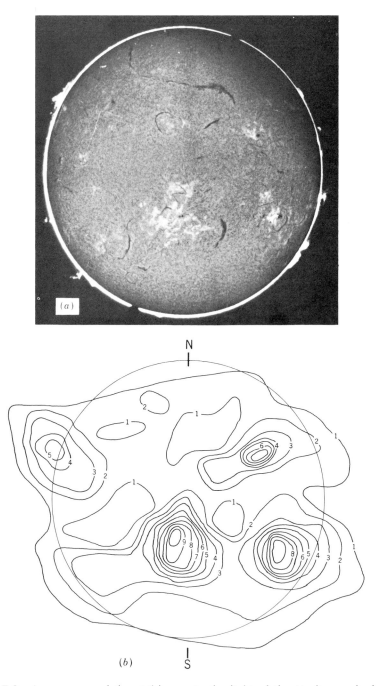

Fig. 7-8 Appearance of the visible sun in the light of the Hα line and of the radio sun on 21 cm on the same day (3 December 1957). The active regions, visible as bright plages on the monochromatic photograph above, correspond closely with radio condensations. One of these is distinctly above the east limb and corresponds to a spot, situated on the limb and hardly visible on the photograph. *(Christiansen.)*

These emission regions, which last for several days or weeks, or even for 1 or 2 months, give out remarkably stable radio emission, whose spectrum covers the whole centimeter and decimeter range. A cursory glance at their positions on the solar disk shows that they always coincide with active regions on the sun's surface containing facular plages and spots (Fig. 7-8). As a result of the sun's rotation about its axis, the spots appear at the east limb, move across the visible disk, and disappear at the west limb in a period of 2 weeks. They may reappear after another 2 weeks, in accordance with the 27-day solar rotation. The centers of emission associated with them do the same, and a center that has already been observed is often seen to reappear after one rotation of the sun. According to Christiansen, their lifetime may reach 3 months. A sequence from the regular daily maps made with the Stanford cross antenna (Fig. 7-9) is shown in Fig. 7-10.

It is interesting to look more deeply into the relations between the spots, the facular plages, and the regions of radio emission which we refer

Fig. 7-9 A cross antenna at Stanford University, used for studying the sun at 9 cm with a 3-minute pencil beam.

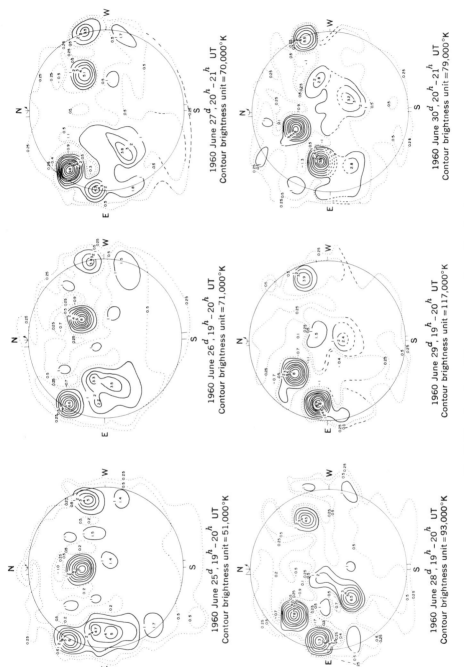

1960 June 25^d, 19^h – 20^h UT
Contour brightness unit = 51,000°K

1960 June 26^d, 19^h – 20^h UT
Contour brightness unit = 71,000°K

1960 June 27^d, 20^h – 21^h UT
Contour brightness unit = 70,000°K

1960 June 28^d, 19^h – 20^h UT
Contour brightness unit = 93,000°K

1960 June 29^d, 19^h – 20^h UT
Contour brightness unit = 117,000°K

1960 June 30^d, 20^h – 21^h UT
Contour brightness unit = 79,000°K

Fig. 7-10   A series of 9-cm maps made at Stanford.

to as *radio condensations*. It is known that their evolution resembles that of the faculae more closely than that of the spots. Furthermore, their average dimensions (several minutes of arc) are like those of the plages, and their intensity is closely correlated with plage area.

As the maximum brightness temperature of radio condensations is around 2×10^6 °K, which is of the order of the electron temperature in the corona, it is probable that it simply represents the thermal emission of regions with higher density and temperature than normal. These regions are situated in the lower corona above the plages (Fig. 7-11). Their altitude can be directly observed by noticing that on 21 cm, for example, the radio condensations corresponding to spots situated on the sun's limb appear outside the optical disk. Such condensations are visible on Figs. 7-8 and 7-10.

On the shortest wavelengths (3 cm, for example) the phenomena get more complicated. In addition to the radio condensations we have just been speaking of, bright regions are observed during periods of strong solar activity with very small diameters comparable with sunspot diameters. The emission exhibits circular polarization, indicating that it originates in a region where the magnetic field is very strong. These condensations, observed by Kundu and Steinberg with the 3-cm Nançay interferometer, are probably regions immediately overlying sunspots where the magnetic field

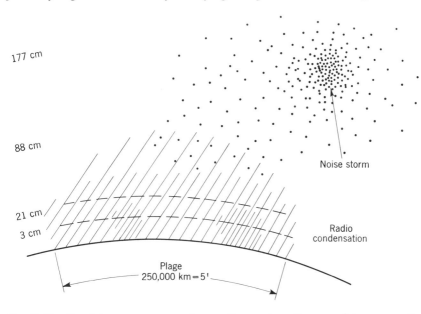

Fig. 7-11 Possible appearance of a radio condensation overlying an active region (facular plage). This structure is essentially determined by the magnetic field (see Fig. 7-15). According to Christiansen, it is the magnetic field that maintains the hot dense gas of the radio condensations in position. (*Minnaert.*)

is particularly strong.[1] They should perhaps be compared with the temporary enhancement of the solar centimeter radiation, referred to as a "gradual rise and fall," which is also circularly polarized.

On the long-wavelength side, the situation is likewise rather complex. Recent observations by Firor in America on 88 cm reveal the existence of a transition range between the centers of slowly varying emission and the noise-storm centers described later. Perhaps the radiation on frequencies around 88 cm comes from a zone lying between the true radio condensation and the coronal region where the noise storm takes place (see Fig. 7-11). According to circumstances, the emission assumes the character of the slowly varying component or of a noise storm.

On the meter wavelengths there also exists a slowly varying component discovered by Boischot and Simon with the large Nançay interferometer on 1.77 m. It comes from very extensive diffuse regions and is apparently thermal. These meter-wave condensations have not yet been definitely correlated with optical observations or with condensations on centimeter and decimeter wavelengths.

The total flux density of the quiet sun on 1.77 m and also its shape vary slowly over intervals of a few months or years. The flux density changes being as much as 20 percent, one might ask whether the very idea of a quiet sun has any meaning on meter wavelengths. Observations that will be made during the period of solar minimum around 1964 will no doubt allow this question to be answered.

As we see, the slow variations of the radio emission which seemed to be well understood some time ago have kept a few surprises for us. It is the same with all the solar phenomena; nothing definite can be said about them except with the greatest caution. Nevertheless, the work carried out by radio astronomers in recent years has led to very interesting interpretations of radio bursts and noise storms, which we shall now discuss.

First we shall recall briefly some of the essential characteristics of chromospheric flares, those phenomena of optical solar activity with which bursts and noise storms are strongly correlated.

CHROMOSPHERIC FLARES

The active regions of the sun in the neighborhood of sunspots frequently produce tremendous local explosions which show up as sudden increases of the light intensity, followed by slow decreases lasting several tens of minutes. The flash of light mainly concerns the spectral lines of hydrogen, which appear strongly in emission above the continuous spectrum. This property enables flares to be brought out by photographing the sun through

---

[1] In the sunspots themselves the magnetic induction often reaches 2,000 to 3,000 gauss.

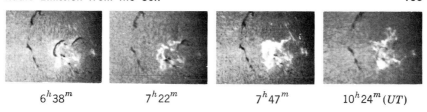

6^h38^m 7^h22^m 7^h47^m $10^h24^m\,(UT)$

Fig. 7-12 A large chromospheric flare. Four successive shots of the class 3+ flare of 3 July 1957 taken at Meudon in Hα with the spectroheliograph, or Lyot filter. Between 6^h38^m and 7^h22^m the sudden disappearance (ejection?) of a dark filament is observed and the start of a bright flare, which reaches its maximum around 7^h47^m and then gradually disappears while a secondary flare visible as a bright point at 10^h24^m develops.

a monochromatic filter which lets through only light of the Hα line, or by means of a spectroheliograph, which leads to the same results by a different procedure. Figure 7-12 shows monochromatic photographs in the Hα line of a group of spots with a flare going on around them. The development of the flare can be followed by cinematography. Unfortunately, flares are rarely visible in white light; this explains why continuous flare observation became practicable only with the introduction of the monochromatic filter invented by Lyot in 1933. Enormous amounts of information on solar flares are available, however, for the solar cycle which is now drawing to a close. This information is far from being fully analyzed, especially as flares are a very frequent phenomenon at times of solar activity.

The mechanism which sets off flares is still unknown. The Soviet astrophysicist Severny is inclined to think that it may be a question of pinch effect in an electrical discharge under the influence of the magnetic field of the spots. Shock waves so produced would raise the temperature locally to 10^7 °K. Then X rays would be emitted and perhaps thermonuclear reactions would set in.

About half of the solar flares are observed to be accompanied by an ejection of matter. Figure 7-13 shows a remarkable case of this phenomenon, generally referred to as a surge, for which no satisfactory explanation has yet been found. The velocity of ascent of the jet is generally of the order of 200 kilometers per second, but rises occasionally to 500 or even 1,000 kilometers per second. After reaching an altitude greater than one-tenth of a solar radius in the corona, the surge sometimes descends slowly toward the surface, following the same path it followed on the way up, but it is possible that some part is ejected from the sun.

It is particularly instructive to study the relations between chromospheric flares and the magnetic field of sunspots. The existence of this magnetic field has been known for a long time; its intensity is measured by

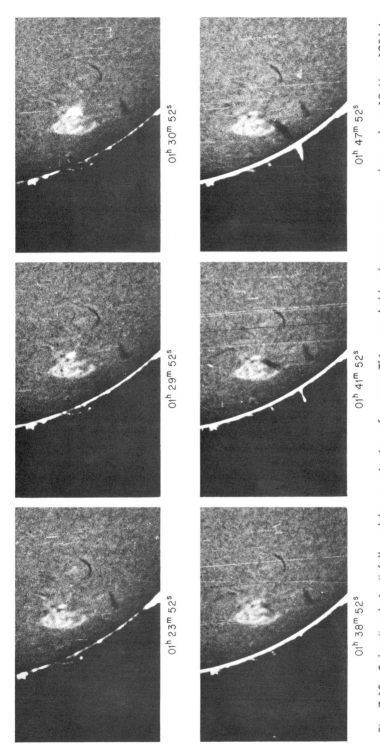

01ʰ 23ᵐ 52ˢ   01ʰ 29ᵐ 52ˢ   01ʰ 30ᵐ 52ˢ

01ʰ 38ᵐ 52ˢ   01ʰ 41ᵐ 52ˢ   01ʰ 47ᵐ 52ˢ

Fig. 7-13 Solar "explosion" followed by an ejection of matter. This remarkable phenomenon was observed on 18 May 1956 in Australia by Giovanelli and McCabe. A bright point develops very rapidly in the heart of a chromospheric flare (photos 1, 2, and 3). Photo 4 shows that this explosion expels a jet of dark matter, whose evolution is shown on photos 5 and 6. These frames also show that matter too transparent to be seen against the solar disk, but visible beyond the limb, was ejected before the dark matter. *(Giovanelli.)*

134

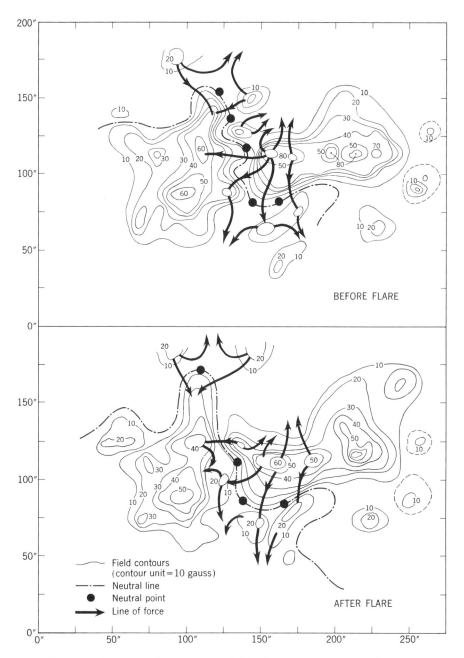

Fig. 7-14 Evolution of the magnetic field of a sunspot group after a large flare (22 August 1958). Contours of equal intensity of the vertical component of the magnetic field are shown with a contour unit of 10 gauss, and the direction of the lines of force is indicated by arrows. The broken curve is the neutral line separating two regions of opposite magnetic polarity, and the large black dots are the neutral points at whose level the flares occur. Note the diminution of the intensity maxima and the simplification of the field structure. *(Severny.)*

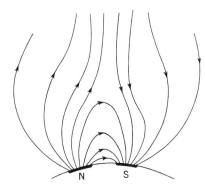

Fig. 7-15 Possible appearance of the magnetic field overlying a sunspot group after a large flare. The lines of force leave the spot N in the direction of the spot S. Part of the field is pulled out into interplanetary space.

observing the Zeeman splitting of certain lines of the solar spectrum. In particular, it has been noted that most sunspot groups are divided into two parts, one of which corresponds to a north magnetic pole and the other to a south pole.

Recently Severny has succeeded in obtaining very detailed maps of the magnetic field in spot groups and plages at the Crimean Astrophysical Observatory, following a method due to Babcock. The flares he observed began preferentially in places where the magnetic field was weak or zero, i.e., at neutral points. After the flare, the structure of the magnetic field was rearranged in detail, and its total intensity was less (Fig. 7-14).[1] Part of the magnetic energy has disappeared, either because part of the magnetic field has been carried off by the material expelled at the time of the flare or because charged particles have been accelerated at the expense of the magnetic field. Of course, both these phenomena could happen simultaneously.

After certain intense flares the magnetic perturbation may have the form represented in Fig. 7-15. Part of the magnetic field of the active region has been ejected into the outer corona in the form of a sort of magnetic tube, which leaves the solar atmosphere and trails off into the interplanetary medium. According to several astrophysicists, e.g., Parker and Piddington, the cloud of gas expelled by the flare carries a certain amount of magnetic field right out of the corona. The magnetic structure we have just described would be capable of persisting for rather a long time, possibly several solar rotations.[2] We shall see that this explains the relation between solar activity and certain terrestrial phenomena as well as the properties of bursts and radio noise storms.

It is not impossible that only active regions having these magnetic tubes can produce bursts and noise storms, disturb the upper atmosphere

---

[1] It should, however, be mentioned that Babcock observes no modification of the magnetic field after flares.

[2] The daily observations of the solar magnetic field made by Babcock at Mount Wilson frequently reveal residual local magnetic fields after the disappearance of the spots with which they were connected.

and terrestrial magnetic field, and finally emit cosmic rays. We shall return to this point later.

This might well be considered a bold hypothesis. Without having any illusions over its essentially provisional character, we have thought it well to say a few words about it. Rather than satisfying ourselves with a simple formal description of the radio phenomena, we always prefer to concentrate on their physical aspect and to give interpretations even though they are very uncertain. This is the spirit in which we shall take up the study of radio bursts.

THE FIRST PHASE: BURSTS OF TYPES III AND V

As we have implied, chromospheric flares are often followed by a group of very intense and complex bursts. Until recent years observations were too incomplete to give a precise idea of the relations between the optical phenomena and the radio bursts and to attempt a general description of the radio events following a solar flare. Now we can localize the center of emission on the sun, follow its movements, and obtain at each instant the spectrum of its radio emission. So our ideas on radio bursts have become much clearer.

As a rule, bursts follow flares. Isolated bursts, which are apparently independent of any visible phenomenon, are now considered much rarer than formerly. Therefore it is logical to try to understand the radio phenomena strictly in relation with optical phenomena. This is what the Australians Giovanelli and Wild in particular have done, and we shall borrow the essentials of what follows from them.

Wild distinguishes two phases in the radio event which follows a flare. The first, which follows immediately after the visible event, consists of a series of very short and very intense bursts (type III bursts) occasionally followed on long wavelengths by emission of appreciable duration (type V bursts). The second phase reproduces the first on a much longer time scale. A large type II burst is followed by a strong increase in radio flux which may persist for several hours (type IV bursts). The phenomenon of which we have just given a glimpse appears in full dress only after the biggest flares. If the flare is small, only the first phase may appear; the second appears, in any case, in only one-third of the strong (class 3) flares. Furthermore, not all type III bursts are accompanied by emission of type V, nor type II bursts by type IV. Nevertheless, we think it is particularly interesting to attempt the description of a complete radio event, since it includes the principal types of known bursts, and we shall be careful not to forget

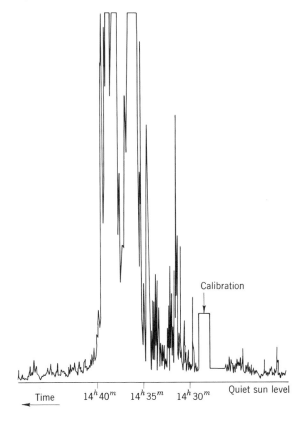

Calibration

Time 14^h40^m 14^h35^m 14^h30^m Quiet sun level

Fig. 7-16 Record of a type II burst preceded by a group of short type III bursts. This observation, made on 169 Mc/s at Nançay on 2 August 1957, shows a series of type III bursts between 14^h30^m and 14^h35^m and a strong double type II burst.

that such phenomena happen only rarely in reality. Let us examine the first phase first.

Among solar bursts the simplest are those of type III. Radiation suddenly increases in a few seconds and then falls back to its initial value. These bursts happen mostly (in 70 percent of cases) during a chromospheric flare, often occurring in groups (Fig. 7-16). A remarkable fact is that each burst occurs first on a wavelength of the order of 50 cm, then appears on progressively longer wavelengths. This led Wild, as early as 1950, to construct a panoramic receiver which takes continuous radio spectra over a large frequency range. The principle of this instrument was described in an earlier chapter. The spectrum of a type III burst obtained this way (Fig. 7-17) is very revealing. The emission at each moment occurs only in a very narrow frequency band some Mc/s wide, which quickly moves toward long wavelengths. If we remember that the emission of a wave of given frequency takes place in principle in regions of the solar atmosphere situated a little above the critical layer, this phenomenon is capable of a very simple interpretation. Suppose that the type III burst is due to a single disturbance which rises very rapidly through the corona. As it passes through, it will excite emission which at each instant involves a definite layer of the solar atmosphere. That the emission is due to plasma oscillations is quite possible and tends to be proved by the narrowness of the frequency band in which the radiation occurs and by the facts that it is frequently accompanied by a double-frequency harmonic and that the

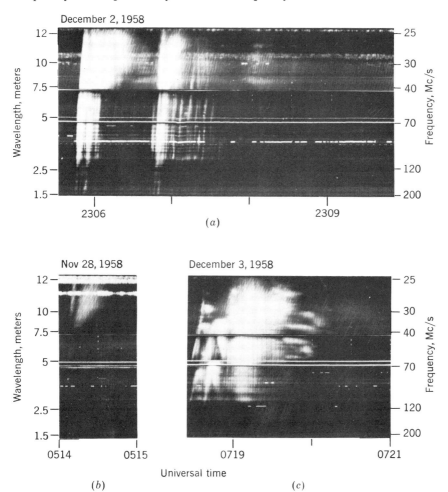

Fig. 7-17 Dynamic spectra of groups of type III bursts. These remarkable records are due to Wild. Note the speed of frequency drift of each burst. Certain type III bursts are followed by brief continuum emission showing up in the form of a sort of diffuse cloud referred to as a type V burst. At c is seen an inverted-U burst, accompanied by a harmonic and followed by a type IV burst. See also Fig. 7-20.

diameter of the source is large.[1] Now, the plasma oscillation takes place at the critical frequency of the medium. As this goes down with increasing height in the solar atmosphere, the emission frequency decreases with time in accordance with observation. For an average type III burst, the frequency drift corresponds to an enormous velocity of ascent of the disturbance, of the order of 60,000 kilometers per second. It would obviously be interesting to measure directly the motion of a type III burst through the solar atmosphere. Wild has recently solved this very difficult problem with the help of an interferometer whose frequency can be swept from 40 to 70 Mc/s each half second. With this equipment, which is unique of its kind, Wild measures an average velocity of 150,000 kilometers per second, which is thus greater than that deduced from dynamic spectra. As it is probable that the disturbed regions where type III bursts originate, and which overlie sunspots, are denser than the rest of the corona, the critical layers are higher there and the velocities obtained from dynamic spectra are underestimated. We can therefore confirm that type III bursts are produced by a disturbance which rises through the corona with an enormous velocity.

The origin of the disturbance responsible for type III bursts now seems clearly established, thanks to the work of Giovanelli. He has demonstrated the simultaneity of type III bursts with brief and violent puffs, which explode from the heart of a flare. A very fine example is shown in Fig. 7-13. We have noted that these phenomena are accompanied by an ejection of matter. They are also certainly the cause of a much faster disturbance which produces the burst.

Certain type III bursts are followed by longer-lasting emission which appears only on wavelengths greater than a few meters. This phenomenon, which was recently discovered by Wild with the help of his panoramic receiver, has been called a type V burst. Figure 7-17 shows a few examples of dynamic spectra obtained by Wild, where it is clearly seen that the type V bursts following those of type III appear in the form of intense continuum emission over a wide frequency range. No fine structure can be seen. Only synchrotron emission from high-speed electrons in a magnetic field, whose characteristics were studied in the last chapter, can explain this emission, which involves a very extensive region in the outer corona. Plasma oscillations and gyromagnetic emission cannot account for the stability and the width of the emission spectrum, which is certainly not thermal. The strong-

---

[1] No doubt we are dealing with a swarm of very fast charged particles which excite plasma oscillations on their way, as Shklovsky suggested in 1947. Other authors, such as de Jager, relate the exciting disturbance to a hydromagnetic wave (longitudinal Alfvén wave) which could propagate in the solar corona at 150,000 kilometers per second, provided the magnetic field reaches 1,000 gauss there. Although high, this value is by no means impossible, and we shall have to wait for future studies to decide finally between these two mechanisms.

est type V bursts require some 10^{33} electrons with energies of the order of 2 million electron volts.

Wild thinks that type III and type V bursts are due to one and the same cause. During the chromospheric explosion, a large number of electrons with speeds very close to that of light are ejected by an unknown mechanism. They rise through the corona with a velocity apparently less than that of light, because their trajectory forms a helix around the lines of magnetic force. On their way, they excite the plasma oscillations required to explain the type III burst.[1] In favorable conditions, which have yet to be clarified, these electrons radiate by the synchrotron mechanism, and their radiation is capable of escaping from the solar corona and being observed on the earth. So much for type V emission.

What happens to the electrons then? In most cases they must leave the solar corona and spread through interplanetary space. In other circumstances, the structure of the magnetic field in the outer corona is such as to force them to return to the photosphere along arched lines of force. Then we observe a burst whose dynamic spectrum resembles an inverted U. The first branch corresponds to the ascent of the disturbance and the second to its descent (see Fig. 7-17*c*). This special burst may also be accompanied by type V emission.

Many points remain to be cleared up. For example, many optical explosions that are probably responsible for radio bursts certainly go unnoticed because of their small dimensions. Then again, type V bursts can still be detected only in Australia and Texas because the panoramic receivers in use elsewhere do not cover the wavelength range where these bursts occur. Finally, J. A. Roberts, using a panoramic receiver covering the range from 400 to 900 Mc/s, has observed a number of brief bursts which somewhat resemble type III bursts, but which occur at unusual frequencies. Many observations are thus still necessary before the problems posed by type III bursts in particular are solved.

THE SECOND PHASE: TYPE II AND TYPE IV BURSTS

During the most intense flares, type III and type V bursts are followed by other more spectacular and longer-lasting radio phenomena. They are much rarer, occurring as already mentioned in only one-third of class 3 flares (the strongest under the international classification) and they are often incomplete. We should repeat that the radio event connected with flares

---

[1] Wild therefore thinks that the disturbance responsible for type III bursts is a jet of electrons and not a longitudinal Alfvén wave as suggested by de Jager. Wild's ideas do not require extremely strong magnetic fields in the corona.

occurs in full only in rare cases. More frequently its appearance is fragmentary.

The second phase of this phenomenon starts with a large burst of type II, often called an outburst (see Fig. 7-16). Like type III bursts, type II bursts drift over the various frequencies of the radio spectrum. They appear progressively over an extensive range reaching from decimeter to decameter waves.

Panoramic receivers show us how type II bursts develop (Fig. 7-18). At each instant the emission is confined to a band about 50 Mc/s wide which slowly moves toward lower frequencies. The band often shows splitting, and it is a remarkable fact that it is often accompanied by a second harmonic which seems to occur only on meter waves. At a given frequency this harmonic appears on the record as a sort of echo of the fundamental, coming 5 minutes later. If it is supposed that type II bursts, like type III's, are caused by a rising disturbance, it can be deduced from the dynamic spectrum that the ascent velocity is of the order of 500 kilometers per second. Wild has succeeded in measuring this speed directly by interferometric observations of the motion of the source. Here again he observes higher values than those given by the dynamic spectra, which can be explained by the fact that the solar atmosphere is denser above sunspot groups than elsewhere. It is now accepted that the outward velocity is from 1,000 to 1,500 kilometers per second.

Giovanelli and Roberts succeeded in identifying the optical phenomena associated with a number of type II bursts. In all the cases they observed, the burst followed an ejection of matter from the level of the visible flare, and the association between the two phenomena is definite. Nevertheless, the rising disturbance responsible for type II bursts cannot be identified with the jet of matter itself. The speeds are too different, amounting usually to 200 or 300 kilometers per second for the ejected matter, whereas the center of the burst usually rises at 1,000 or 1,500 kilometers per second. This difficulty disappears if one adopts Westfold's suggestion that the disturbance causing the burst is a shock wave created in the corona by the matter ejected from the flare. Plasma oscillations are set up by the passage of this wave and produce radio emission. We may note that the ejections of matter associated with type II bursts always take place with speeds greater than the speed of sound in the corona (about 170 kilometers per second), which is the condition for the production of a strong shock wave.[1]

[1] The speed of surges seen optically nevertheless seems a little low to explain the high velocity of propagation of a shock wave. And it is not impossible that the flare ejects material which is generally invisible but has a speed of the order of 800 to 1,000 kilometers per second. These figures have been sometimes measured for visible ejections. Furthermore, although the surges often fall back toward the photosphere after reaching a certain height, it is probable that some of the material sometimes escapes from the sun (see Fig. 7–22).

As the shock wave and ejected material pass through the solar atmosphere, its local structure is completely upset. We shall return to this point later. In particular, it is possible that conditions favorable to charged-particle acceleration are created, the source of the type II bursts then behaving like a genuine particle accelerator. This idea is based on recent observations. By careful examination of the dynamic spectra of type II bursts, J. A. Roberts and Haddock have found that they often possess a fine structure. The wide spectral range of the type II contains in this case a large number of short bursts which rather resemble type III bursts. Now we have seen that these no doubt result from plasma oscillations set up by the passage of fast particles. The charged particles accelerated by the shock wave responsible for the type II bursts might play an exactly comparable role. The emission of the large bursts would thus be accompanied by individual type III bursts. Roberts observes in some cases a more complex fine structure corresponding to type III bursts going both up and down (the frequency of the latter increases very rapidly with time). It is almost obvious that the particles are ejected in several directions simultaneously from the place where the shock wave passes.

We are still far from explaining all the peculiarities of type II bursts. The presence of a harmonic in more than 60 percent of these bursts is no great difficulty. It arises from the fact that the plasma oscillations generating the emission are not sinusoidal and have very large amplitudes. The second harmonic is also often found with bursts of type III. The splitting of each band, both the fundamental and the harmonic, which is very frequently observed (see Figs. 7-16 and 7-18), is more puzzling. It is most unlikely that this phenomenon corresponds to two distinct disturbances. The only reasonable explanation is that given by Roberts, who invokes Zeeman splitting of the emission frequency, under the influence of the sunspot magnetic field, but there is nothing certain about this.

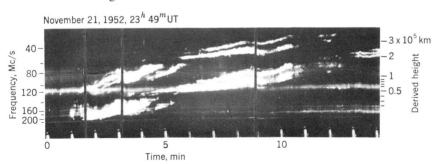

November 21, 1952, $23^h 49^m$ UT

Fig. 7-18 Dynamic spectrum of a large type II burst. This very complex burst shows splitting and is accompanied by a harmonic which exactly reproduces the characteristics of the fundamental. The emission at 120 Mc/s is due to a terrestrial transmitter. *(Wild.)* See also Fig. 7-20.

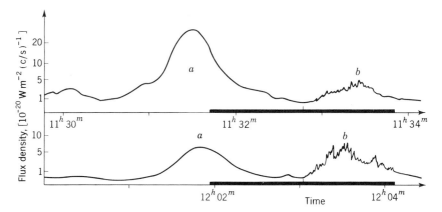

Fig. 7-19 (a) Type IV source and *(b)* noise storm, 20 November 1956. These records show the transit of the radio sun through two lobes of the great Nançay interferometer on 169 Mc/s. The visible disk is indicated by the heavy line. The type IV source situated beyond the west limb of the sun is very wide and shows intense but steady emission. The noise storm situated on the east of the sun, however, is greatly disturbed. *(Boischot.)*

The big type II bursts are sometimes followed by a further increase in intensity, lasting from 10 minutes to a few hours, and are often circularly polarized. These long-lasting bursts were originally identified with noise storms, and their study was undertaken in France on the installation of the big Nançay interferometer. It was soon seen that this conception had to be revised. The burst shows no rapid changes, and the emission remains very stable over the course of time. Its intensity is very high, much greater in general than that of a noise storm. Finally, a characteristic that was discovered only later is that the emission takes place simultaneously on centimeter, decimeter, and meter waves. These facts led Boischot to distinguish a new type of emission that he called a type IV burst. Figure 7-19 shows an interferometric record of a type IV burst and noise storm taking place simultaneously. The difference between the two phenomena is clearly seen. Also, the dimensions of the source of type IV emission are found to be very large, equal to one-third of the diameter of the visible disk.

Using panoramic receivers working from 100 to 600 Mc/s, Haddock and Maxwell succeeded in obtaining dynamic spectra of this type of emission. Figure 7-20 shows one of these records, which is very different from other bursts. The emission covers an extremely wide range of frequencies quite uniformly, and its continuous spectrum shows no rapid variation with time. One other phenomenon is no less remarkable: on meter wavelengths at least, the same region of the corona simultaneously emits a very wide range of wavelengths.

The type IV source, which is a cloud of considerable dimensions, first rises through the corona with a high velocity comparable to that of a type II (1,500 kilometers per second), then comes to rest, and disappears .at very great altitudes above the photosphere, sometimes 4 or 5 solar radii.

It is obvious that type IV bursts, whose brightness temperature reaches 10^{11} or even 10^{12} °K, are not thermal in origin. As early as 1957 Denisse and Boischot thought that the continuous spectrum of these bursts, which is very wide and stable, comes from synchrotron emission. This idea was later taken up by Wild to explain type V bursts, whose characteristics are somewhat similar to type IV, but last a shorter time and involve a more restricted range of frequencies. The synchrotron mechanism is the only one capable of explaining a stable burst involving a wide frequency range. The fact that all frequencies of a type IV burst come from the same point also supports this hypothesis. Furthermore, it can be shown that in the coronal regions where the emission takes place a relativistic electron can radiate for several hours before losing its energy by collision with another particle. This is just the duration that is observed in most cases.

Type IV bursts often follow a chromospheric flare and frequently accompany type II bursts, as we have mentioned. In our present state of knowledge, it is difficult to get a general idea of the behavior of type IV bursts, since they seem to come in wide variety. Therefore we shall simply

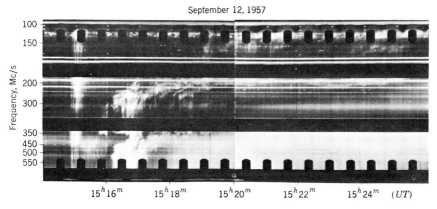

Fig. 7-20 Dynamic spectrum of types III, II, and IV. This historic spectrum, obtained on 12 September 1957 at the University of Michigan, shows the complex of radio phenomena connected with a large solar flare. From left to right are seen successively a group of type III bursts, a large type II burst (compare with Figs. 7-17 and 7-18), then a strong enhancement of the emission throughout the band from 550 to 300 Mc/s. This continuum emission free from all structure is characteristic of type IV bursts, of which this photograph is perhaps the first spectral recording. *(Haddock.)*

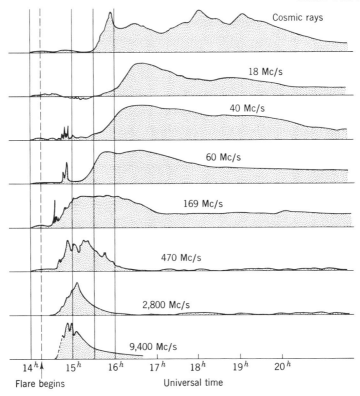

Fig. 7-21 Type IV burst connected with a flare of 22 August 1958 and the cosmic-ray event observed by balloon.

describe an interesting case of a burst associated with the flare of 22 August 1958 (Fig. 7-21). About 20 minutes after the start at the flare at 14^h17^m UT, a very rapid increase in radio flux was observed simultaneously on centimeter and decimeter wavelengths as far as 169 Mc/s. The type IV burst disappeared after 1½ hours on these wavelengths, but the emission persisted on 169 Mc/s and set in progressively on meter and decameter wavelengths. In this range of frequencies, its duration was very long, more than 6 hours. It is remarkable that the phenomenon was accompanied by an enhancement of cosmic radiation observed by Anderson and Winckler 45 minutes after the start of the type IV, which corresponds to particles with energies of the order of 100 million electron volts.

The type IV burst was preceded by a type II burst, which just appears at 169 Mc/s and is clearly visible on the lower frequencies.

At the present time, two successive phases are distinguished in the event of 22 August 1958 and about 20 known similar cases: (1) the type IV burst itself, which occurred simultaneouly on all frequencies above

169 Mc/s and lasted 1½ hours; (2) continuum emission limited to meter and decameter waves, differing from the type IV not only spectrally, but also by its smaller diameter of a few minutes of arc and its long duration (a few hours to some days), which relates it to the noise storms studied below; hence the name *continuum storm*.

Like noise storms, a continuum storm shows great radial directivity, being rarely observed when the flare occurs near the limb of the sun. The source of emission lies relatively low in the corona, between 0.2 and 0.4 solar radius at 1.77 m, near critical frequency. This second part of a type IV burst is more difficult to explain by the synchrotron mechanism than the first. J. F. Denisse proposes to explain the emission by a plasma Čerenkov process. High-energy particles which have been accelerated at the beginning of the flare would remain trapped somewhere near the sun in a magnetic configuration. These particles, slowly diffusing outside, would excite plasma longitudinal waves when entering higher-density regions, and these waves could transfer their energy to radio radiation. The magnetic configuration also stores cosmic rays from the flare, which slowly leak away.[1]

We must now try to understand the relation between type II and type IV bursts as well as the relation between the two parts of the complete radio event associated with an intense flare. As we have said, an initial explosion ejects both high-energy electrons and a mass of much slower material. The electrons rise rapidly through the corona, causing one or several type III bursts, possibly followed by a type V burst which lasts a few minutes. The jet of matter, which occasionally is visible optically, is much slower, although it moves faster than sound in the corona and creates a shock wave. Diagrams *A* and *B* of Fig. 7-22, due to the Australian McLean, represent the first two phases of the phenomenon. At *A* the explosion *e* occurs, and at *B* the jet of matter *j* is seen to rise, preceded by the shock wave *c*. As it is strongly ionized and therefore highly conducting, it takes with it part of the magnetic field of the sunspot group *tt*. In addition, high-energy electrons from the flare are captured in the magnetic field and cannot escape. At *C* the jet of matter preceded by the shock wave continues to rise, increasing in volume, dragging behind it the cloud of relativistic electrons *n*. The type II emission takes place at *c*, and the cloud *n* generates type IV radiation. Later on, the shock wave recedes into interplanetary space, together with the jet of ionized matter (diagram *D*), while the cloud of relativistic electrons comes to rest in the outer corona and emits synchrotron radiation for several hours. This requires the structure of the magnetic field to be such that the electrons remain trapped, although in a region of very large size.

We see that this phenomenon results in a complete rearrangement of the magnetic field overlying the sunspot group. Lines of force are pulled

[1] This explanation should be taken as provisional.

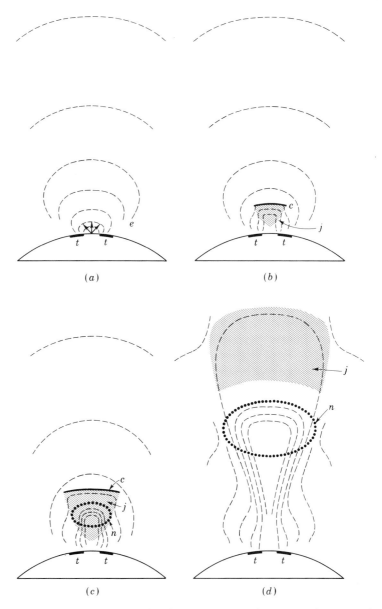

Fig. 7-22 Ejection of matter and radio burst. Lines of magnetic force are shown broken. The cloud of ejected matter is represented by cross-hatching, and *n* represents the center of the type IV source. *(McLean.)*

out of the solar atmosphere, and the final stage of the phenomenon is a tube of magnetic force which loses itself in interplanetary space. Figures 7-15 and 7-27 suggest its possible appearance. Perhaps this structure can be related to the coronal streamers seen optically during total eclipses, for the general appearance is rather similar.

We see that the study of radio bursts has led to considerable progress in solar physics. It was already known that the appearance and development of a center of activity was a phenomenon of magnetic origin. According to Kiepenheuer's striking picture, the development of an active center is simply the history of a magnetic bubble issuing from the depths of the star and appearing at the surface. What was less suspected was the importance of the electromagnetic phenomena associated with flares (which, we wish to emphasize, are very frequent events during active periods). Although they are difficult to study optically, still they are a preferred area of radio astronomical research. Yet another hurdle is the true nature of the chromospheric flares.

RADIO NOISE STORMS

These often very violent phenomena, which are one of the most spectacular manifestations of solar activity, were discovered in 1942 by Hey, one of the pioneers of radar. Noise storms can, in fact, be so intense that occasionally they completely jam radars working on meter wavelengths.

A noise storm differs from all other solar radio emission by two features: it occurs only on meter wavelengths, and it appears as a considerable enhancement of the total radiation of the sun together with very numerous and very short superimposed bursts. Records of this phenomenon, such as Fig. 7-23, fully justify the term *radio noise storm*. Storms may last some hours or even a few days, and the radiation exhibits strong circular polarization as regards both the continuous background and the short bursts, which are referred to as type I bursts.

The violence of noise storms and their considerable repercussions at the surface of our earth soon led radio astronomers to give them special attention. They have been the subject of many studies aimed especially at connecting them with sunspots and other optical manifestations of solar activity. We have to recognize that the results for a long time were deceptive, as long as interferometric measurements could not localize the emitting regions. It was to fill this gap that the big Nançay interferometer was constructed on a wavelength of 1.77 m (169 Mc/s), which was considered particularly favorable for studying noise storms. Daily positions of noise storms can be measured with a resolution of 3.8 minutes of arc in the east-west direction and about 7 minutes of arc in the north-south direction. The results are published in the form of a diagram giving the position of the

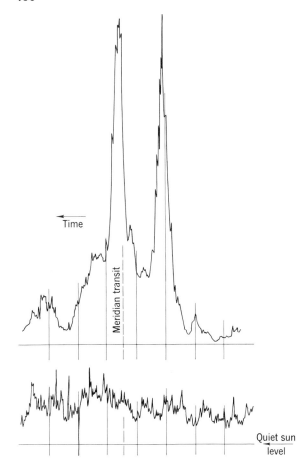

Fig. 7-23 Recording of a radio noise storm on 169 Mc/s on 17 August 1958. Above, record of the total radio flux density of the sun obtained with a single reflector at Nançay. Below, passage of the sun through the central lobe of the great interferometer at Nançay; two sources are simultaneously present, one on the west limb and the other near the central meridian. The time marks are generated automatically each minute.

emitting regions in the east-west direction plotted against the date (Fig. 7-24). Intensities are indicated by cross-hatching.

This equipment has brought considerable progress to the study of noise storms. It has been confirmed that they are more or less associated with a visible spot, but they do not necessarily fall vertically above the spot and appear to drift within the solar atmosphere. They certainly rotate with the sun as a whole, but their rotation curve is almost always different from what a stationary region would give. Height determinations lead to very high values: on 1.77 m the height varies between 0.5 and 1 solar radius above the photosphere, i.e., 350,000 to 700,000 kilometers. This altitude is well above the critical layer corresponding to the observed frequency.

The apparent diameter of noise storms is always quite small, less than 6 minutes of arc at 169 Mc/s. It is remarkable to see that a phenomenon which occurs at such a great height involves only such a small region of the solar atmosphere, a region which is often smaller than the facular plages and the radio condensations which overlie the plages. It should also be noticed that the emission from a noise storm is very strongly directive, and it is generally strongest when the storm is in the vicinity of the central meridian of the sun.

As was mentioned above, a noise storm is a superposition of two components both coming from the same region of the sun but apparently of different natures: the background continuum and the short type I bursts. Their relative strength is also quite variable as Boischot and Simon have shown. There are noise storms which are almost quiet, and others with unceasing bursts. In the range of wavelengths between the meter and decimeter waves, it is not easy to distinguish an almost quiet storm from the slowly varying component, and all gradations exist between these two types of emission, as observed by Firor on 88 cm. This does not help to simplify the interpretation of noise storms, and no definitive theory has been established.

It is nevertheless obvious that the emission is not thermal in character, as brightness temperatures above 10^9 °K are often observed, while the electron temperature in the solar corona hardly exceeds 10^6 °K. It clearly

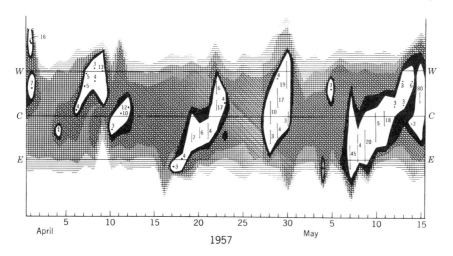

Fig. 7-24 Location of noise storms on the sun. This diagram is based on observations with the big Nançay interferometer. Each day the position of the sources is marked by points, or lines if the diameter is considerable, and the intensity is shown. Intensities outside the noise storms are indicated by cross-hatching. The east and west limbs and the center of the visible sun are indicated by *E, W,* and *C.* Note the simultaneous presence of two noise storms on 1 April, 22 April, and from 27 to 30 April.

originates in a region where there is a strong magnetic field, as proved by its conspicuous circular polarization. This field is certainly connected with the sunspot fields.

Knowing the magnetic field at the surface of the sunspots themselves makes it possible to calculate it at different heights in the overlying coronal region. It appears that the calculated field at the height of noise storms, which ranges from 350,000 to 700,000 kilometers, is too weak to exercise much influence over the propagation of radio waves. This appears to be in contradiction with observation, which shows pronounced refraction and strong circular polarization. We are thus led to think that the storms originate in a disturbed region of the corona where the magnetic field could be particularly strong. We shall return to this point later.

Unfortunately this gives us no information about the noise-storm emission mechanism itself. There is one feature that may lead us to the mechanism: the fact that the storm bursts are always very narrow-band. The only possible processes are those which generate well-determined frequencies and not a broad continuum, namely, plasma oscillations or gyromagnetic radiation. Twiss and Roberts in Australia assumed that a swarm of relatively fast electrons spiraling in the magnetic field reach the inside of the storm for each type I burst.

The gyromagnetic emission from these electrons can hardly account for the very high intensities that are often observed during noise storms. It would be more acceptable to assume that these electrons are capable of amplifying a preexisting radio wave by stimulated emission, but only in sharply defined frequency bands around the gyrofrequency.

We think it is interesting to make some comments on this admittedly bold hypothesis because of its considerable theoretical importance. It is actually the first time that such a possibility of amplification of natural radio waves has been indicated, although it has now been achieved in the laboratory with molecular amplifiers, or masers. Suppose that the corona contains high-energy electrons with an energy distribution as shown in Fig. 7-25. These electrons could exchange a fraction of their kinetic energy with the

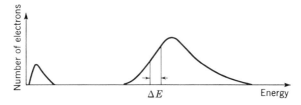

Fig. 7-25   Possibility of high-energy electrons amplifying by stimulated emission. If the electrons have an energy distribution of the type shown in the figure, those with energies corresponding to the heavy line can amplify radio waves by energy jumps such as ΔE.

radio-frequency radiation present in the medium. They could lose energy by emitting radio photons and gain it by absorbing them. These transitions obey the general laws of radiation enunciated above. Electrons with energies in the range indicated by the heavy line in Fig. 7-25, i.e., those whose number density increases with increasing energy, are particularly interesting. In fact, such a population of particles (which may be characterized by a negative excitation temperature) is capable of amplifying radio waves, since the stimulated emission outweighs the absorption as we have already shown. On condition that these are the only electrons to interact with the electromagnetic wave, this process can be sufficiently effective to explain the intensity of noise storms. We may point out that there is no difficulty in explaining the polarization of noise storms by this amplification mechanism, for the amplified wave exhibits the same polarization characteristics as the incident wave.

Although Twiss's theory is not based on a really solid foundation, it has the interest of showing that noise storms are apparently associated with the presence of high-energy electrons in the solar atmosphere. The acceleration of charged particles in the corona thus seems to be one of the fundamental manifestations of solar activity.

This remark takes on renewed interest when we study the relations between radio noise storms and other solar bursts as Avignon and Pick-Gutmann recently did. It is found that noise storms occur frequently above active regions which are also producing flares and radio bursts, especially type IV bursts. Although the observations bear on only a limited number of cases so far, it is probable that the correlation is rather close, and in all cases distinctly better than could be established between noise storms and the number, dimensions, and general appearance of sunspots. We have also seen above that type IV bursts may be followed by a continuum storm, which is very much like a noise storm; the only important difference is the absence, not necessarily total, of short bursts. If we agree with Twiss that noise-storm radiation is due to electrons with more than average energy, the only difference between this type of emission and the synchrotron mechanism for type IV bursts and continuum storms is the greater or lesser energy of the electrons involved.

We therefore believe that certain special spots, which could be called *radio spots,* may be capable of producing the family of rapidly varying radio phenomena described in the present chapter. Others, on the other hand, may not be the cause of any emission except the slowly varying component.[1] Radio spots are possibly characterized by the presence of the magnetic structure described above (see Fig. 7-15). The radio noise storms are

[1] It should be noted again that the intensity of the radio condensation seems to depend in part on burst activity of the spot according to Kundu's observations on 3 cm.

located in the tube itself. All the charged particles accelerated after a flare probably stay trapped inside this magnetic bottle and can escape only by diffusing downwards or upwards along the channel formed by the lines of force.[1]

In all probability, this structure persists for rather a long time, possibly several solar rotations. Indeed, the same radio spot frequently emits several consecutive type IV bursts and is overlain by a rather long-lived noise storm.

The sun also often has several active spots at the same time, each with its noise storm (see Figs. 7-23 and 7-24) and each emitting type IV bursts during the same period.

Let us hope that the coming years will clarify these still very confused problems and will finally give us a clear picture of solar radio-frequency activity. At present, it is certain that the magnetic field plays an absolutely fundamental role in solar phenomena. Very efficient charged-particle acceleration processes are likewise seen to be at work, and we shall find that the same is the case in many celestial sources of radio-frequency emission.

RADIO ASTRONOMY AND SOLAR-TERRESTRIAL RELATIONS

In addition to its theoretical interest, the sun also possesses exceptional practical interest. It does not restrict itself to furnishing the earth with the energy necessary for the life of its inhabitants, but exercises its influence in all sorts of ways, profoundly affecting the structure of the earth's upper atmosphere in particular. The study of the relation between solar and terrestrial phenomena is at the present time an extremely important branch of astronomy and geophysics, one that we can give only a brief glimpse of here.

The importance of the emission of radiation and corpuscles from the sun will have been suspected from what we have said above. It has been known for quite a long time that the ionized layers of the upper atmosphere, the ionosphere, are created by the ultraviolet and X radiation of the sun, these photons having enough energy to chip electrons off the atmospheric molecules.[2]

The solar origin of the ionosphere can be in no doubt. Furthermore,

[1] According to Denisse, it is also possible that noise storms, like continuum storms, can be explained by Čerenkov radiation from high-energy particles which are produced at the time of the flare and then trapped in the high corona by suitable magnetic configurations. They continue to fall back on the sun for several days down the magnetic tubes and radiate on reentering dense regions.

[2] This physical effect of solar short-wave radiation is always accompanied by photochemical effects which lead to the formation of molecules such as O_3, OH, and numerous ions (O_2^-, O^+, O_2^+, N_2^+, etc.) whose existence has been proved either directly by means of rockets or indirectly by the light emitted as the ions recombine.

the lowest ionospheric layer, at a height of 80 kilometers (D layer), exists only during the day and disappears at night. The E layer, which also vanishes during the night, is found at heights from 90 to 140 kilometers. Only the upper layers (F_1 and F_2) persist at night, although their electron density has a daily variation. All the layers show annual variations also. It is particularly interesting to note that the properties of the ionosphere undergo considerable modifications during the period of a total eclipse; this is a direct demonstration of the influence of the sun. When a flare occurs on the sun's surface, the structure of the ionosphere is strongly modified by the enhancement of the ultraviolet radiation. It has now been directly observed that the ultraviolet intensity goes well up during a flare. There may also be X-ray emission. These practically instantaneous flare effects are felt mainly in the D layer, where the electron density greatly increases and complete absorption sets in on radio wavelengths greater than about 10 m.[1] The practical consequences of this phenomenon are very important. In fact, the decameter waves used for long-distance communication pass through the D layer and are reflected by higher layers before reaching the receiver. Propagation is impossible when the D layer becomes totally absorbing and a large flare is accompanied by a complete fade-out of short-wave reception. This very annoying phenomenon involves the whole sunlit hemisphere and may last for several hours. Figure 7-26 shows an example of a fade-out accompanying a large radio burst.

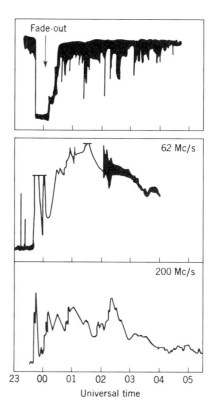

Fig. 7-26 Fade-out and large radio burst connected with the flare of 21–22 February 1950. This large flare observed in Australia was followed by a type II burst and a long, intense enhancement of radio-frequency emission (no doubt a type IV burst). Above, the disappearance of echoes obtained with an ionosonde whose transmissions are completely absorbed by the D layer. (*Christiansen et al.*)

[1] The absorbing properties of the D layer are associated with its relatively high density of 10^{-6} gram per cubic centimeter. Energy losses at collisions between electrons and other particles are high; the electrons reradiate only part of the energy held in store from the incident wave; the rest is lost in the collision.

Along with these spectacular phenomena, the sudden ionospheric disturbances, the state of the ionosphere can vary more slowly in step with solar activity. In fact, the ionizing X rays and ultraviolet vary slowly over the course of the solar cycle, and the electron density of the E and F layers is a strict function of solar activity, which is thus fundamental to the work of the ionospheric prediction services which have developed in several countries for the forecasting of radio-propagation conditions. Radio astronomy makes a valuable contribution to this field, as it appears that the centimeter or decimeter flux density of the sun correlates much better with the state of the E layer, for example, than with other criteria of solar activity, such as sunspot area or intensity of the green coronal line. This was found by Denisse and Kundu from their own observations on 3 cm and Covington's on 10.7 cm. Also, Davies has shown that fade-outs seem to be more closely connected with bursts than with flares (not all flares have bursts).

The repercussions from solar-particle emission are rather sharply distinguished from the X-ray and ultraviolet effects. In fact, the charged particles which reach the vicinity of the earth are deviated by the earth's magnetic field and can reach regions that are not in sunlight. As they more or less follow the lines of force of the earth's field, they are especially numerous in polar regions. Thus there are important latitude effects. Finally, the emission of charged particles by an active center is usually directive, in general taking place in the interior of the tube of magnetic lines of force which comes out of the sun following the flare, while X rays or ultraviolet are emitted in all directions.

Geophysicists have supposed that certain disturbances of the magnetic field are due to the arrival of solar particles in the neighborhood of our earth. In particular, sudden-commencement magnetic storms, which are always connected with solar flares and take place 1 or 2 days after the flare on the average, could result from a jet of particles emitted at the time of the flare. A theory of sudden-commencement storms has been given by Chapman and Ferraro. A stream of electrically neutral charged particles is acted on by the earth's magnetic field with opposite effects on the positive and negative particles. The electric currents so produced in the upper atmosphere then induce the observed variations of the magnetic field.

Denisse and Simon in France have investigated these relations between geomagnetic and solar activity. They have found that the flares causing sudden-commencement magnetic storms are almost always the same ones that cause type II and type IV bursts. This observation prompts an interesting remark. We recall that the shock wave responsible for a type II burst rises through the solar atmosphere with a speed of some 1,500 kilometers per second. Now, the disturbance that gives rise to the magnetic storm travels through space with a speed of this order (1,200 to 1,900 kilometers per second), as can easily be calculated by measuring the time difference between the flare and the start of the magnetic storm if, as is not very common, there is no ambiguity. The agreement is striking. Either the stream of particles from the sun is responsible, or it is the shock wave alone, traveling through an interplanetary medium that is dense enough to propagate it, and disturbing the earth's magnetic field on its arrival. Recent observations of the upper atmosphere, carried out by means of artificial satellites and cosmic probes, have revealed the existence of two belts of particles surrounding the equatorial regions of the earth at a great altitude. In these regions a considerable number of electrons with energies from 10 to 100 kev are trapped by the earth's magnetic field. The arrival of the solar disturbance changes their structure and a certain number of electrons will be freed to move into the earth's atmosphere, causing a magnetic storm according to the process outlined by Chapman and Ferraro.

The polar auroras are another consequence of this phenomenon. The particles released from the radiation belts or coming directly from the sun concentrate in the polar regions and ionize the upper atmosphere, where the recombination of ions and electrons separated by ionization emits light containing the lines and bands of nitrogen and oxygen. Störmer is responsible for a detailed study of the aurora, which is closely related to magnetic storms and solar radio bursts.

The sun also emits particles with much higher energy, in fact, cosmic rays. The relationships between the cosmic radiation and solar activity are beginning to be fairly well understood, thanks mainly to observations taken on board sounding balloons, rockets, and artificial satellites. In some cases, a significant increase of cosmic radiation is noted less than 1½ hours after the start of the flare. This phenomenon occurred, for instance, after the great flare of 23 February 1956, when particle energies greater than 20 or 30 Gev were observed.

This flare, however, was exceptional in many ways; the observed cosmic-ray energies usually do not exceed 500 Mev.[1] A quite typical case is that of the flare of 22 August 1958, which caused a type IV burst that was described above (see Fig. 7-21). In this case, we can be certain that the acceleration of the cosmic rays (which seemed to be composed essentially of protons) happened at the same time as that of the relativistic electrons responsible for the type IV burst. More than 50 similar cases are now known. These cosmic particles are protons whose energy is too low (30 to 100 million electron volts on the average) to reach the surface of the earth. Spiraling around the lines of force of the earth's magnetic field, they arrive above the polar regions where they disappear as they give rise to ionization in the lower ionosphere. The ionosphere then becomes absorbing

---

[1] A single observation of solar gamma rays with energies of 0.5 Mev was made by Peterson and Winckler at the exact time of the unique flare of 20 March 1958.

for radio waves, and causes the echoes from ionospheric sounders to fade out; this phenomenon is called polar-cap absorption (PCA).

One might imagine that the cosmic rays diffuse away from the sun in the channel formed by the tube of magnetic field which we have already referred to several times. If the earth is located inside the extension of this tube into interplanetary space, the cosmic radiation can reach it. This appears to be the case when we are dealing with very-high-energy particles such as those of 23 February 1956. The magnetic tube being curved by solar rotation as shown in Fig. 7-27, flares occurring on the west limb of the sun will have more chance of producing particles that can be received on earth than those occurring in the east, and this in fact is what is observed. Conversely, if we select the flares giving the lower-energy protons responsible for PCA's, they occur as commonly on the east as on the west of the sun, and the interpretation given above cannot be retained. We picture these protons of average energy forming clouds dense enough to force their way through the interplanetary magnetic field without too much resistance, as will happen if the kinetic pressure of the particles is higher than the pressure exerted by the magnetic field. Moving as a group they sweep the magnetic field before them. Therefore, in a way that is at first sight paradoxical, the propagation of particles with average energies, provided they are numerous, is interfered with less by interplanetary space than are the rare high-energy particles which must be considered as acting independently.

In spite of the sun's contribution, the largest part of the cosmic radiation is of galactic or extragalactic origin, a matter to which we shall return in due course. Solar activity influences this radiation in a peculiar fashion, by modulating the intensity of the cosmic-ray flux (Forbush effect). For example, certain solar flares are followed by a decrease instead of an increase in cosmic rays. Most astrophysicists are in agreement in thinking that this phenomenon is due to a screening effect of the magnetic tube coming out from the active region of the sun. This tube can extend through space to distances much greater than the radius of the earth's orbit. When the earth is inside this magnetic tube, the magnetic field that everywhere

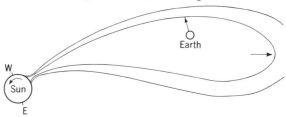

Fig. 7-27 Magnetic disturbance coming from the sun and extending into interplanetary space. The disturbance, which is ejected at the time of a strong flare, can extend beyond the earth's orbit with a speed of 1,000 to 2,000 kilometers per second. Note the deformation resulting from the sun's rotation.

surrounds it cannot be penetrated by the cosmic rays, which then cannot reach the earth's atmosphere, and so a decrease in cosmic rays is observed. This phenomenon may recur for a certain time with a 27-day period equal to the sun's rotation period.

To sum up, the study of solar terrestrial relations confirms that the sun ejects two sorts of particle, in agreement with the results of radio astronomy. Particles of one kind, with speeds equal to 1 or 2 thousand kilometers per second, leave the sun after large flares and carry with them part of the magnetic field. They are probably connected with the strongest type II bursts. The magnetic disturbance so produced is in the form of a magnetic tube which extends well beyond the earth's orbit and persists for a long time. In this channel solar cosmic-ray particles of high energy, probably accelerated simultaneously with the relativistic electrons responsible for type IV bursts, can propagate. The particles with the lowest energy, which are responsible for polar-cap absorption and so are created by flares corresponding to type IV bursts and continuum storms, travel as a tight cloud through interplanetary space virtually unaffected by the magnetic field. As regards the high-energy particles which seem to be responsible for type III and type V bursts, they have not been directly observed.

We wish to emphasize the fact that comparison of the solar cosmic rays and radio emission has at last led to some information about interplanetary space, about which practically nothing was known before. The big magnetic disturbances originating in solar flares here seem to play a fundamental role. A more coherent picture of solar phenomena and their geophysical impact has been built up in these recent years, but much still remains unexplained. Thanks to the observations of all kinds carried out during the International Geophysical Year 1957–1958, most of which have not yet been published or even analyzed, and which constitute a corpus of experimental data that is unique in the annals of science, it is probable that the picture will become still clearer in the rather near future.

BIBLIOGRAPHY

General

Goldberg, L.: The Photosphere of the Sun, "Handbuch der Physik," vol. 52, Springer-Verlag, Berlin, 1959.
de Jager, C.: Structure and Dynamics of the Solar Atmosphere, "Handbuch der Physik," vol. 52, Springer-Verlag, Berlin, 1959.
Kuiper, G. P.: "The Sun," The University of Chicago Press, Chicago, 1952.

Quiet sun

Pawsey, J. L., and R. N. Bracewell: "Radio Astronomy," Clarendon Press, Oxford, 1955. A new edition is in preparation.

Slowly varying component

Christiansen, W. N., et al.: *Ann. Astrophys.,* **23:** 75 (1960).

Kundu, M. R.: *Ann. Astrophys.,* **22:** 1 (1959).

Moutot, M., and A. Boischot: *Ann. Astrophys.,* **24:** 171 (1961).

Bursts, noise storms

A good deal of information will be found in R. N. Bracewell (ed.), "Paris Symposium on Radio Astronomy," Stanford University Press, Stanford, Calif., 1959, and in the lectures by de Jager, Kiepenheuer, Minnaert, Wild, and others in "Rendiconti della Scuola Internazionale di Fisica," Società Italiana di Fisica, Ist. di Fisica, Bologna, 1959. See also numerous articles in the *Australian Journal of Physics,* and the following:

Avignon, Y., and M. Pick-Gutmann: *Compt. Rend.,* **248:** 368 (1959).

Boischot, A.: *Ann. Astrophys.,* **21:** 273 (1958).

Boischot, A., and M. Pick-Gutmann: *J. Phys. Soc. Japan,* **17:** Suppl. A-II: 203 (1962).

Pick-Gutmann, M.: *Ann. Astrophys.,* **24:** 183 (1961).

Simon, P.: Thesis, Paris, 1956.

Solar-terrestrial relations

Publications are extremely numerous and widely dispersed. They will be found mainly in *Journal of Atmospheric and Terrestrial Physics, Journal of Geophysical Research, Geophysical Journal, Annales de Géophysique, Report of Ionosphere and Space Research in Japan.* For solar cosmic rays see:

Warwick, C.: *Sky and Telescope,* **24:** 133 (1962).

RADIO EMISSION FROM THE SOLAR SYSTEM

8

To speak of radio waves from the planets recalls, of course, the more or less serious, but always fruitless, efforts which have been made to communicate with their hypothetical inhabitants. The facts are quite different. This emission is usually only the thermal radiation of the planets and is, furthermore, very weak. The exception is an irregular and intense meter-wave emission from Jupiter. Although its origin is not understood, it is certainly not a signal emitted by any inhabitants. The temperature of $-140°C$ which exists on the planet seems as unfavorable to life as it is possible to be.

THE THERMAL RADIATION FROM THE MOON

It is relatively easy to detect the centimeter-wave emission from the moon. It was discovered in 1946 by Dicke and Beringer on 1.25 cm, and then investigated in detail by Piddington and Minnett in Australia on the same wavelength with a 44-inch paraboloid, by Gibson on 1.6 mm, and by Coates on 4.3 mm. Lunar radiation has also been detected on decimeter wavelengths by Seeger in the Netherlands on 75 cm, in France on 33 cm, and by several observers on 21 cm. However, it is practically impossible to observe it on meter wavelengths, where much less directive antennas are available, the gain is lower, and the emission is interfered with by a number of stronger sources. Comparison between brightness temperatures measured on the different radio wavelengths and in the infrared shows that our satellite behaves on the whole like a black body at 250°K. Nevertheless, the thermal radiation of the moon in the infrared, as measured by Pettit

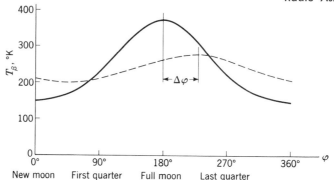

Fig. 8-1 Variation of the moon's brightness temperature in the infrared (full line) and at 1.25 (broken line). The amplitude of variation is less on 1.25 cm than in the infrared and exhibits a phase relay $\Delta\varphi$ behind the phase of the moon. *(Piddington and Minnett.)*

and Nicholson with a thermocouple at the focus of a telescope, varies a good deal with the phase of the moon. At full moon the observed temperature is $383°K$, but only $105°K$ at new moon.

On 1.25-cm and 8.6-cm wavelengths, the amplitude of this variation is greatly attenuated, and at the same time it is noticed that the intensity maximum comes several days late with respect to the maximum in the infrared (Fig. 8-1). Then on decimeter wavelengths the lunar radiation does not vary with time. This curious phenomenon can easily be explained if it is realized that the actual surface temperature is being measured in the infrared, whereas the radio emission comes from deeper layers, the optical thickness of the material decreasing with frequency. The temperature of the deeper layers rises and falls less than that of the surface layers because of the thermal inertia of the lunar material, and the phase retardation observed on centimeter wavelengths stems from the fact that the solar radiation reaches the deeper layers only after a certain delay associated with the thermal conductivity of the surface materials, which is probably rather low.[1]

Attempts have been made to deduce the character of the lunar surface from these measurements. Unfortunately the results are rather contradictory, but it is probable that a detailed investigation of the thermal properties of the moon's surface will lead to the solution of the problem while we are waiting for astronautics to progress to the point where a rocket can be landed on the moon.

[1] The diurnal and annual temperature variations at different depths in the earth obey similar laws.

THERMAL EMISSION
FROM THE PLANETS

It is much more difficult to detect the thermal radiation from the planets than from the moon, because of the small angular diameter of these bodies. Measuring the thermal emission from Venus requires a sensitivity 3,000 times greater than is needed for the moon, and 10,000 times for Mars.

In spite of these difficulties, investigators at the Naval Research Laboratory in Washington succeeded in measuring the brightness temperature of Mars on 3.15 cm in 1956, when the planet was rather close to the earth. This temperature of $218 \pm 76°K$ gave an antenna temperature of only $0.24°K$, and 71 observations with the big 50-foot paraboloid had to be averaged in order to measure it. The value obtained agrees with the infrared temperature of $260°K$ and is a little below the melting point of ice ($273°K$).

The thermal emission from Venus was detected by the same authors (Mayer, McCullough, and Sloanaker) on 9.4 cm and 3.15 cm. The temperatures obtained were $580 \pm 230°K$ and $560 \pm 73°K$ respectively, while the infrared temperature is much less, of the order of $240°K$. The radio astronomical value is no doubt the real temperature of the surface of the planet. Gibson and McEwan have also detected the emission from Venus on 8.6 mm (about $410°K$) and on 4 mm. The thermal emissions from Saturn (about $134°K$) and Mercury (about $1000°K$) have been observed at the University of Michigan.

Finally, at the Naval Research Laboratory again, the thermal emission of Jupiter on 3.18 cm has been measured by means of a maser amplifier, in its first radio astronomical application (see Fig. 3-21). This instrument was placed at the focus of the 50-foot paraboloid in April 1958 and yielded an increase in sensitivity of about 16 times. The antenna temperature is only $0.5°K$, corresponding to a planetary temperature of $177 \pm 22°K$. This value is in very good agreement with the infrared measurements (143 to $173°K$). Jupiter is a very cold world, where life is certainly impossible, especially as the atmosphere is composed mainly of methane and ammonia. On 10.3 cm the radio emission from the planet measured by McClain and Sloanaker with the new 84-foot radio telescope of the Naval Research Laboratory seems to vary from moment to moment, corresponding to brightness temperatures between 400 and $860°K$. On 30 cm, Roberts and Stanley likewise measure a variable temperature of the order of $5500°K$, and on 60 cm an even higher temperature. This curious fact seems to be connected with the nonthermal emission of the planet on meter wavelengths, which we shall now refer to.

NONTHERMAL EMISSION
FROM PLANETS

In 1955 a publication by Burke and Franklin in America caused a big stir in the astronomical world. It announced the discovery of an intense and variable emission coming from Jupiter that they had observed on 13.6 and 8.6 m. This news was received with some skepticism, which, however, did not stop Shain in Australia from investigating old recordings obtained in 1950–1951 on 16.2 m. There he found the evidence of very strong emission that had been previously attributed to interference of solar bursts. This emission was recorded when Jupiter passed through the 17-degree beam of his antenna (Fig. 8-2).

Later Kraus detected the emission from Jupiter on various wavelengths between 11.3 and 7 m at Columbus, Ohio. The emission is not observable on shorter wavelengths. It is clear that we are dealing with a nonthermal phenomenon recalling solar noise storms but with a spectrum which decreases even more rapidly toward longer wavelengths.[1]

Shain and Kraus succeeded in localizing a source on the surface of Jupiter by comparing the time of arrival of the bursts with the rotation of the planet. The rotation speed does not vary uniformly from the equator to the poles and probably refers to clouds of solid ammonia. The source appeared to coincide with the South tropical disturbance.

The mechanism of production of the bursts is still absolutely unknown, and Warwick even questions whether they are real and whether they do not more probably originate through the influence of the earth's

[1] The flux density appears to vary as the −5 power of the frequency.

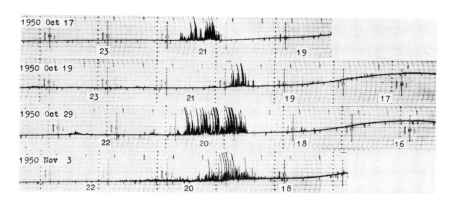

Fig. 8-2 Observations of radio emission from Jupiter at 16.2 m wavelength. These recordings made in Australia by Shain show the disturbed nature of the emission. The time of transit through the beam is indicated by the arrow. (*Shain.*)

ionosphere. On the other hand, some ideas on the origin of the distinctly nonthermal emission on decimeter waves are emerging. This emission is strongly polarized, indicating the presence of a magnetic field on Jupiter. Synchrotron radiation immediately suggests itself.

It is, indeed, not impossible that the magnetic field of Jupiter could trap and retain charged particles of solar or cosmic origin. It is known that the earth is surrounded by two radiation belts of solar origin which are trapped in its magnetic field. In each case the particles, which are high-energy electrons, may emit radio waves by the synchrotron mechanism. In the case of the earth, the emission is not easy to study directly, but that of the particle belts no doubt surrounding Jupiter is certainly much more intense and takes place on higher frequencies. In support of this theory, we may quote the observed polarization of the Jupiter emission and also the fact that its intensity depends on solar activity, the sun being no doubt the source of the particles. On the other hand, it is not yet clear what the value of the magnetic field or the electron energy is.

It is also not known whether the meter-wave emission takes place by the same process. Nevertheless, it is also found to be polarized and also seems to be connected with solar activity. It is thus tempting to attribute all the nonthermal radio emission from Jupiter to the synchrotron mechanism.

There is no a priori reason to think that Jupiter is the only planet with nonthermal emission. But radio astronomers have not yet succeeded in reliably detecting nonthermal emission in the solar system excepting that of Jupiter and the sun itself.

RADAR ECHOES FROM THE MOON, METEOR TRAILS, AND THE AURORA

Radio astronomers are usually content to study celestial objects by receiving their natural radiation. However, one can consider sending strong radio waves out to them and collecting what they reflect, in accordance with the principle of radar. Radar echoes were first obtained from the moon in 1946 by DeWitt and Stodola in the United States and by Bay in Hungary with rather low transmitter powers. At the present time the experiment has been carried out on many frequencies, and the big 250-foot radio telescope at Jodrell Bank is at present being used as a radar for this purpose. This special astronomical technique, which is perhaps not a part of radio astronomy proper and is commonly described as radar astronomy, must be referred to here, if only because of its philosophic and practical interest. It is the first time that direct contact with a body outside the earth has been established, and it represents a true *experiment* in the realm of astrophysics in which man, until now, has had to be content with a passive role. The

Fig. 8-3 The 150-foot steerable reflector at Stanford University, constructed for studies of the solar system by radar. *(Stanford Research Institute photo.)*

practical aspect is that serious thought is being given to the use of the reflections from the moon to set up long-distance radio communication.[1]

Unfortunately radar echoes from the moon are afflicted by fading. The long-period fluctuations are apparently due to passage through the earth's ionosphere because they depend on the altitude of the moon above the horizon. However, they are important only on meter wavelengths. Other fluctuations, with periods of about a second, occur on all frequencies. They probably depend on the way in which reflection takes place from the surface irregularities of the moon. The moon librates in such a way that the topography of the central region where the waves are being reflected changes from one moment to the next. It is obvious from these remarks that the best system for communication by moon reflections would employ frequency modulation on centimeter wavelengths.

In addition, by measuring the time interval between transmission and reception of the reflected wave train (about 2.4 seconds) we can determine the distance from the observatory to the surface of the moon to about 1

[1] On 27 January 1959 legible signals were transmitted from the United States to Holland on 2 m by reflection from the moon.

kilometer. This result will no doubt be useful to astronomers and geophysicists.

On 20 March 1959, it was officially announced in the United States that similar radar echoes had been obtained from the planet Venus in February 1958 at the Lincoln Laboratory. The time of transit was about 2.5 minutes. No doubt it will be possible to obtain echoes also from Mars, and such studies form part of the research program for the big Jodrell Bank telescope and many other instruments.

More recently, echoes have been obtained on the sun, the radio waves being reflected in the corona by the critical layer which corresponds to the frequency. These experiments, which were carried out at Stanford University, open a new field of investigation of the solar corona.

Another area of radar is devoted to the ionized regions of the upper atmosphere. The most convenient method of studying the ionosphere is by ionospheric sounding, which is simply radar. The earth's atmosphere can also be ionized by particles coming from the sun and by the passage of meteorites through it. The particle streams give rise to the aurora, of which we have already spoken, and radar methods permit the determination of its altitude and electron density. Auroras are found to be produced at considerable altitudes, usually above 100 kilometers (this explains why they are visible from so far away). They show high electron densities, of the order of 10^5 to 10^7 electrons per cubic centimeter, which are thus much higher than those normally observed in the ionosphere.

The ionization produced by meteorites, which are solid particles of extraterrestrial origin, usually less than a gram in weight, is revealed by a visible trail which we know as a shooting star or fireball and which is highly reflecting for radio waves.

The observation of radar echoes from the meteor trails is an excellent way of studying meteors; it gives their distance, height, velocity, etc. This work, which was especially developed in England, has led to a clear proof that meteors belong to the solar system, but the major interest is geophysical, leading to information about the structure of the upper atmosphere. Observations of the distortion and motion of persistent meteor trails (which, like most meteor studies, can also be done optically) have shown that violent winds with speeds up to 40 meters per second exist at altitudes as high as 100 kilometers.

BIBLIOGRAPHY

Hanbury Brown, R., and A. C. B. Lovell: "The Exploration of Space by Radio," Chapman & Hall, Ltd., London, 1957.

Giordmaine, J. A.: *Proc. Nat. Acad. Sci. U.S.,* **46:** 267 (1960).

Lovell, A. C. B.: "Meteor Astronomy," Clarendon Press, Oxford, 1954.

Mayer, C. H.: Radio Emission of the Moon and Planets, in "Planets and Satellites," The University of Chicago Press, Chicago, 1961.

GALACTIC
RADIO EMISSION

9

The Milky Way, from the remotest antiquity, has never ceased to capture man's imagination. It has been the object of multitudes of legends and has evoked many fantastic and poetical explanations. It was quite late when its true nature was realized. Its bright band can be resolved into a myriad of stars.[1] Sir William Herschel first tried at the end of the eighteenth century to determine its boundaries and learn its structure by star counts in different parts of the Milky Way. He founded the subject of stellar statistics, but did not solve the problem he had posed. It was only much later, when it was generally accepted that the Milky Way—the galaxy—is a system like the spiral nebulae revealed by photographs, that studies of it began to make real progress.

If we consider only optical astronomy, the situation is still rather discouraging. The parts of the galaxy that are most densely populated with stars are often blotted out by huge clouds of absorbing material, which are particularly numerous in the vicinity of the plane of symmetry of the system. In fact, optical astronomy gives us hardly any information on the parts of the galaxy which are situated more than 3,000 light-years from the sun, and the interstellar matter conceals even details that are relatively quite close to us. It is only by constant comparison of the very fragmentary data in our possession with what we know about external galaxies such as the great Andromeda nebula and the Magellanic clouds that our knowledge of galactic structure can advance.

The existence of radio emission by the galaxy gives rise to new hopes.

---

[1] Galileo seems to have been the first to suspect that the Milky Way could be composed of star clouds.

Nevertheless, Jansky's discovery of 1931, which is the foundation of radio astronomy, went unnoticed for a long time. A decade passed before Reber drew the first maps of the radio galaxy, on two different wavelengths, and noted that its appearance depended strongly on the wavelength. While it was wide and very bright on meter waves, it was narrow and fainter on decimeter waves, suggesting that several distinct mechanisms enter into the radio-wave emission. The existence of a powerfully emitting region in the constellation Sagittarius, which cannot be discerned optically because interstellar absorption is strong in that direction, shows that the interstellar matter absorbs radio waves much less than it does light. We can therefore hope to study regions that are quite invisible in the telescope, thanks to radio astronomy. We shall see that since Reber's time progress in our knowledge of the galaxy has been extremely rapid. The unveiling of its spiral structure by means of the 21-cm line of neutral hydrogen is, without doubt, one of the most remarkable scientific achievements of the last half century.

Before commencing the study of the radio galaxy, we shall recall some of the principal characteristics of spiral galaxies and give a brief description of our own galaxy.

GALACTIC STRUCTURE

Figure 9-1 shows one of the most beautiful and best-known galaxies, the Andromeda nebula. It is one of the best examples of what a distant observer looking obliquely at our galaxy would see.

This object is characterized by two bright arms, starting from the central region. These are the spiral arms, which were seen for the first time about 1845 by Lord Rosse, with a telescope that he had built himself, in the constellation Canes Venatici. Photographs taken with large instruments show that these arms are composed of a mixture of stars and diffuse matter. Between the arms stars are also found, but they are generally less bright. The structure of the central condensation is much less well known than that of the arms. Nevertheless, it has been resolved into stars in some of the brighter galaxies. Finally, in the exact center of the galaxy there is a small nucleus which is usually hidden on photographs (which are overexposed the better to bring out the arms) but which is visible to the eye and then has the appearance of a bright star (Fig. 9-2).

Examination of a spiral galaxy thus shows a rather simple structure with a very bright central nucleus surrounded by a condensation from which two spiral arms start.

The spiral arms lie in a very flattened disk, as revealed by the edge view of a galaxy in Fig. 9-3. The central condensation appears on this photograph as much thicker than the arms and is spheroidal. Note the

Fig. 9-1 The great nebula in Andromeda (M 31). On this 48-inch Schmidt photograph the spiral arms and absorbing matter in the galaxy are seen as well as the two satellite elliptical galaxies NGC 205 and 221. *(Mount Wilson and Palomar Observatories photo.)*

presence of a band of absorbing material closely concentrated along the galactic plane of symmetry.

More advanced studies show that the whole of the disk and the central condensation are embedded in an almost spherical halo whose dimensions have not been very well determined and which is essentially composed of globular clusters of stars. Numerous globular clusters have been found in the Andromeda nebula, distributed practically isotropically around the galaxy.

This is probably the structure of our own galaxy, which is sketched diagrammatically in Fig. 9-4. We shall briefly summarize the various investigations of classical astronomy which have confirmed this structure.

1 That the galaxy is a flattened system is apparent when we look at the Milky Way. Star counts have verified that the sun is situated not far from the galactic plane of symmetry and is rather a long way from the center of the galaxy, which is located in the constellation Sagittarius, the place where the number of stars per square degree of sky is much higher than elsewhere. Stellar statistics have dealt with different types of stars, especially the *O*- and *B*-type blue supergiants, which are the brightest of all and can be seen from a great distance. But it has not been possible from optical observations to determine the position of the spiral arms with certainty, except that apparently the sun is located inside one of these arms.

2 In our galaxy we also find the absorbing matter mentioned in connection with Fig. 9-3. It is closely concentrated along the galactic plane

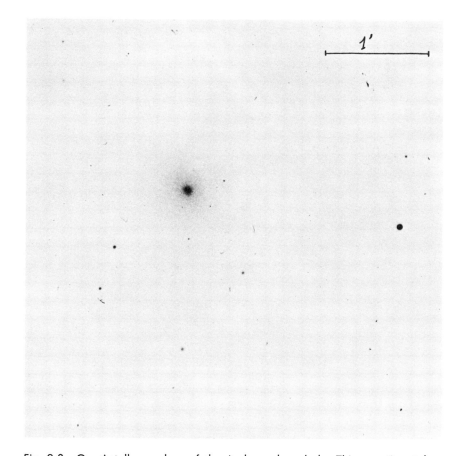

Fig. 9-2 Quasi-stellar nucleus of the Andromeda nebula. This negative, taken by Baade on the 100-inch telescope, and kindly provided by R. Minkowski, is greatly underexposed in order to bring out the nucleus of the galaxy, which on the scale of this picture would have dimensions on the order of several meters.

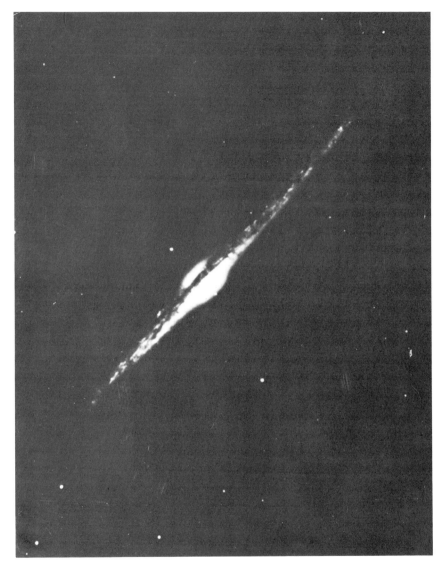

Fig. 9-3 The galaxy NGC 4565. *(Mount Wilson and Palomar Observatories photo.)*

and takes the form of a dark band which seems to divide the Milky Way in two, particularly from Cygnus to Sagittarius. It is a very curious fact that the light of the stars that can be seen through this obscuring material is linearly polarized, as first shown by Hiltner and Hall in 1949. This remarkable observation can be explained only by supposing that the interstellar matter is composed of elongated ferromagnetic or paramagnetic dust particles all oriented in the same sense under the influence of a galactic magnetic field. This field, whose strength is estimated at 10^{-5} gauss, would be generally parallel to the galactic plane and would be of fundamental importance in cosmic phenomena, as we shall see below.

3 This dust is not the only stuff found in interstellar space. We also find highly rarefied gas (from 1 to 100 atoms per cubic centimeter) composed mainly of hydrogen. For comparison, we recall that 1 cubic centimeter of gas at atmospheric pressure contains 2×10^{19} atoms. This interstellar gas is not accessible to optical observation in regions which are remote from any star, but in the vicinity of the hotter stars it may be ionized by the ultraviolet emission. Under these conditions, it becomes luminous and emits the spectral lines of hydrogen (as well as some lines of ionized oxygen and certain metals which also occur in small amounts in the interstellar gas). These HII regions (in contrast to HI regions where the hydrogen is neutral and invisible) appear in the form of bright nebulosities, of which a fine example is shown in Fig. 9-5. These clouds are often so numerous that they give the impression of a continuous background.

4 Optical observations of the central regions of the galaxy hardly allow their structure to be determined. Very numerous stars having a distance of the order of 26,000 light-years and apparently belonging to the central condensation are all that it has been possible to catch sight of between the clouds of absorbing matter.

5 The study of the galactic globular clusters shows that they possess no concentration toward the galactic plane and are essentially contained within a sphere of 130,000 light-years diameter. This is the halo of the galaxy, whose center of symmetry can be shown to coincide with the central regions of our spiral.

To sum up, the following schematic picture of our galaxy can be given,

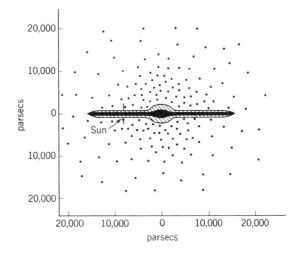

Fig. 9-4 Diagram showing the structure of our galaxy. The central disk, which contains the bulk of the stars and interstellar matter (in black), is surrounded by a halo containing many globular clusters (dots).

Fig. 9-5   The galactic nebulosity NGC 5146. Complex association of absorbing clouds and ionized hydrogen. *(Haute-Provence Observatory photo.)*

and we here express the dimensions in parsecs, and not in light-years, following the custom of astronomers.[1]

A central nucleus about which little information is given by optical observations is surrounded by a stellar condensation with a diameter of about 4,000 parsecs and a thickness probably half this. Emerging from this condensation are spiral arms composed of a mixture of stars and interstellar matter, defining a galactic disk whose diameter is about 30,000 parsecs and whose thickness is not more than 500 parsecs. The whole is immersed in an approximately spherical halo 40,000 parsecs in diameter.

These immense dimensions will be better appreciated by noting that the diameter of the earth's orbit is only five-millionths of a parsec. The sun

[1] One parsec = 3.26 light-years. A parsec is the distance from which the earth's orbit would be seen to subtend an angle of 1 second of arc.

is only one of 80 billion stars composing the galaxy. The interstellar matter amounts to at least 1.5 percent of the total mass of the galaxy, which is about 10^{11} times that of the sun.

Optical observations have long since shown that the stars of our galaxy are in relative motion. As early as the eighteenth century the study of proper motions, i.e., the motion of stars over the celestial sphere, was undertaken. This is long-winded and difficult work which requires instruments for very precise positional measurement, because the apparent motions are very small. Proper motions can also be determined by photography, and the results are of higher accuracy. Moreover, the speed with which the stars approach or recede from the earth, their radial velocity, is easily deduced by observing the displacement of their spectral lines. The displacement $d\lambda$ is given by $d\lambda = \lambda v/c$, where λ is the wavelength, v is the radial velocity of the star, and c is the velocity of light, according to the Doppler effect. If the proper motion and radial velocity of one and the same star have both been measured, the magnitude and direction of its velocity through space can be deduced. These data show that the stars of the galaxy possess random velocities. The sun, for example, is moving with respect to the nearby stars toward a point known as its apex, located in the constellation Hercules, with a speed of 20 kilometers per second. But the bodily motion of the stars in any given region of the galaxy is much greater. The local group of stars, of which the sun is a member, is moving at 220 kilometers per second toward a point near the star α Cygni. This new apex is located approximately in the galactic plane, at 90 degrees from the center of the galaxy. This mass movement can be interpreted as a rotation of the local stellar group about the galactic center with a period of 220 million years. It has been shown that all parts of the galaxy are rotating about the center with a speed that depends on their distance from the center. If the whole mass of the galaxy was concentrated at its center, the motion, which is controlled by the laws of universal gravitation, would obey Kepler's laws; i.e., the angular velocity would be inversely proportional to the square root of the distance from the center. In fact, the mass is distributed throughout the central condensation and galactic disk, and the rotation does not obey such simple rules.[1] The study of this rotation leads to a determination of the distribution of mass inside the galaxy.

If a star relatively close to the sun is considered, it is found that the magnitude and direction of its rotation velocity are slightly different from that of the sun. In general, the star possesses a radial velocity with respect to the sun. This is what is called *differential rotation,* and its study is associated with the name of the Dutch astronomer Oort. Differential rotation is very important because it allows the calculation of distances starting from

---

[1] In any case, the rotation of the galaxy, which can be detected on all the external galaxies, produces progressive distortion, which is, of course, very slow.

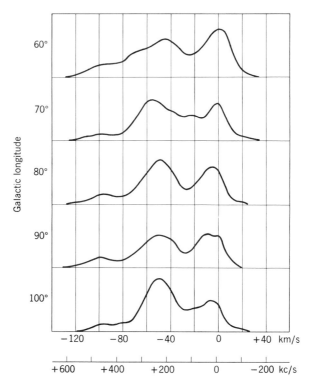

Fig. 9-6   Some 21-cm line profiles in the galaxy. These profiles refer to different galactic longitudes on the galactic equator. *(Muller and Westerhout.)*

radial velocity. The optical measurements which revealed the galactic rotation unfortunately can be applied only to regions relatively close to the sun, other regions being more or less obscured by interstellar dust. This difficulty does not exist in radio astronomy, and we shall now see how the Dutch radio astronomers succeeded, on Oort's initiative, in determining the distribution of neutral interstellar hydrogen and the position of the spiral arms.

THE 21-CM LINE AND SPIRAL
STRUCTURE OF THE GALAXY

The measurement of radial velocities depends, as we have said, on the Doppler shift of a spectral line emitted by the source under study. In radio astronomy, the shift of the neutral-hydrogen line on 21.1 cm is used. For this purpose a very-narrow-band receiver is needed, with a bandwidth of the order of 5 to 40 kc/s, whose center frequency can be varied between rather wide limits around the central value of 1,420 Mc/s by exactly known amounts. We have seen in an earlier chapter various ways of constructing such equipment. It is found that the frequency can be considerably shifted (occasionally by 500 kc/s) and that the line is almost always strongly widened. This is explained by supposing that the waves arriving from the direction viewed by the antenna originate in different regions of the galaxy more or less remote from the sun and are thus affected by greater or less radial velocities.

Observations on 21 cm are generally made with a single antenna. At the present time, the most important being used for this purpose are two 25-meter paraboloids, one located at Dwingeloo in the Netherlands and the other at Bonn in Germany. But observations of 21-cm galactic emission are also being made at many other stations, notably in America, Australia, England, and soon in France. As a rule, the antenna tracks the part of the sky to be studied while at the same time the frequency is varied. The result of a frequency sweep is a line profile, some examples of which are shown in Fig. 9-6 for different values of galactic longitude. The galactic longitude is an angle measured along the galactic plane from an arbitrary origin. This coordinate, together with the galactic latitude measured in a direction perpendicular to the galactic plane, is convenient to use in galactic work.

As the sun and earth possess proper motions with respect to the group of local stars, it is necessary to correct the observation for these factors. Then the intensity of the continuous radiation of the galaxy has to be subtracted to obtain the corrected line profile from which the properties of the region in the line of sight can be deduced.

Suppose that 21-cm radiation is received from a neutral-hydrogen region P situated at a distance R from the galactic center, about which it is rotating with an angular velocity ω (Fig. 9-7). The sun S is at a distance R_0 from the center and has angular velocity ω_0. It is easy to calculate the radial velocity V_r of the point P. The velocities v and v_0 of S and P are respectively $v = R\omega$ and $v_0 = R_0\omega_0$. Now, from the triangle CSP we have $R \sin \alpha = R_0 \sin l'$, and the radial velocity, which expresses the differential rotation, is given by

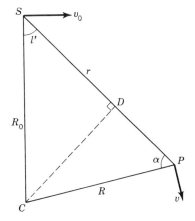

$$V_r = v \sin \alpha - v_0 \sin l'$$

or $\quad V_r = R_0(\omega - \omega_0) \sin l'$

The angle l' is, within an additive constant, just the galactic longitude of the point P. If l is the galactic longitude, we have $l' = l - 327.7°$.

Fig. 9-7 Explaining differential galactic rotation.

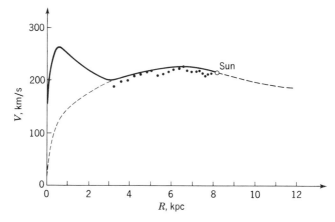

Fig. 9-8 Rotation curve of the galaxy. The points indicate rotation-velocity values obtained by the method of maximum velocity. *(Oort, Muller, and Westerhout.)*

If we know R_0, ω_0, and l', we can deduce the velocity of rotation of each point of the galaxy by measuring its radial velocity. This is what is done for the regions near the sun, starting from stellar radial velocities. It is possible to carry out the same operation for neutral-hydrogen clouds, but there is an ambiguity in position of the emitting region when regions closer to the galactic center than the sun are viewed. As appears from Fig. 9-7, a given radial velocity corresponds to two points situated on either side of D. Only the point D, whose radial velocity is a maximum since it is the closest to the galactic center, is free from confusion. By measuring the largest observable radial velocity in a line profile, the rotation velocity of the point D, i.e., the nearest point to the center of the galaxy on the line of sight, can thus be calculated without ambiguity. This method is applicable to all the regions of the galaxy which are closer to the center than the sun, and it allows the rotation curve (Fig. 9-8) of the galaxy to be determined as well as the map of differential galactic rotation (Fig. 9-9).

Nevertheless, it is not valid for the outer regions of the galaxy, whose rotation it is impossible to determine from the 21-cm line. One has to put up with rather imprecise models based on stellar observations and the results of galactic dynamics. But in these regions the study of the distribution of neutral hydrogen is easier, because a given radial velocity corresponds to a single point on the line of sight (see Fig. 9-9). Assuming that the rotation velocities are given by the broken line in Fig. 9-8 as determined from Doppler-shift measurements on stars,[1] we can determine in

[1] This hypothesis is justified by the fact that radial-velocity measurements on stars and neutral hydrogen in the same galactic region have generally given concordant results.

what region the part of the emission corresponding to a given radial velocity is generated, by choosing a given frequency in the line profile. This radiation is not absorbed by the nearby neutral hydrogen, whose radial velocity is not the same and which therefore absorbs and emits on a different frequency. The determination of the density of hydrogen atoms is then relatively easy. If an antenna temperature T_a is observed at a certain frequency, the corresponding emitting region with an excitation temperature T_e has an optical depth τ such that

$$T_a = T_e(1 - e^{-\tau})$$

It is generally supposed that the excitation temperature T_e of neutral hydrogen is uniform throughout interstellar space. Various independent determinations of this temperature give a value of the order of $100°$K. The optical depth has then only to be determined in order to characterize the emitting region.

It is easy to deduce from this the density of the neutral hydrogen taking part in the emission. It is generally low (1 to 100 atoms of hydrogen per cubic centimeter) and the optical depth is low. In spite of this, inter-

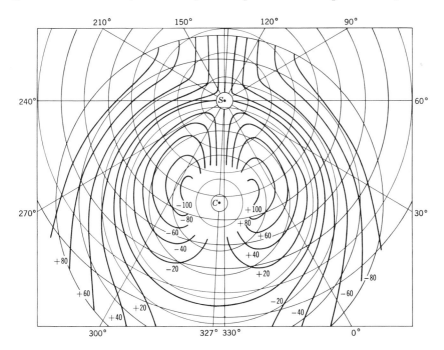

Fig. 9-9   Chart for differential rotation in the galaxy. At each point in the galactic plane the calculated value of the radial velocity is shown in kilometers per second. C is the galactic center, and S the sun. The velocities are positive for recession, and the circles are spaced at 2,000 parsecs. (Coutrez.)

stellar space is so vast that the mass of hydrogen in the galaxy is far from being negligible relative to the stars, amounting to 1 or 2 percent of the total mass.

The results of observations made in 1957 by the Dutch radio astronomers, notably van de Hulst, Muller, and Oort, are plotted on Fig. 9-10. It is seen that the neutral hydrogen is distributed in spiral arms separated by regions where the density of interstellar matter is lower. In the principal outside arm, the mean density of hydrogen is of the order of 1 atom per cubic centimeter. The regions near the sun are rich in neutral hydrogen and have a complex structure. The high density of hydrogen in the solar neighborhood is visible on most of the line profiles, where a maximum is often seen at low radial velocities.

The interpretation of certain profiles, such as that referring to galactic longitude 100° (see Fig. 9-6) is easy even for a beginner. The line of sight first encounters a nearby region of high density, then a strong spiral arm, and finally another weak and distant arm corresponding to the highest radial velocities. This arm can be located on Fig. 9-10.

The study of the inner regions of the galaxy runs into great difficulties. Indeed, we have noted that a given frequency in the line corresponds to emission from two zones of the galaxy, the nearer partly absorbing the emission from the farther. Moreover, the neutral-hydrogen clouds can possess turbulent motion which upsets the line profile. Nevertheless, study of the experimental rotation curve given in Fig. 9-8 yields some information on the inner structure of the galaxy. It will be seen that the experimental points do not fall on a smooth curve but exhibit a series of peaks. We recall that these velocities were determined by measuring the maximum radial velocity of the profile with respect to the point D in Fig. 9-6. If there is very little neutral hydrogen at D, the maximum velocity observed does not really correspond to D but to remoter or closer points where the emission is appreciable, and the velocity measured is less than would have been given by D. On the other hand, if there is plenty of hydrogen at D, the maximum velocity corresponds satisfactorily to this point. In the first case the experimental points are below the smooth curve, and in the second case they fall on the curve. A simple study of the rotation curve thus leads us to think that the line of sight is tangent to one arm of matter about 5,000 parsecs from the center and to another at about 6,500 parsecs.

We can try to improve these results by studying the line profiles, but we may mention again that the interpretation encounters enormous difficulties. The thickness of the spiral arms perpendicular to the galactic plane is estimated at 220 parsecs approximately. The flattening of the galactic disk is thus extremely pronounced.

While the Dutch were studying the structure of the part of the galaxy visible from the latitude of their country, Kerr and Hindman in Australia were completing their observations, and in 1957 they published a map of the galactic neutral hydrogen whose features agree rather well with those determined by their Northern Hemisphere colleagues. Figure 9-10 is a composite diagram of the galactic arms revealed by these observations. Practically the whole of the galaxy can be explored by means of the 21-cm line of neutral hydrogen. Only the regions situated in the direction of the galactic center and anticenter, where differential rotation is imperceptible (see Fig. 9-9), are not easy to study. The progress in our understanding of the galaxy that has been permitted by the 21-cm line is obvious. Not only has it been possible to reveal the existence of spiral structure, but the arms

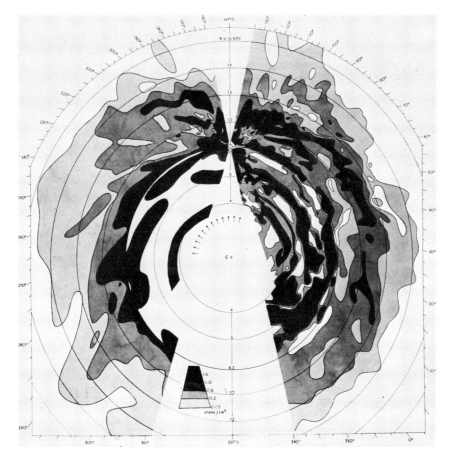

Fig. 9-10 Distribution of neutral hydrogen in the galaxy. This map is based on Dutch observations for the right-hand side and Australian observations for the left. The galactic center is marked *C*, the sun *S*. The spiral arms are rather irregular. *(Oort, Kerr, and Westerhout.)*

themselves are now known in quite rich detail. In addition, we see that their outline is far from being regular as is the case in certain external galaxies.

It is satisfactory to note that optical determinations of the arms are in good agreement with radio. Baade and Morgan in America have noticed that the arms of galaxies contain a population of special stars, known as population I, characterized essentially by associations of very hot giant stars of spectral types *O* and *B* which are often surrounded by clouds of ionized hydrogen. The *O* and *B* stars and the ionized clouds, presumably indicators of spiral arms in our galaxy, always coincide in distance and direction with the arms determined by radio astronomers. Consequently the results obtained on 21 cm can be taken as practically conclusive.

Nevertheless, further refinements could result from improvements in the law of galactic rotation. Recent work by Kerr gives strong support to the suggestion that the galactic matter moves on slightly spiral orbits, expanding as it rotates. If this idea is verified by observations, it will be necessary to correct the positions of the arms. On the other hand, the distance scale in the galaxy is not well known and might be increased by as much as 50 percent.

The 21-cm line has also recently allowed it to be shown that the outer regions of the galaxy are not situated in the same plane as the inner regions. These curious distortions are interpreted by Woltjer as due to hydrodynamic effects of the intergalactic medium on the galaxy, which is moving through it with a speed of 100 kilometers per second in the direction of the Andromeda nebula.

Finally, the 21-cm line has given information of the greatest interest on the structure of the central condensation of the galaxy. This point is so important and so interesting for astrophysics that we shall deal separately with it at the end of the chapter.

CONTINUOUS GALACTIC EMISSION

The 21-cm line of neutral hydrogen stands out above continuous radio emission which also comes from the galaxy but whose nature and properties are essentially different. This radiation has a spectrum which extends without discontinuity over the whole range of wavelengths observable in radio astronomy. On meter wavelengths it is extremely strong and the Milky Way appears rather wide. On shorter wavelengths it reduces to a more or less narrow ridge getting weaker and weaker as centimeter wavelengths are approached.

Much progress has been made since the first maps of the galactic continuum were made on 160 and 480 Mc/s by Reber, so marking the starting point of galactic radio astronomy. On meter waves many maps have been drawn in England, Australia, and the United States, using antennas of low resolving power. Those showing the greatest detail were obtained by Blythe in England on 38 Mc/s with a beamwidth of 2.2 degrees and by Kraus and Ko on 242 Mc/s with a beam $1.2° \times 8°$. On decimeter wavelengths we have the maps of Seeger and of Large et al. near 400 Mc/s, of Piddington and Trent on 600 Mc/s, of Bolton on 910 Mc/s, and of Altenhoff et al. on 2,700 Mc/s. On decameter waves, we have the 19.7-Mc/s survey of Shain, Komesaroff, and Higgins with a beamwidth of 1.4 degrees.

Two contour maps excelled over all others, at the time they were published, by their fine resolution and represented considerable progress in the study of galactic radiation. The first, which mainly concerns the southern sky, was made by Mills in Australia on 85 Mc/s (3.5 m wavelength) with the well-known cross antenna which bears his name (Fig. 4-28), whose beamwidth is 0.9 degree. This map, which is reproduced in part in Fig. 9-11, shows that the meter-wave emission of the galaxy is rather concentrated along the galactic equator, much more than was thought from studying the earlier maps, which were not sufficiently detailed. The second map was obtained in the Netherlands by Westerhout, who observed the galaxy on 22 cm, just outside the hydrogen line, with the 25-meter paraboloid at Dwingeloo (Fig. 5-3). The beamwidth of this instrument (0.57 degree) is comparable with that of Mills, and the 22-cm map, part of which is shown in Fig. 9-12, possesses an important region of overlap with the Australian map. It is very interesting to compare these two observations in this common portion, as Mills and Westerhout have done, deducing important properties of the radio galaxy that we shall now review.

On Mills's map, and better still on the cross sections of the galaxy such as those of Fig. 9-13, we note the existence of two main components of galactic emission. On the one hand there is a relatively narrow band a few degrees wide, which essentially follows the galactic equator, and on the other a weaker component which extends over the whole sky, with an intensity which slowly diminishes away from the galactic plane. Numerous radio sources are superimposed on this continuous background and constitute a serious hindrance to the interpretation of the extended emission. On decimeter wavelengths, the galactic ridge is even narrower, and its apparent temperature of about 20°K is much less than the several tens of thousands of degrees observed on 3.5 m. As for the extended component, it has almost completely disappeared.

The enormous galactic brightness temperatures on meter waves (exceeding 250,000°K on 15 m) demonstrate that the radiation on these frequencies is of nonthermal origin. This fact is confirmed by studying the spectrum of the continuum radiation whose brightness temperature varies as $\nu^{-2.7}$. We have seen in Chap. 6 that this law cannot correspond to thermal emission.

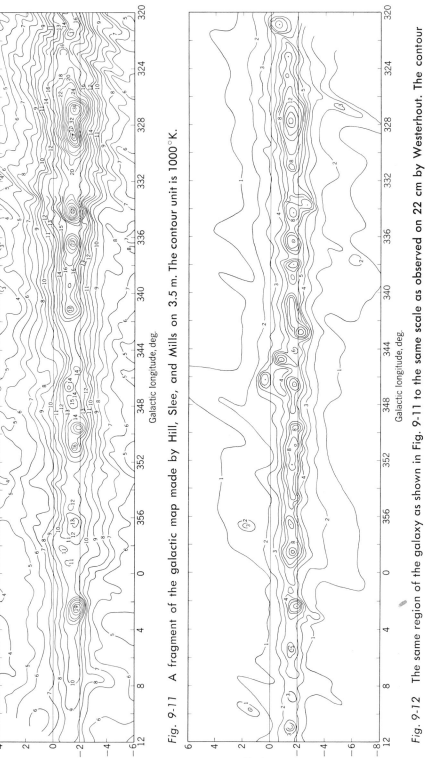

Fig. 9-11 A fragment of the galactic map made by Hill, Slee, and Mills on 3.5 m. The contour unit is 1000°K.

Fig. 9-12 The same region of the galaxy as shown in Fig. 9-11 to the same scale as observed on 22 cm by Westerhout. The contour unit is 3.25°K. Compare the two maps in the regions of the galactic center (longitude 327.7°); also note the large number of discrete sources superimposed on the background, some of which appear on both maps.

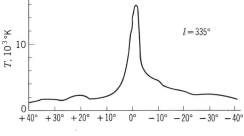

Fig. 9-13 Transverse scans over the galaxy on 3.5 m at galactic longitudes 335 and 350°. (*Mills.*)

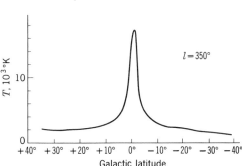

The origin of this emission has remained obscure for quite a time. It is certain that it may not be attributed to stars, whose integrated emission is certainly several orders of magnitude too low, or to unresolved radio sources. The possibility of emission by high-energy electrons in a magnetic field has finally solved this problem. It is probable that almost all the continuum emission of the galaxy comes from the synchrotron mechanism. The presence of high-energy particles in interstellar space is absolutely certain since they can be observed on the earth in the form of cosmic rays. Furthermore, the existence of magnetic fields in the galaxy has been revealed by observations of the polarization of starlight. If we adopt the synchrotron mechanism, proposed by Alfvén and Herlofson in 1950, Mills's observations show that the narrow ridge of the galactic continuum comes from a disk which probably corresponds with the optical disk. Its thickness perpendicular to

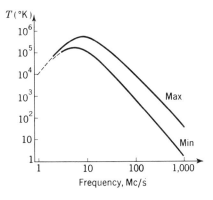

Fig. 9-14 Spectra of the hottest and coldest parts of the galaxy. The relative values at frequencies less than 10 Mc/s are extremely uncertain. The two spectra are identical and have a slope of −2.7. (*De Vaucouleurs.*)

the galactic plane is 500 parsecs, which is the same as is deduced from optical observations. The magnetic field existing in this disk is of the order of 10^{-5} gauss, and radiation is well explained by assuming that the distribution of high-energy electrons (of the order of 10^9 electron volts) is analogous to that of the primary cosmic rays. The number of electrons having a given energy is then inversely proportional to the 2.4 power of the energy.

The same type of emission should take place also in the galactic halo and produce the wide component observed on meter wavelengths as proposed by the Soviet astrophysicist Shklovsky in 1952. The magnetic field could be two or three times weaker than in the galactic disk. Mills assumes that the halo is not spherical but rather spheroidal, with its major axes greater than 30,000 parsecs and a minor axis of 20,000 parsecs perpendicular to the galactic plane.

Nonthermal radiation on decimeter wavelengths, as we have just been saying, gives very low brightness temperatures, so much so that it becomes difficult to detect the halo and the narrow component appears rather faintly. On these wavelengths a good part of the observed radiation comes from a very concentrated zone along the galactic plane, even narrower than the narrow component on meter wavelengths. In this case we are certainly dealing with thermal emission from ionized interstellar hydrogen whose brightness temperature varies as ν^{-2}, while the brightness temperature of the nonthermal component varies as $\nu^{-2.7}$. The importance of thermal emission was long overestimated. The galactic ridge observed on meter waves was ascribed to it before synchrotron radiation was thought of. Westerhout's observations on 22 cm restored it to its right place. On this wavelength ionized hydrogen and relativistic electrons contribute equally to the total emission of the galactic ridge. On longer wavelengths the nonthermal emission predominates. According to Westerhout, the thermal component comes from a disk of ionized interstellar hydrogen which is symmetrical with respect to the galactic plane whose thickness is only 200 parsecs. It is essentially equal to that of the neutral-hydrogen arms and less than half that of the nonthermal disk. The density of ionized hydrogen varies greatly from the center to the periphery of the galactic disk, as Fig. 9-15 shows, and its excitation temperature is estimated at 10,000°K.

It is interesting to compare this value with the brightness temperature of the nonthermal component. On decimeter wavelengths it is considerably below 10,000°K, and the ionized gas appears in emission above the nonthermal component in accordance with the general laws of radiation that we established in Chap. 6. On meter wavelengths the brightness temperature of the nonthermal radiation is of the order of 10,000°, and thus of the same order as the excitation temperature of ionized hydrogen, and the presence of the latter is not noted. The situation on decameter wavelengths

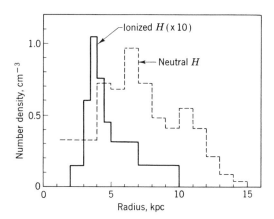

Fig. 9-15 Relative distributions of neutral and ionized hydrogen with distance from the galactic center. (Westerhout.)

is quite the opposite. Indeed, the brightness temperature of the nonthermal component reaches 100,000°K in places, and the nearby ionized hydrogen appears to be everywhere in absorption and not in emission.

This is what Shain observed in Australia on 19.7 Mc/s (15.2 m wavelength). This investigator constructed a cross interferometer similar to Mills's with a beamwidth of only 1.4 degrees. If his observations are compared with those of Westerhout and Mills, it is noticed that most of the emission regions observed on decimeter wavelengths appear in absorption on decameter waves, particularly on the galactic ridge itself. The appearance of the galaxy on these frequencies somewhat recalls its visible appearance of an absorbing band splitting the galactic ridge in two.[1] In certain regions, particularly in the direction of the galactic center, the ionized hydrogen absorbs more than 99 percent of the nonthermal emission. It is certain that galactic observations on decameter waves, apart from fully confirming the role of ionized hydrogen in the galaxy, constitute a powerful technique for studying the structure of the ionized-hydrogen regions.

We have so far contemplated only the broad picture of the various components of galactic emission. But examination of the contour maps reproduced here shows a considerable number of details, some of which are most interesting even without mentioning the discrete sources which are the concern of Chaps. 10 and 11. A very important feature was discovered by Mills on the longitudinal profile of the galactic ridge as observed on 3.5 m (Fig. 9-16). A certain number of well-marked, regularly spaced steps can be seen. The edges of these steps coincide approximately in position with the outer edges of spiral arms determined by the 21-cm line. This seems to show that the nonthermal emission from the galactic ridge originates in spiral arms. These can be imagined as tubes in which the magnetic field is particularly strong. Inside these tubes relativistic electrons circulate,

[1] The similarity is only apparent, since the causes of emission and absorption are essentially different in the two cases.

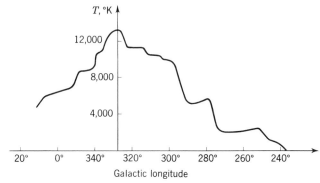

Fig. 9-16 Scan along the galactic equator on 3.5 m. On this figure, in which the contribution from discrete sources has been eliminated as far as possible, the steps corresponding to the outer edges of the galactic arms are clearly visible. *(Mills.)*

channeled along the lines of force about which they spiral (Fig. 9-17). Thus the synchrotron emission takes place mainly inside the arms. The staircase appearance of the ridge is found also on other galactic maps, especially on one made in France on 33 cm. It is not so obvious on 22 cm; this led Westerhout to think that the thermal emission does not come from well-defined arms, as in the case of the nonthermal component, but that the ionized hydrogen responsible is really distributed continuously throughout the disk referred to above. This opinion has been disputed, particularly by Shain, who pointed out that the ionized hydrogen in the Andromeda nebula is essentially confined to the arms.

Plenty of problems still remain to be solved before all the characteristics of the radio emission from the galaxy can be explained. Nevertheless, even now we can give a fairly complete idea of the radio galaxy, whose features are comparable with those of the optical galaxy.

1 The interstellar neutral hydrogen is essentially distributed along spiral arms and gives out 21-cm emission.

2 Part of this hydrogen is ionized by the radiation of hot stars and is also probably concentrated in the spiral arms, but this latter point is much argued.

3 High-energy electrons, as well as heavy cosmic-ray particles, are circulating in the galaxy. Some are in the galactic halo in a magnetic field of 10^{-5} gauss and emit radio waves by the synchrotron mechanism; the others are confined to the galactic arms, which are magnetic tubes with field strengths two or three times higher than in the halo.

The hypothesis of synchrotron emission in galactic space is supported, as already mentioned, by the existence of cosmic rays. But it cannot yet be said to be conclusively established. Many difficulties remain, the principal one being the mechanism of accelerating the particles to energies of at least 10^9 electron volts. The great physicist Fermi proposed a very ingenious explanation which invokes the turbulent motion within the galaxy; consequently we are anxious to study these motions. Several investigators have tried to detect the existence of polarization in the galactic continuum. These measurements which are particularly delicate because of very complex instrumental effects have recently given a positive result. C. L. Seeger, G. Westerhout, and C. A. Muller in the Netherlands, working at a wavelength of 75 cm, have discovered an extensive region of the galaxy in the constellation Perseus where the polarization reaches 10 percent. The direction of polarization is approximately perpendicular to the galactic plane. This region which has otherwise nothing special about it seems to be the only one where polarization is pronounced. This extremely interesting observation, now confirmed by more recent measurements made in Great Britain, firmly establishes the effectiveness of the synchrotron mechanism in the galaxy. Detailed comparisons between the radio polarization and the polarization of starlight by interstellar dust, which seem to be perpendicular (thus making the direction of the magnetic field parallel to the direction of polarization of starlight), will certainly be very fruitful, and a possibility can be seen of directly determining the strength of the galactic magnetic field, independently of theoretical considerations. But measurements of Zeeman splitting of the 21-cm line, which we shall consider in the following chapter, give an even more direct determination.

It remains for us to deal with the center of the galaxy. Here again, we shall see how radio astronomical observations have come to the aid of optical astronomy, powerless because the absorption due to interstellar dust is so great in that direction.

THE CENTER OF THE GALAXY

Optical astronomy teaches us almost nothing about the galactic center. In that direction the light of the stars is almost totally absorbed by the intervening interstellar dust. Photographs of the Sagittarius region, where the galactic center is located, clearly show a stellar cloud known as the great

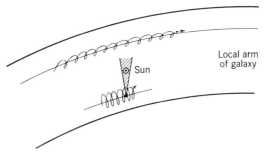

Fig. 9-17 Synchrotron emission in galactic arms.

Sagittarius star cloud, but it is not certain that it is part of the actual central condensation; it could equally well belong to one of the spiral arms between the galactic center and the sun, the same arms which elsewhere are responsible for the absorption. Apart from this cloud, everything is obscured. The screen can be penetrated by light only in the rare places that Baade has sought with the Schmidt camera on Mount Palomar. Through one of these holes, about the size of the moon, a great number of stars were observed to be at a distance of about 8,000 parsecs, and they certainly form part of the central condensation.[1] Sensitive infrared receivers can be considered for the purpose of improving the situation, such as image converters, photomultipliers, and photographic plates. In fact, the absorption of light by interstellar dust decreases strongly with increasing wavelength, being 23 times less in the near infrared (0.983μ) than in the blue (0.426μ). Kaliniak, Krassovsky, and Nikonov in the Soviet Union and J. Dufay and Berthier in France have studied the region of the galactic center in the infrared and observed another stellar cloud symmetrical with the star cloud mentioned above. Between the two is a dark band in the place where the galactic center itself would be expected to appear. Dufay and the Soviet authors agree in thinking that the two star clouds belong to the central condensation. It is quite possible, but can the galactic center itself be observed optically? Does the galaxy possess a small but extremely luminous nucleus comparable with that of the Andromeda nebula which it closely resembles in all its other aspects? This is what astronomers cannot tell us, faced as they are by an impenetrable wall of interstellar matter in front of the region which is certainly the most interesting in our galaxy.[2]

The interstellar matter is only very slightly opaque to radio waves, and it may be expected that radio astronomy will succeed in determining the structure of the galactic center about which classical astronomy gives us so little information. But it should not be thought that this work is easy. Although very strong emission is received from these regions (the radio source Sagittarius A is one of the strongest in the sky), we have no direct means of determining the distance of different emission regions which may occur on the line of sight, even with the 21-cm line, which is unaffected by differential rotation in the direction of the center, as Fig. 9-9 shows. Only indirect data are available, such as the line profiles at different distances from the center, data which can be extrapolated toward the galactic center

---

[1] The figure of 8,200 parsecs which is usually given for the distance of the galactic center cannot be considered as certain, and radio astronomy can give no information on this point. For rather firm grounds for estimating this distance at 10,000 parsecs, see G. E. Kron and N. U. Mayall, *Astron. J.*, **65:** 581 (1960).

[2] Nevertheless G. Courtès and P. Cruvellier have recently observed at the Haute-Provence Observatory weak Hα emission showing a high radial velocity of -190 kilometers per second in interstellar clouds which could well belong to the galactic center.

itself. In fact, it is only recently that these complicated problems have been disentangled, and the description that we are about to give of the central regions of the galaxy cannot yet be considered as conclusive.

If we examine again the contour maps of the central region of the galaxy shown in Fig. 9-12, we see a very compact and very intense central source situated at galactic longitude 327.71 ± 0.03° and latitude −1.47 ± 0.03°; its diameter is less than half a degree, but it seems larger because of the effect of the antenna beam. This source is superimposed on a more extended emission region, whose angular dimensions are estimated as 2° × 1° and whose center coincides in position with the compact source.

On 3.5 m, Mills's map has a quite different appearance. Westerhout's extended source appears to be much the same, allowing for antenna smoothing and errors, but in the position of the compact source a minimum is now found. Obviously, there is absorption where previously on decimeter waves there was emission. This absorption effect is even more noticeable on the map obtained on 15.2 m by Shain, on which the central region is much less intense than the neighborhood (Fig. 9-18).

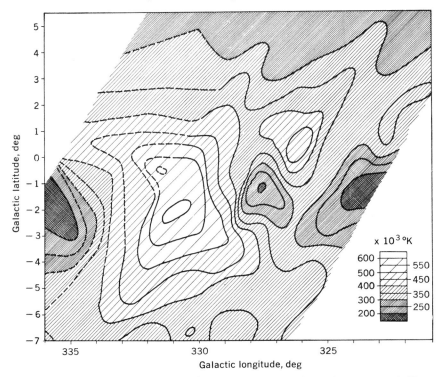

Fig. 9-18 Contour map of the galactic center on 15.2 m. Compare with Figs. 9-11 and 9-12. In the position of the galactic center (longitude 327.7°) strong absorption is seen. *(Shain.)*

Comparison of these observations shows beyond doubt that the extended source at the galactic center is nonthermal, as its flux density varies as the -0.7 power of the frequency; i.e., it is much more intense at meter wavelengths than on shorter wavelengths such as, for example, 22 cm.

On the other hand, the more compact central source cannot be of the same nature, for it shows up, at least in part, in absorption at very long wavelengths, a property which is characteristic of the galactic ionized hydrogen. We can therefore state that all or part of the compact source is thermal, i.e., is composed of ionized interstellar hydrogen. The position of this source with respect to the center of the galaxy has been much discussed. In 1955 Davies and Williams, as well as McClain, thought they had localized the thermal source in a relatively close spiral arm only 3,000 parsecs away from the sun, and they identified it as a cloud of ordinary ionized hydrogen. This hypothesis should not be rejected, although the intensity of the 22-cm source and the absorption it produces on meter wavelengths are rather exceptional. Starting from this argument and taking into account the coincidence of the source with the direction of the center of symmetry of the galaxy, which is difficult to ascribe to chance alone, Westerhout believes that it is really part of the central condensation and is located at the galactic center itself.

Until lately this is all that the study of the continuum emission from the central regions of the galaxy had revealed, under the handicap of insufficient resolving power. Great progress was made when Drake succeeded in observing the galactic center on 3.7 cm with the 85-foot reflector of the National Radio Astronomy Observatory at Green Bank, West Virginia. He used a receiver with a traveling wave tube having a passband of 1,000 Mc/s, which gives high sensitivity. The excellent resolution of this equipment (about 6 minutes of arc) enabled Westerhout's central source to be resolved into a group of four small sources lined up along the galactic plane (Fig. 9-19). The strongest source, which is also the most compact, is located exactly at the galactic center of symmetry, and there is no doubt that we are here dealing with the galactic nucleus itself. Using the two-antenna interferometer at Nançay (see Fig. 4-16), we have been able to fix the diameter of this source at 3.5 minutes of arc. It is interesting to compare the linear dimension of 8 parsecs with the nucleus of the Andromeda nebula (Fig. 9-2). They are found to be much the same. Furthermore, we have compared the flux density on 21 cm with Drake's value and also with measurements by Pariiskii, who has also resolved the central nucleus on 3 and 9 cm with the large radio telescope at Pulkovo. The source is found to be thermal, with no less than 1,000 hydrogen atoms per cubic centimeter.

Although it is tempting to identify this extraordinary object with the nucleus of the Andromeda nebula, we have as yet no proof because our knowledge of the two objects is not of the same kind for each. On the one

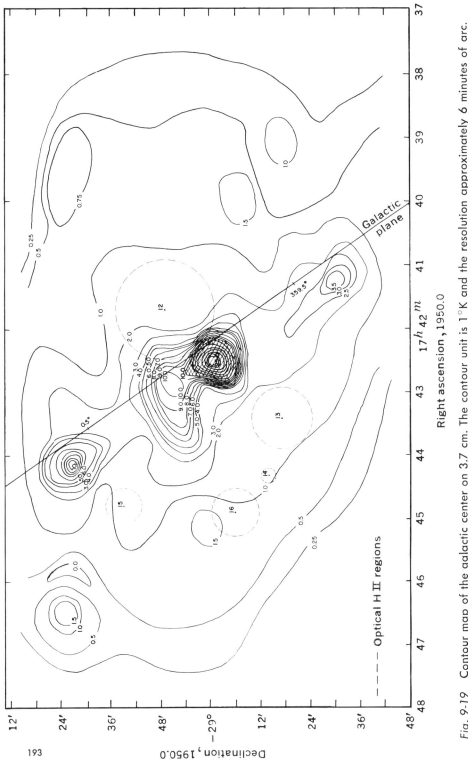

193

Fig. 9-19 Contour map of the galactic center on 3.7 cm. The contour unit is 1°K and the resolution approximately 6 minutes of arc. (Drake.)

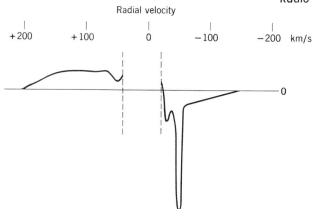

Fig. 9-20   The 21-cm line profile in the exact direction of the galactic center. *(Rougoor and Oort.)*

hand, we know from the recent observations with Lallemand's electronic camera that the nucleus of the Andromeda nebula is a particularly dense cluster of stars in rapid rotation and, on the other hand, that the nucleus of our galaxy contains ionized hydrogen. To take the comparison further, it would be necessary to know whether there is interstellar matter in the nucleus of the Andromeda nebula; work is already in progress for this purpose. The recent observations of Courtès and Cruvellier, which we have already mentioned, also introduce a very interesting element. Nevertheless, it is improbable that the Hα line that they observe comes from the nucleus itself. Little is known about the other three sources observed by Drake but not yet detected on other frequencies. Consequently it is not known whether they are thermal or not, but we hope that this problem will soon be solved and will at the same time shed light on the question of the meter-wave absorption at the galactic center. In fact, it does not seem that the central thermal nucleus can be capable on its own of producing all the absorption.

The 21-cm line has also led to progress in the study of the inner regions of the galaxy by revealing their remarkable and unexpected expansion. It had already been noticed in 1953 that the 21-cm line profiles in the central regions show extensions corresponding to velocities much greater than would be expected from galactic rotation alone. This phenomenon had been interpreted by assuming that the neutral-hydrogen clouds possessed violent turbulent motions. This explanation not being very satisfactory, the question was taken up again in 1957–1958 with the big 25-meter radio telescope at Dwingeloo, and it was quickly perceived that it could not be retained.

In the actual direction of the galactic center the hydrogen line is very wide and complex, whereas it should be narrow and unshifted if the galactic motion is limited to rotation about the center. Figure 9-20 shows the line profile obtained by Rougoor and Oort. The right-hand side, which corresponds to velocities of approach (negative), appears in absorption on the continuous background of the galactic nucleus. Consequently we are dealing with neutral hydrogen lying in front of the nucleus. Its continuum emission is strong, corresponding to temperatures higher than the excitation temperature of neutral hydrogen, which is about 100°K. On the left-hand side the line appears in emission and originates in regions situated behind the nucleus which are receding from us. Thus the whole of the neutral hydrogen existing in the central condensation is in expansion with velocities reaching 200 kilometers per second.

The regions which are expanding with a velocity of 50 kilometers per second are densest. The line profiles observed in different parts of the central condensation show that we have two fragments of spiral arms situated about 3,000 parsecs from the galactic center, taking part in the rotation at a normal speed of 200 kilometers per second and also having an expansion velocity of 50 kilometers per second, as shown in Fig. 9-21.

The cosmological and astronomical importance of this expansion will not be lost on the reader. If we suppose that the expanding arm has a thickness of 150 kiloparsecs and a density of 0.3 atom of hydrogen per cubic centimeter, a mass of hydrogen slightly greater than the mass of the sun is leaving the central regions of the galaxy per annum. At this rate, the central disk will be depleted of hydrogen in less than 100 million years, which is very short compared with the age of the galaxy, estimated to exceed 10 billion years. Consequently it is necessary for this matter to be replaced as the expansion progresses, probably at the expense of the galactic halo. The magnetic field no doubt plays an important role in these large-scale movements of matter.

Still more recently, Oort and Rougoor have investigated the distribution of neutral hydrogen quite close to the very center of the galaxy. Here there is no longer expansion, but enormous rotation velocities reaching 265 kilometers per second. The hydrogen seems to be distributed in a very dense annulus 550 parsecs from the center and in a central disk, as shown in Fig. 9-21. This leads to a complete revision of the rotation curve of the galaxy; this has been done in Fig. 9-8.

The surprising appearance of this rotation curve can be explained by a very high concentration of mass in the central parts of the galaxy. It is also very instructive to compare the distribution of neutral hydrogen just described with the nonthermal emission of the same regions as determined by Mills. He observes a certain number of spiral-arm segments corresponding, as we have said, to steps in the longitudinal profile of the galactic ridge, as observed on 3.5 m; it is interesting to superimpose Mills's arms on Fig. 9-21. We find, not without surprise, that with a single exception, all the segments are good continuations of the arms drawn by Rougoor and Oort

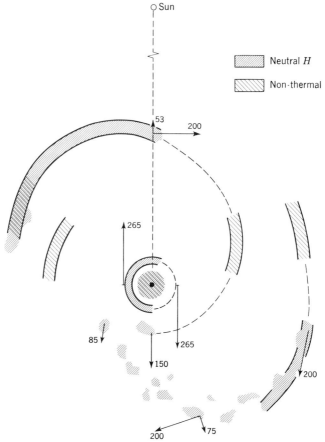

Fig. 9-21 Diagram of the central parts of the galaxy, of which we still have only fragmentary knowledge. The arms observed in the 21-cm line and by Mills on 3.5 m generally seem to overlap. The arrows indicate velocities in kilometers per second.

at 21 cm. In addition, the big central nonthermal source, whose existence is generally agreed on, coincides in dimensions with the rapidly rotating neutral-hydrogen disk. All this is still far from being explained, but it seems that it may well be the magnetic field playing the fundamental role in these structures.

Apart from right in the center, it does not seem that there is much ionized hydrogen in the inner regions of the galaxy. Westerhout thinks that ionized hydrogen appears only outside the expanding arm, at about 3,500 parsecs from the center (see Fig. 9-15). It is strongly concentrated there, and probably a physical connection between the two structures exists.

For instance, it might be supposed that the strong ionization is caused by the presence of a large number of hot young stars being formed in this region of especially favorable conditions; but this belongs to the realm of speculation.

There is nothing final yet in what we have just said about the central regions of the galaxy. Nevertheless, it can be considered as broadly understood, and in our opinion it is one of the main successes of radio astronomy. To sum up, radio astronomers have succeeded in demonstrating:

1 A very small and very intense central nucleus corresponding, no doubt, to the nucleus of the Andromeda nebula.

2 Up to 600 parsecs from the center, regions in which the neutral hydrogen is in very rapid rotation. Of particular interest is a small disk

Fig. 9-22   The galaxy NGC 5364. (Mount Wilson and Palomar Observatories photo.)

which appears to be related to the rather strong magnetic fields revealed by the existence of a source of synchrotron radiation. According to Woltjer, this source is a confined magnetic system; i.e., the lines of magnetic force are completely contained, with no external connections.

3 Farther out, the neutral hydrogen is expanding and seems to be contained mainly in two spiral arms. It is probably replenished by matter coming from the galactic halo and is no doubt channeled along magnetic lines of force. We can explain why no expansion is detected in the regions very close to the center by supposing that these lines of force do not penetrate into the central closed system. The neutral-hydrogen arms could then show up by synchrotron emission.

4 At 3,000 parsecs from the center special phenomena of unknown character are found. The hydrogen concentration is very high; it is neutral inside the arms and ionized outside. It does not appear that the magnetic field is stronger in these regions than in the rest of the galaxy.

Such is the situation. The description we have just given is conjectural on several points and also rather incomplete because radio astronomy gives us no information on the distribution of stars in the central regions of the galaxy. In some regards, the galaxy strongly recalls the Andromeda nebula, especially as concerns its outer regions. Its arms are rather tightly wound, with complex and fragmented structure. In its central regions, it reminds us rather of certain galaxies possessing a ring, like NGC 5364 (Fig. 9-22). In this object two arms can be seen leaving the center and ending in a very bright ring in which two outer arms are rooted. The bright ring might correspond to the dense galactic zones 3,000 parsecs from the center.

It is a pleasure for us to conclude this chapter by paying our respects to the Dutch team of radio astronomers who, since our branch of science began, have continually astonished us by the numerous and original results they obtain. Thanks to them, the study of the galaxy has progressed more in 10 years than it had perhaps done since Herschel.

BIBLIOGRAPHY

General

Bok, P. F., and B. J. Bok: "The Milky Way," 3d ed., Harvard University Press, Cambridge, Mass., 1957.

Oort, J. H.: Radio-frequency Studies of Galactic Structure, "Handbuch der Physik," vol. 53, Springer-Verlag, Berlin, 1959.

Oort, J. H., F. J. Kerr, and G. Westerhout: *Monthly Notices Roy. Astron. Soc.,* **118:** 379 (1958).

Shklovsky, I. S.: 'Cosmic Radio Waves," Harvard University Press, Cambridge, Mass., 1960 (Russian edition, 1956).

The 21-cm line

Kerr, F. J., J. V. Hindman, and M. S. Carpenter: *Nature,* **180:** 677 (1957).

Kerr, F. J.: *Monthly Notices Roy. Astron. Soc.,* **123:** 327 (1962).

Schmidt, M.: *Bull. Astron. Inst. Neth.,* **13:** 247 (1957).

Westerhout, G.: *Bull. Astron. Inst. Neth.,* **13:** 201 (1957).

Continuum emission

Altenhoff, W., et al.: *Veröff. der Univ. Sternwarte zu Bonn,* No. 59 (1960).

Large, M. I., D. S. Mathewson, and C. G. T. Haslam: *Monthly Notices Roy. Astron. Soc.,* **123:** 113 (1961).

Mills, B. Y., E. R. Hill, and O. B. Slee: *Observatory,* **78:** 116 (1958).

Shain, C. A., M. M. Komesaroff, and C. S. Higgins: *Australian J. Phys.,* **14:** 508 (1961).

Continuum polarization

Westerhout, G., C. L. Seeger, C. A. Muller, W. N. Brouw, and J. Tinbergen: *Bull. Astron. Inst. Neth.,* **16:** 187, 213 (1962).

Galactic center

Rougoor, G. W., and J. H. Oort: *Proc. Nat. Acad. Sci. U.S.,* **46:** 1 (1960).

GALACTIC RADIO SOURCES

10

On top of the galactic background continuum dealt with in the preceding chapter, various radio sources are superimposed, some compact, some extended, and some of relatively high intensity. In 1946 Hey, Parsons, and Phillips deduced the existence of the first of these discrete sources, situated somewhere in the constellation Cygnus. Shortly afterwards, Bolton and Stanley in Australia located the Cygnus source, and, with Ryle and Smith in England, discovered others and established the first catalogues, containing respectively 22 and 50 objects. Since that time, much effort has been given to the detection of radio sources, and tremendous radio telescopes and interferometers have been built for the purpose. Progress has been rapid, and today several hundreds of radio sources are known, the strongest being observable over the whole range of wavelengths used in radio astronomy, from a few tens of meters to a few centimeters.

Establishing a catalogue of radio sources is a tedious and difficult job, requiring antennas with well-known radiation patterns, stable receivers, and patient investigators endowed with good physical insight. The problems that have to be solved are indeed extremely complicated. First the radio sources have to be detected, then their positions on the celestial sphere have to be measured, together with their flux densities and if possible their angular dimensions. To detect and measure the flux, it is an advantage to use a large but simple antenna, with low sidelobes to reduce the risk of confusion, but this way out is unfortunately always a trouble, and on meter wavelengths often impossible. Furthermore, these antennas do not give the position and diameter with high accuracy. This is why interferometers have been much used in the study of radio sources, in spite of their inconveniences mentioned in an earlier chapter. These are the impossibility of measuring the absolute flux density of a source and especially the risk of confusion by overlap with the interference fringes of neighboring sources. In addition, large-diameter sources may go unnoticed.

Under these circumstances, it is not surprising that some divergence exists between the two principal source catalogues, that of Mills on 3.5 m and the Cambridge catalogue at 1.88 m. In the part of the sky which is visible to both groups of radio astronomers, one observing in the Southern Hemisphere and the other in the Northern, the agreement between the sources of the two catalogues is not always good, although the wavelengths are comparable. This stems in large part from the fact that the instruments used are of very different types. Mills's aerial, the celebrated "cross" that he invented, is intermediate between a simple antenna and an interferometer; the English team uses a four-element interferometer.

At the present time, only the 500 strongest sources can be considered as certain. It will be understood that in these circumstances it is premature to try to deduce certain properties of the universe from statistics bearing on radio sources, as several radio astronomers have attempted to do in a way that, in our opinion, is a little arbitrary. Nevertheless, a quick look at a map of the sky on which the positions of the strongest radio sources are plotted will show that their distribution over the celestial sphere is far from being uniform. It appears that a large proportion of the radio sources are localized in the galaxy, because an obvious concentration of sources along the galactic plane can be noticed.

Of course, radio astronomers have striven to identify sources of radio emission with optical objects. The fact that the sun is a powerful source of radio waves led them at first to suppose that the stars might be radio sources. They very quickly had to face the facts—no star is a sufficiently strong radio emitter to be detectable in the largest radio telescopes, at least in the present state of receiving technique.[1] The identification of radio sources with visible objects is usually difficult. Indeed, a very strong radio source may very well correspond with a very faintly luminous object. Cygnus A, for example, which is hardly any weaker than the quiet sun at 100 Mc/s, is identified with an optical object of the eighteenth magnitude. Furthermore, there is no a priori proof that the luminous and radio emissions of an extended source come from the same part of the object. Finally, and most importantly, only the positions of the 100 strongest sources are known with an accuracy of the order of a minute of arc. In most cases the

[1] It is easy to see that the radio emission of the sun would not be observable if it were placed at the distance of the nearest star, 3.6 parsecs away. There is a good chance, however, of detecting radio emission corresponding to the tremendous outbreaks of flare stars. Three or four sources have been thought to be radio stars, including the strong source 3C 48, whose apparent diameter is the smallest known (less than 1 second of arc). Some are now known, however, to be remote extragalactic objects.

error is up to 5 minutes of arc which, as a rule, does not allow identification.

Nevertheless, at the present time the optical counterpart of a rather large number of radio sources is known. Out of about 500 sources that are known for certain, about 50 have been identified with galactic objects and 60 at least with external galaxies. These are still too few for precise statistics, and it is uncertain whether the identifications are representative of the majority of radio sources. But the astrophysical and cosmological interest of the sources that have been identified is very great and sufficient for our consideration in this chapter and the next.

We may possibly be reproached with confining ourselves to the identified radio sources. Nevertheless, it appears preferable to us within the framework of this book to deal with physical mechanisms for the generation of radio waves in radio sources, rather than their statistical properties, which are more or less subject to caution. Furthermore, the strength and even the existence of the weak sources in the catalogues is rarely certain.

About half the identified sources correspond to galactic objects. Many of them are gaseous nebulae such as the Orion nebula or the Omega nebula. They are clouds of ionized hydrogen emitting thermal radio waves as well as the lines of hydrogen in the optical region. Other obviously nonthermal sources are very peculiar nebulosities, the best-known example being the famous Crab nebula. Still others appeared to belong to an intermediate type and are still hardly touched. An example is the source coinciding with the nebulosity M 20, not far from the galactic center.

As was mentioned in an earlier chapter, it is possible to distinguish thermal from nonthermal sources by the appearance of their spectra. The flux density of thermal sources does not change with frequency, while that of nonthermal sources does, being proportional to a power of the frequency ranging from -0.3 to -2. By observing the one source at different frequencies, it should be possible in principle to determine its character. Unfortunately, absolute flux-density measurements are still too infrequent and too inaccurate to yield definite results concerning the spectrum. Only the spectra of the strongest sources can be considered to be well known. We see that much progress remains to be made in this sphere.

GALACTIC SOURCES
OF THERMAL RADIATION

We shall begin with a few comments on the thermal radio sources. Table 10-1a gives the data on the main thermal sources, whose optical counterparts are well known since we are dealing with galactic nebulosities that are visible in the light of the Hα line of hydrogen. Figure 10-1 shows an example. About 35 of these objects are known. It is rather difficult to get a general idea of this type of object, as their characteristics vary greatly from one to another. Nevertheless, we now have rather definite ideas on the mechanisms by which they emit luminous and radio waves.

The interstellar hydrogen which is located in the vicinity of the galactic plane is not distributed uniformly, but in clouds of various dimensions. When there is no exciting source in the vicinity of the cloud, the hydrogen it contains remains in the neutral state, the lowest energy state, and emits only the 21-cm line. The galactic emission observed on this wavelength, which was dealt with in the preceding chapter, comes from these clouds. It is not usually possible to observe each cloud individually on 21 cm, for there are always several of them in the line of sight, giving the impression of continuous patches of emission.

When a hot star happens to be in the immediate neighborhood of a hydrogen cloud, or inside one, its ultraviolet radiation ionizes the gas and raises it to a temperature of the order of $10,000°K$, within a sphere whose radius varies with the temperature of the star. According to Strömgren, this radius ranges from 1 parsec for an exciting star of type $A0$ to 150 parsecs for an exceptionally hot star of spectral type $O5$. This mass of ionized

Fig. 10-1 The great Orion nebula M 42. *(Haute-Provence Observatory photo.)*

hydrogen emits radio waves by the purely thermal mechanism referred to above. Free electrons passing near protons undergo acceleration and radiate a continuous radio-frequency spectrum. This spectrum is flat; i.e., the energy radiated in unit frequency interval does not depend on the frequency.[1] There is also emission of light; some of the free electrons are captured by protons to form new excited atoms. They cascade down through the different energy levels of the atom, emitting characteristic lines of hydrogen. The spectra of ionized-hydrogen clouds therefore contain hydrogen lines, especially the Balmer series in the visible. The other elements which are present in these clouds in smaller concentrations (helium, oxygen, nitrogen, sulfur, etc.) also emit lines, mostly forbidden lines.[2]

In certain cases these lines are superimposed on a continuous spectrum which originates either from the recombination of hydrogen ions with free electrons (Balmer and Paschen continua), or from the scattering of starlight by dust contained in the nebula, or from still other causes.

The dimensions of most of the hydrogen clouds located near the galactic plane seem rather small, of the order of 10 parsecs on the average. They contain about 10 atoms of hydrogen per cubic centimeter. For the same reasons that we have given above in connection with neutral-hydrogen clouds, the radio emission of those of the clouds that are ionized gives the impression of spatially continuous emission, with only small variations. This is how the thermal part of the general emission of the galaxy originates; this was dealt with at length in the preceding chapter. But the giant clouds having especially high electron densities, and the relatively close ones, can stand out on their own. Examples are the great Orion nebula, the Omega nebula, and the Rosette nebula. Their angular diameters are relatively large because of their proximity in spite of the fact that their linear dimensions only rarely exceed 50 parsecs.

A study of Table 10-1 shows that the thermal radio sources have, on the whole, a diameter of the order of 1 degree. This circumstance greatly interferes with their study, because the resolution of most simple radio telescopes is also of this order of magnitude and it is difficult to use such equipment to measure their diameter.

The first extensive investigation of thermal sources carried out with a

---

[1] In studying radio sources, it is convenient to deal in flux density measured per unit frequency interval instead of brightness temperature as hitherto. As the flux density is proportional to $T\nu^2$ according to the Rayleigh-Jeans law, where T is the brightness temperatures and ν the frequency, it is seen that the dependence on frequency is different in the two cases. If the flux density varies as ν^{-n}, the brightness temperature varies as $\nu^{-(n+2)}$. For a thermal source, $n = 0$: the flux density is independent of frequency, but T is inversely proportional to the square of the frequency.

[2] Forbidden lines correspond to transitions excluded by the selection rules; i.e., their probability of occurrence is very low. Nevertheless, in the interstellar "vacuum" physical conditions are such that they readily occur; however, it is difficult to observe them in the laboratory.

single antenna is that of Westerhout in the Netherlands; he succeeded in detecting radio emission from about 35 gaseous nebulae on a wavelength of 22 cm.[1] Certain unidentified sources that he observed with the 25-m paraboloid at Dwingeloo are certainly thermal. The fact that they are not visible optically is explained by remembering that the absorption of light by the interstellar dust blots out anything happening at more than 1,000 or 2,000 parsecs away in the plane of the galaxy. These invisible sources are no doubt hidden behind clouds of absorbing material. Thanks to the good resolving power of the radio telescope at Dwingeloo (0.57 degree), Westerhout has been able to estimate the diameter of these radio sources approximately, and in general they coincide quite well with those of the optical nebulosities. The accuracy of diameter measurements, however, could still be improved.

One might hope to increase the accuracy by interferometry. For this purpose the authors have used the variable-spacing interferometer at Nançay, which works on the same wavelength as the Dwingeloo radio telescope. It has become possible to state the size and shape of the strongest thermal sources and to get information on the distribution of emitting regions within the body of some of them; most of these emitting nebulae possess a central dense core, which is sometimes double.

Flux-density measurements allow the number of electrons per unit volume of the nebula to be determined. Here again the estimates agree rather well with optical measurements. On the average, the electron density is of the order of 10 to 50 electrons per cubic centimeter, but the central region of certain nebulae is much denser, the density being a few thousand electrons per cubic centimeter.

The field of research on gaseous nebulae is being actively extended in both the radio and optical regions. Indeed, they possibly contain the key to the problem of the formation of the stars. The Soviet astronomer Ambartsumian discovered that the hottest stars, which are also the youngest, are almost always organized in groups of identical objects. These stellar associations of *O*- and *B*-type stars are very often situated in gaseous nebulae, although they can occasionally exist in empty regions of the sky.

It seems that there is a close relationship between the *O* and *B* associations and the nebulosity surrounding them. It may be supposed that the nebulae originate in matter ejected by the stars. This is unlikely in view of the enormous masses of the gaseous nebulae, which very often reach several thousand times that of the sun. The opposite explanation is more plausible—that the stars are created from the interstellar matter. The problem is an important one, and we may hope that the next few years may give us a conclusive answer.

[1] An identical series of observations has also been completed at the California Institute of Technology on 31 cm by R. W. Wilson and J. G. Bolton, and on 10 cm in West Germany and the U.S.S.R.

TABLE 10-1a

Some identified galactic thermal sources

Object	α(1950.0) h	m	δ(1950.0) °	′	Flux density at 22 cm, watts/m²(c/s) $\times 10^{-26}$	Diameter, degrees	Distance, pc	Remarks
Cygnus X	~20	27	~+42	09	~4,900	Complex	800 or 1,500	Complex of H II regions
Omega nebula (M 17, NGC 6618)	18	17.8	−16	52	1,030	0.1	1,700	H II region
North America nebula (NGC 7000)	20	53.4	+43		550	2.5	900	H II region
Orion nebula (M 42, NGC 1976)	05	32.8	−5	27	520	0.08	500	H II region
Rosette nebula (NGC 2244)	06	29.3	+4	57	260	1.33	1,400	H II region
Lagoon nebula (M 8, NGC 6523)	18	01.0	−24	22	260	0.8	1,200	H II region
M 16, NGC 6611	18	17.8	−16	09	260	0.41	2,000 ?	H II region
Horse's Head nebula (NGC 2024)	05	38.4	−1	54	95	0.35	500	H II region

TABLE 10-1b

Some identified galactic nonthermal sources

Object	α(1950.0) h	m	δ(1950.0) °	′	Flux density at 100 Mc/s, watts/m²(c/s) ×10⁻²⁶	Dimensions	Distance, pc	Remarks
Cassiopeia A	23	21.2	+58	32	19,000	$4' \times 4'$	3,400	Type II supernova remnant
Puppis A	8	20.3	−42	48	7,000	33′	?	Type II supernova remnant
Crab nebula (M 1, NGC 1952)	5	31.5	+21	59	1,700	$3.5' \times 5.5'$	1,100	Remnant of type I supernova of 1054
Hanbury Brown 21 (2C 1725)	20	44	+50	20	510	$2° \times 2.5°$	?	Type II supernova remnant
IC 443	06	13.7	+22	31	500	0.8°	2,000	Type II supernova remnant
Cygnus loop (NGC 6960, 6992, 6995)	20	49.5	+29	50	300	2.7°	770	Type II supernova remnant
Tycho's supernova	00	22.6	+63	52	250	6′	360 ?	Remnant of type I supernova of 1572
Auriga A	04	57	+46	30	140	1.4°	?	Type II supernova remnant
Kepler's supernova	17	27.7	−21	26	80	2.5′	1,000	Remnant of type I supernova of 1604

Fig. 10-2 The Crab nebula M 1. (Mount Wilson and Palomar Observatories photo.)

THE CRAB NEBULA

Galactic nebulae have been known for a long time. The first catalogue of these objects was established as early as the eighteenth century by the French astronomer Messier, who was struck by the hazy, nonstellar appearance of certain objects. In this catalogue, which is still in use, we find a jumble of galactic nebulae and spiral galaxies whose true nature was realized only much later. One of the galactic nebulosities struck Messier particularly by its strange and quite unique appearance, and he put it at the top of his list. We refer to the Crab nebula (M 1, NGC 1952) located in the constellation Taurus near the star ζ Tauri. This small filamentary mass is of the ninth magnitude and so is visible in a medium-size instrument (Table 10-1b and Fig. 10-2).

Since the time of Messier, the Crab nebula has never ceased to arouse interest. Its spectrum has often been photographed, for example, by Mayall at the Lick Observatory around 1937 (Fig. 10-3). It is characterized by an abnormally strong continuum with strongly doubled lines of the usual emission spectrum of interstellar matter (hydrogen lines, forbidden lines of oxygen and nitrogen, etc.) standing out. One of the components of each line comes from the filaments situated in front of the nebula, the other from behind. The line splitting, which is obviously due to Doppler effect, is the clue revealing that the front is approaching us with a speed of about 1,100 kilometers per second, while the back is receding at a similar speed. The Crab nebula is thus rapidly expanding.

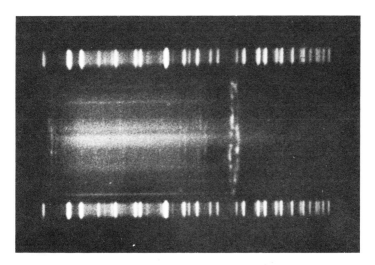

Fig. 10-3 Spectrum of the Crab nebula. The emission lines (in white) are strongly split and their structure is irregular. The strongest is from O II at 3,727 angstroms. Note the strong continuum. *(Mayall.)*

This expansion is also revealed by motion of the filaments near the edges, which Lampland discovered in 1921 by comparing photographs taken a few years apart. The annual expansion reaches 0.23 second of arc per annum along the major axis of the nebula; this is a quite measurable amount.

Knowing the angular expansion and the actual velocity of the gas measured spectroscopically, we obtain, on certain assumptions about the symmetry of the object, an approximate estimate of its distance, which is about 1,100 parsecs. This value may be subject to revision. Better still, we can calculate the approximate date of the start of the expansion by supposing that it has always gone on at the same speed. This phenomenon must have occurred in the course of the eleventh century.

Now on 4 July 1054 a spectacular explosion took place in the heavens. Not far from ζ Tauri an extremely bright star suddenly appeared, so bright that it was visible in full daylight. For some extraordinary reason, no traces of this remarkable phenomenon have been discovered in European chronicles; but the Chinese astrologers in the service of the emperor were keeping records of celestial occurrences such as comets, meteors, and new stars, and did not miss this one. The sinologist Édouard Biot, son of the famous astronomer Jean-Baptiste Biot, discovered in the imperial annals a fundamental text whose translation, revised by Duyvandak, is as follows:

"Period Chih-ho, first year, fifth moon, day Chi-ch'ou [4 July 1054], an unusual star appeared to the southeast of T'ien-kuan [ζ Tauri?]. It could be a few tenths of a degree away. After more than a year, it gradually became invisible." Other texts establish that the star disappeared in the month of April 1056 and improve some of the detail. One of them describes the new star as follows: "It was as visible in full daylight as Venus, with spikes leaving it in all directions. Its color was reddish-white. It was perfectly visible for 23 days." This last sentence no doubt means that it was visible in full daylight for 23 days after the first observation.

As we have mentioned, no one in Europe seems to have recounted this event. Yet it was observed in Japan and possibly also by the Indians in Arizona, who have left us cave drawings which very likely represent a conjunction of the new star with the crescent moon, which took place on 5 July 1054.

Everything in the Chinese and Japanese descriptions leads us to believe that we are dealing with a supernova explosion, such as is sometimes observed in external galaxies (Fig. 10-4).

For reasons still not well understood, a star, suddenly becoming unstable, explodes, probably as a result of nuclear chain reactions, and ejects a gaseous envelope at high speed. At this moment its absolute magnitude may go beyond the staggering figure of -16.5 (the brightest known stars are only of magnitude -6 and the magnitude of a complete galaxy is around −17). Its brightness then decays steadily by 1½ magnitudes in 23 days at the beginning. The total energy dissipated during the explosion reaches 10^{44} joules. It is no exaggeration to say that we are acquainted with few phenomena as grandiose as the appearance of a supernova.

The Crab nebula has the great interest of being a relatively young remnant, that is close and easy to study, of such a catastrophic explosion. Discoveries of the highest interest were to be made in it from 1940 on. In 1942 Baade published remarkable photographs of the nebula (Fig. 10-5). The first, which was obtained with a narrow-band colored filter letting through the light of a few strong spectral lines, shows that this light all comes from a filamentary structure. The other photograph was made by means of a filter letting through a wide band situated in a spectral region containing no lines, and so refers to the continuous part of the spectrum. It shows only an amorphous mass and no trace of filaments. We are therefore dealing with two entirely distinct regions, whose properties must be very different.

It seemed impossible a few years ago to explain the origin of the continuous spectrum which is, as we have said, exceptionally strong. The hypothesis proposed in the beginning envisaged temperatures of several hundreds of thousands of degrees throughout the amorphous mass, tem-

Fig. 10-4 Extragalactic supernova in the galaxy NGC 5668. These photographs, kindly supplied by C. Bertrand, were taken at Meudon Observatory on 9 and 26 May 1954. The first photograph was taken at maximum luminosity when the magnitude of the supernova was approximately equal to that of the whole galaxy, which appears as a diffuse cloud.

peratures that we could not see how to produce or maintain. In 1953 Shklovsky in the Soviet Union suggested that the radiation might come from very-high-energy electrons moving in magnetic fields. Luminous emission of this kind (which is just the synchrotron effect) had already been

Fig. 10-5 Photographs of the Crab nebula in two different spectral regions. The first, taken in the range 6,300 to 6,750 angstroms, mainly responds to the Hα line of hydrogen and the line of singly ionized sulfur at 6,724 angstroms. The second was taken in the range 7,200 to 8,400 angstroms and shows no filaments. *(Mount Wilson and Palomar Observatories photo.)*

observed in the General Electric synchrotron, but how could it possibly occur in nature? At the time, Shklovsky's idea appeared revolutionary. Nevertheless it was completely confirmed when Dombrovsky discovered in the following year that the light in the continuous spectrum possessed strong linear polarization. We have, in fact, seen that one of the principal characteristics of synchrotron emission is the linear polarization of the electromagnetic waves emitted. This polarization, which has been studied in great detail by Oort and Walraven in the Netherlands and Madame Martel in France, is clearly visible on the photographs obtained by Baade with polarizing screens in different orientations (Fig. 10-6).

Only one step remained to be taken to establish the radio emission from the Crab nebula as synchrotron emission. The radio object, which is one of the strongest sources in the sky, has dimensions quite comparable with those of the optical object ($6' \times 4'$) and closely resembles it. To verify the hypothesis, several investigations were undertaken to show that the radio emission is also polarized. The detection of linear polarization by Vitkevich on 3 cm, at the sensitivity limit of his equipment, was confirmed in 1957 by Mayer, McCullough, and Sloanaker using their 50-foot reflector at 3.15 cm. The position angle of the direction of polarization (149 degrees) and the degree of polarization (7 percent) agree well with the values determined by Oort in the visible (160 degrees and 9.2 percent). The continuous optical and radio emissions are certainly due to the same cause; the continuous optical spectrum is indeed the prolongation of the radio spectrum (Fig. 10-7).

According to Oort, the magnetic field permeating the Crab nebula is of the order of 10^{-4} gauss, or rather more than in interstellar space, where it is only 10^{-5} gauss. Probably electrons with very high energies (about 10^{11} electron volts) are responsible for the optical emission, while energies of 10^9 electron volts are sufficient to explain the radio emission.

The peculiar appearance of the filaments surrounding the nebula has not yet received a completely satisfactory explanation. Woltjer in the Netherlands supposes that they are a manifestation of large-scale electric currents related to the magnetic field. Certainly the matter in these filaments is not ionized by a central star (the nebula contains only two small stars too faint to maintain ionization) but by the ultraviolet light coming from the amorphous mass itself. It might be thought that the filaments give out considerable power in the form of thermal radio emission, but recent determinations of the diameter of the radio object, especially work of the authors on 21 cm, show that this is not so. The radio-emitting region is smaller than the filamentary structure.

We have dealt at some length with the Crab nebula because it is of the highest importance, and many investigators have devoted a large part of their activity to it. On the one hand, the Crab nebula is the best-known

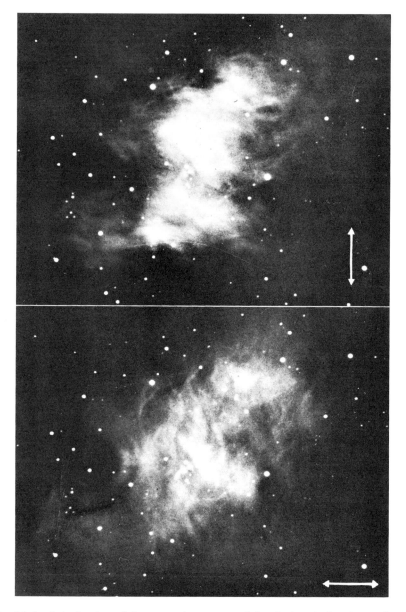

Fig. 10-6 Polarization of the amorphous mass of the Crab nebula. These photographs were taken with the 200-inch Mount Palomar telescope through polaroid screens. The orientation of the plane of polarization is shown by the arrows. *(Baade.)*

example, and the easiest to study, of a supernova remnant, and on the other hand, it has proved that synchrotron emission of electromagnetic waves is a very efficient mechanism, which occurs in nature on a large scale. Finally, the presence of high-energy particles in the heart of the nebula leads us to think that it may be a powerful emitter of cosmic rays. Some investigators have supposed that objects analogous to the Crab nebula, which should be rather numerous in the galaxy as we shall see later, could be sufficient to explain the whole of the observed cosmic radiation. Although it is very difficult to evaluate, even roughly, all the parameters needed to confirm or deny this theory, it now seems probable that the contribution of the supernovae is not enough, but, with the exception of flares which, as mentioned in connection with the sun, occasionally eject particles with medium energies, no other sources of cosmic rays are yet known. It would also be highly desirable to determine directly by measurements of the direction of arrival of high-energy particles reaching the solar system, whether the Crab nebula is indeed a source of cosmic rays. Such a project is very difficult because the particles, being charged, are deflected by the galactic, solar, and terrestrial magnetic fields, but with the advances in the field of artificial satellites and cosmic probes it is not inconceivable.

The origin of the high-speed electrons radiating in the Crab nebula is still uncertain. It is difficult to decide between the several suggestions that have been made:

1 They are left over from the explosion itself.

2 They are still being supplied. This idea depends on the fact, observed

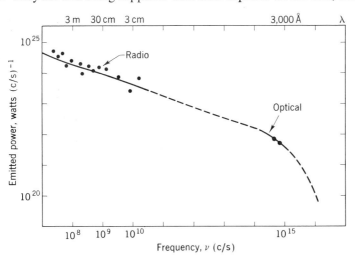

Fig. 10-7 Continuous spectrum of the Crab nebula. The radio spectrum is a good continuation of the optical spectrum. The points refer to the observational data. *(Woltjer.)*

by Baade in particular, that the central regions of the nebula still periodically eject small clouds of high-velocity matter.

3 They come from nuclear reactions caused by collisions between cosmic rays and gas atoms of the nebula. According to G. R. Burbidge, this phenomenon should be quite general and might be the cause of the high-energy electrons responsible for the nonthermal radio emission of the galactic arms and halo.

In any case, the electrons must be partly accelerated by collisions with strongly turbulent matter or shock waves in the nebula.

What finally happens to these electrons after their creation or acceleration? They gradually lose their energy in the form of radio or optical radiation. Many of them succeed in escaping from the nebula and spreading through the galaxy. According to Woltjer, the supernova remnants in the galaxy taken together might be enough to create sufficient high-speed electrons to explain the whole of the nonthermal emission of the galaxy. This would make the Fermi acceleration mechanism in interstellar space superfluous.

It is obvious that much work remains to be done to bring everyone into agreement and to construct a complete and satisfactory theory of the Crab nebula. Even so, its study has already led to surprising progress in our understanding of astrophysics.

NONTHERMAL RADIO SOURCES
IN THE GALAXY

Though it was exceptionally bright, the supernova of 1054 is not the only one whose appearance has been noticed in the Milky Way.[1] It is fascinating to pore through ancient chronicles for information on so rare a phenomenon, but it is a thankless task, because the objects reported are much more likely to be comets than new stars.

The Chinese texts contain numerous and valuable data, but they are not the only source. A new star was observed in the constellation Scorpius by two Arab astronomers in 827. Again in Scorpius, another was noted in 1006 by the monk Epidanus of St. Gallen as well as by Bar-Hebraeus in Syria. It is also mentioned in the Chinese journals for 3 April 1006, as well as in the Japanese chronicles. For lack of precise positions, it is not known whether these two supernovae can be identified with two of the radio sources belonging to the constellation Scorpius. On the other hand the position of the two latest supernovae to have appeared in our galaxy are known quite exactly. One was observed by the famous Danish astronomer Tycho Brahe in 1572, and the other by Kepler himself in 1604. Both were also well observed in the Far East and in several European observatories.

[1] On the average, one supernova appears every 30 years in a normal galaxy.

Now two quite strong radio sources correspond exactly in position with these two supernovae (Table 10-1*b*). The optical remnant was more difficult to discover. That of the supernova of 1604 was photographed by Baade on 18 June 1941 by means of the 100-inch telescope on Mount Wilson in the form of filamentary nebulosities arranged around the position given by Kepler (Fig. 10-8). The overall diameter is of the order of 2.5 minutes, and a spectral-line shift corresponding to an expansion has been observed. The remnant of Tycho's supernova is even harder to see. It was recently photographed with the Palomar telescope by Baade and Minkowski (see Fig. 10-8), and no measurements of expansion velocity could be made. Probably the faint luminosity of these objects is due to their location in highly absorbing regions of the galaxy. Still, it is possible that physical conditions in the two nebulosities are rather different from those in the Crab nebula, either because of the high density of the surrounding interstellar matter or because of their less advanced age (350 years instead of 900). Also, the spectrum of their radio emission, which we have recently been able to establish by measurements around 21 cm, is different. Whereas the flux density of the Crab nebula varies as $v^{-0.2}$, that of our two sources varies as $v^{-0.7}$, which corresponds to emission from electrons with a different energy

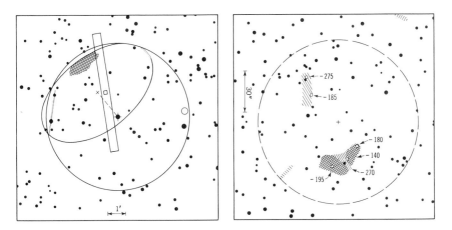

Fig. 10-8 The supernovae of 1572 and 1604. The position given by Kepler for the supernova of 1604 is shown by a cross in the drawing on the right. Filaments (crosshatched) whose radial velocities have been measured and indicated in kilometers per second can be distinguished among the field stars. The center of the radio source is inside the circle. On the left, the position given by Tycho Brahe for the supernova of 1572 is indicated by a small circle and the radio object is contained within the elongated rectangle. A few very faint filaments comprise the visible remnants of the supernova, whose general shape may be elliptical or circular. Tycho Brahe probably made a substantial error in measuring the right ascension of this supernova. (*Minkowski.*)

Fig. 10-9 The radio source Cassiopeia A. The few filaments visible among the stars are probably the remnants of a supernova explosion. Close observation shows that they are arranged in a circular arc. This very faint object has been identified with the strongest radio source in the sky. *(Mount Wilson and Palomar Observatories photo.)*

spectrum. In this case, there are few high-energy electrons. This spectrum is also close to that of several other galactic radio sources which we shall now examine.

Cassiopeia A, the strongest radio source in the sky, was identified in 1954 by Baade and Minkowski, again with the Palomar telescope. It is now very well known, and it is certain that we are dealing with a circular nebulosity more or less fragmented, whose diameter is about 4 minutes and which possesses an enormous expansion velocity of 7,440 kilometers per second (Fig. 10-9). It has also been possible to observe its proper motion, which gives a distance estimate of 3,400 parsecs. In spite of the faint luminosity of the object, excellent spectra have been obtained which show the characteristic lines of interstellar matter strongly displaced by Doppler effect. It does not seem, as with the Crab nebula, to emit in the continuum. The excitation of the gas, which corresponds to a temperature of nearly 20,000°K for a relatively high density of 1,000 electrons per cubic centimeter, is doubtless due not to the effect of ultraviolet radiation but to collision of the rapidly expanding gas with the surrounding interstellar medium, which is dense in this part of the galaxy. The total mass of gas ejected is of the order of magnitude of the sun's mass, whereas the mass of the Crab nebula amounts to hardly a tenth of this.

There can be no doubt that we are again dealing with a supernova remnant. But this object is rather different from the Crab nebula both in mass of ejected matter and in expansion velocity, which is extremely high. The supernova of 1054, like those of 1572 and 1604, was of type I, which is characterized by the regularity of its light curve and by its high luminosity at maximum. On the other hand, Cassiopeia A seems to be the remnant of a supernova of type II, which is characterized by less luminosity (the absolute magnitude at maximum reaching only −12) and a generally irregular light curve. This classification is not arbitrary, and it has been possible to associate most of the supernovae observed in external galaxies with one group of phenomena or the other. According to Minkowski, the type II supernovae correspond to the explosion of very massive stars, and it should not be surprising that a mass equal to the sun's is ejected in the course of the phenomenon.

The explosion of the supernova involved is relatively recent. It can be placed around the year 1700. Although astronomical observations were seriously and assiduously pursued at this period, it is not surprising that the supernova went unnoticed, both because of its remoteness and because of the strong extinction of light in the intervening interstellar medium. At the time of maximum, the magnitude of the new star could hardly have exceeded +5, not much more than the eye can detect without instruments.

The physical nature of Cassiopeia A is today reasonably well understood, thanks to the theoretical work of Shklovsky. This author, like his predecessors, thinks that the emission is synchrotron radiation. At the time of its explosion the supernova ejected an ionized gaseous mass containing magnetic field and relativistic particles responsible for the emission. In this expanding mass, the magnetic field should decrease roughly as the inverse square of the dimensions of the cloud, and the energy of the particles inversely as the dimensions, in an adiabatic expansion, the energy loss by radiation being relatively low. The flux density due to synchrotron emission should thus decrease in the course of time, and in the case of Cassiopeia A the calculation gives a decrease of 2 percent per annum. Observations of the ratio of the flux density of Cassiopeia A to that of Cygnus A (the latter should vary only very slowly with time) now go back far enough for such a decrease to be quite measurable. In fact, Högbom and Shakeshaft at Cambridge and Findlay at Green Bank have found a slow decrease in flux density of about 1 percent per annum. Shklovsky's idea is thus confirmed, and it is probable that a refinement of his theory would lead to better quantitative agreement with observation. It should be mentioned in this regard that it is a pity that Cassiopeia A has been used as a flux-density standard in radio astronomical observations. It would be better to take an extragalactic source whose time scale is necessarily longer. Recent work by the authors has shown that the radio emission of Cassiopeia A originates in a spherical shell, nearly 4 minutes in diameter and 0.6 minute in thickness.

Apart from this exceptional object, about 10 other nonthermal galactic radio sources have been identified, all with probable supernova remnants, which may be recognized by their filamentary spherical structure. In Table 10-1*b* we give the characteristics of a few of them.[1] Because of its large dimensions (about 3 degrees) and its high luminosity, the Cygnus loop has been much studied in recent years. Here again, the expansion velocity has been measured both by the Doppler shift of its spectral lines and by position measurements of the filaments. The speed averages 90 kilometers per second. The distance to the Cygnus loop is relatively low, 770 parsecs, and its average diameter is 40 parsecs.

The nature of these radio sources is no doubt the same as that of Cassiopeia A. But they must be of more advanced age, in view of the fact that their present flux density is much less. Shklovsky's theory, which we have spoken of above, predicts that the rate of decrease of flux density depends strongly on the spectrum of the source, i.e., ultimately on the energy spectrum of the electrons responsible for the emission. The higher the spectral index, i.e., the more the flux density varies with frequency, the faster the decrease of flux density. In fact, all the large supernova remnants such as the Cygnus loop, which are relatively ancient, have a very small

---

[1] Several other very extended but less well-known radio sources could be added, among them Vela X whose radiation is strongly polarized.

spectral index of the order of 0.4 or 0.5. Conversely, the supernovae of Kepler and Tycho, whose spectral indexes are very high, as likewise that of Cassiopeia A, have already become rather weak sources, while the Crab nebula, which is three times older, is still extremely bright because its spectral index is very small, hardly 0.3.

Here again, Shklovsky's theory receives good qualitative confirmation. It can nevertheless be criticized for not taking account of the effect of the interstellar matter which efficiently retards the expansion of supernova remnants. The appearance of the optical spectrum of these objects shows that the luminous emission is essentially excited by collision. Again, these odd-shaped filamentary nebulae usually have an irregular appearance and are fragmented into several pieces, reflecting the inhomogeneities in the distribution of interstellar matter. Finally, the electrons can be continually accelerated by encounters with the shock wave that accompanies the expansion of the envelope, whereas Shklovsky supposes that there is no acceleration after the initial explosion. These little-known phenomena all make the quantitative study of supernova remnants very difficult, especially age estimates. The age of 50,000 years which has been suggested for the Cygnus loop seems to us a little high. It is also not known why the energy spectrum of the relativistic electrons varies so much with the radio source.

In any case, the frequency of supernova explosions in the galaxy is high enough to maintain a large number of objects resembling Cassiopeia A or the Cygnus loop. Although only a few of them are known at present, it is not absurd to suppose that there may be several hundreds, even a thousand, most of which are optically invisible because of interstellar absorption. One may also wonder whether all the nonthermal radio sources in the galaxy are not supernova remnants. Even further, these supernova remnants no doubt finish up by occupying such large volumes as to intrude upon one another and to be no longer distinguishable by radio telescope, thus making an important and perhaps essential contribution to the general nonthermal emission of the galaxy.

GALACTIC RADIO SOURCES
AND THE 21-CM LINE

We now come to the contributions made by studies of the 21-cm line to galactic radio sources. Some of them contain neutral hydrogen, and it is natural to try to deduce from the observed emission line profiles information on internal motion revealed by Doppler shifts. Using the 60-foot radio telescope of the Agassiz station of Harvard College Observatory, Menon showed that the expanding Cygnus-loop envelope (see Fig. 10-10) has a neutral-hydrogen region on the inside. This same author and van Woerden in the Netherlands have also studied Orion, a complex structure whose main feature is the great ionized nebula M 42, which is a very strong radio source. A great ring of bright nebulosities, Barnard's ring, may also be seen; it could well be a supernova remnant of very great age. Line profiles at different positions in this object show that it is in expansion with a speed of

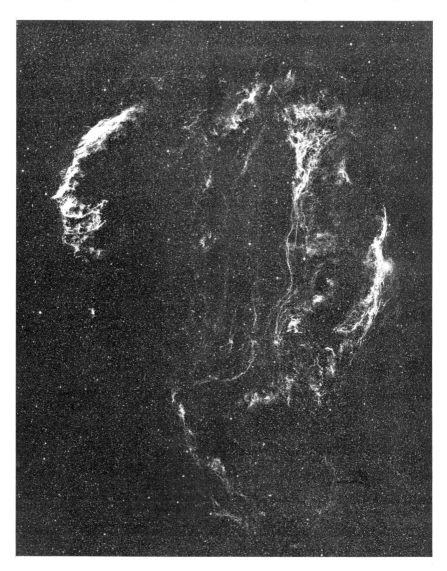

Fig. 10-10 The Cygnus loop. This remarkable filamentary nebulosity occupies about 9 square degrees of the sky. It is probably a supernova remnant. *(Mount Wilson and Palomar Observatories photo.)*

about 10 kilometers per second. Barnard's ring, whose mass would be equal to 110,000 times that of the sun, thus has more than one similarity with the Cygnus loop.

In general, and in spite of a few exceptions, the 21-cm emission regions essentially coincide with optically absorbing regions. The neutral hydrogen and interstellar dust thus seem to be closely associated, as foreshadowed in the preceding chapter. Furthermore, the absorption lines of calcium and sodium observed in the optical spectrum of certain stars and attributed to interstellar matter, appear to be formed in regions where the neutral-hydrogen density is high. This indicates once again that the neutral hydrogen, which can be observed only by radio astronomers, is to be compared with the interstellar matter of optical astronomy. The 21-cm line will no doubt permit very detailed study of interstellar matter. Investigations of neutral-hydrogen clouds far from the galactic plane have been undertaken by van Woerden at Dwingeloo. It is laborious work, and the interpretation of the observed profiles is often delicate.

In these investigations the hydrogen line is observed in emission. But if certain especially strong radio sources are studied on 21 cm, it is occasionally noted that the line appears in absorption. The continuous emission of the source is absorbed by intervening neutral-hydrogen regions. Each hydrogen cloud absorbs on the frequency corresponding to its own radial velocity, and the profile of the absorption line can be very complex. We have seen how observation of the galactic center on 21 cm allowed the structure of the neutral hydrogen to be determined and in particular revealed an arm in expansion 3,000 parsecs from the center. Hagen, Lilley, and McClain in 1955, and then C. A. Muller in 1957, made similar studies on Cassiopeia A, with 50- and 82-foot paraboloids respectively. The result is shown in Fig. 10-11, which shows the line profile in the direction of Cassiopeia A in a direction just away from the source. It will be seen that the parts of the profile which are in absorption in front of the source show up in emission away from it. This signifies that the brightness temperature of the source on 21 cm is higher than the excitation temperature of the neutral-hydrogen clouds which absorb the radiation, say about 100°K. This will easily be understood by reference to the laws of radiation transfer established in Chap. 6. Also note that some parts of the line profile show up in emission outside the source but do not correspond to absorption when the source is pointed at. These are due to clouds situated behind the source. The two maxima of the emission line in the direction of Cassiopeia A correspond, according to the Dutch observations, to two galactic arms situated 500 and 3,000 parsecs respectively from the solar system. As these two arms show absorption, it is certain that Cassiopeia A is farther away than 3,000 parsecs. As no trace of absorption can be detected at the highest radial velocities, which still correspond to the 3,000-parsec arm, it may be

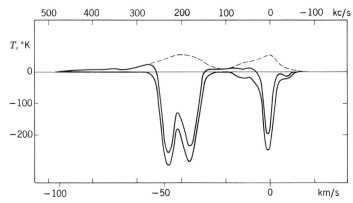

Fig. 10-11 The 21-cm line profile in the direction of Cassiopeia A. The broken line shows the emission profile for neighboring regions. The middle line is the profile observed on the radio source itself. From the difference between these curves we deduce the lower line, which represents the contribution to absorption by neutral-hydrogen clouds closer to us than the radio source. *(Muller.)*

deduced that Cassiopeia A belongs to it. There is nothing surprising in this, for it is known that type II supernovae like the one that gave rise to this source form part of the population characteristic of spiral arms (population I). We may conclude that the distance to Cassiopeia A lies between 3,000 and 4,500 parsecs. This estimate agrees remarkably well with the distance of 3,400 parsecs obtained optically by Minkowski by a totally independent method.

The 21-cm line thus offers for the first time a way of evaluating the distances of radio sources without reference to optical observations. It is probable that the distance of many other radio sources will be successfully determined with instruments that are sufficiently sensitive and have sufficiently narrow bands, especially sources whose optical counterpart is invisible. It will then be possible to tell whether a particular radio source belongs to our galaxy or is extragalactic, thus solving one of the fundamental problems in the statistics of radio sources. The study of absorption line profiles will also lead to very valuable information on the dimensions and random velocities of the neutral-hydrogen clouds.

The most spectacular result obtained from the 21-cm line in absorption is the first direct measurement of the galactic magnetic field. The Zeeman effect splits the line into two oppositely polarized circular components, but because the splitting is extremely weak, amounting to only a few tenths of cycles per second, which is much less than the line width, it is very difficult to measure. Nevertheless, after several years of effort, R. D. Davies, G. L. Vershuur, and P. A. T. Wild at Jodrell Bank have succeeded in observing the splitting of the absorption line in the radiation from Taurus A. The splitting occurs in a cloud where the magnetic field is 3×10^{-5} gauss. In front of Cassiopeia A and Cygnus A a weaker field of about 5×10^{-6} gauss is observed. In order of magnitude, these values are about what is generally assumed in the galactic disk. But one difficulty of interpretation remains: the field so measured by Zeeman effect is the field inside the hydrogen cloud producing the absorption, and there is nothing to show that it is equal to the general magnetic field of the galaxy in which the cloud is immersed.

BIBLIOGRAPHY

General

Shklovsky, I. S.: "Cosmic Radio Waves," Harvard University Press, Cambridge, Mass., 1960 (Russian edition, 1956).

Thermal sources

Osterbrock, D., and E. Flather: *Astrophys. J.,* **129:** 26 (1959).
Westerhout, G.: *Bull. Astron. Inst. Neth.,* **14:** 215 (1958).

Nonthermal sources

Baade, W., and R. Minkowski: *Astrophys. J.,* **119:** 206, 215 (1954).
Shklovsky, I. S.: *Astron. Zh.,* **37:** 256, 369 (1960); English translation in *Soviet Astron.-AJ,* **4:** 243, 355 (1960). See also R. N. Bracewell (ed.), "Paris Symposium on Radio Astronomy," Stanford University Press, Stanford, Calif., 1959.

Crab nebula

Oort, J. H., and T. Walraven: *Bull. Astron. Inst. Neth.,* **13:** 285 (1956).
Woltjer, L.: *Bull. Astron. Inst. Neth.,* **14:** 39 (1958).

EXTRAGALACTIC RADIO SOURCES

11

As our galaxy is a very flattened system, the radio sources it contains are all very close to the galactic plane. But there are also a large number of sources away from this part of the sky, and their effectively isotropic distribution suggests that we are dealing with objects outside the galaxy. Since our galaxy generates strong radio emission, we can expect to receive measurable radio-frequency power from the closest spiral nebulae. This is indeed what has been observed, and a rather large number of radio sources have now been identified with relatively nearby galaxies. More surprising has been the identification of certain sources like Cygnus A, which is one of the strongest of all, with galaxies that are very remote and consequently very faint. It seems, therefore, that a distinction should be drawn between these objects and the normal galaxies that we are now going to study. Nevertheless, all the extragalactic radio sources have one characteristic in common: their flux density always varies approximately as the -0.3 to -1.0 power of the frequency and is generally attributed to synchrotron emission.

NORMAL GALAXIES

Among external galaxies, the great Andromeda nebula (see Fig. 11-1) is the first whose radio emission was detected. This important discovery is due to Hanbury Brown and Hazard and was made with the fixed 220-foot paraboloid at Jodrell Bank in 1950 on 1.9 m. In spite of the relatively low resolving power of this instrument, it was immediately noticed that the radio emission came from a much more extended region than the physical object occupied. This conclusion was confirmed by later observations, especially those of Seeger on 75 cm and of Large, Mathewson, and Haslam with the large steerable radio telescope at Manchester on the same wavelength (Fig. 11-1). Thanks to this instrument, Hanbury Brown and Hazard were also able to observe the great extent of the galaxy on 1.9 and 1.27 m.

The fact that the radio galaxy is much more extended than the optical object may be explained by supposing that the Andromeda nebula possesses a halo analogous to our galaxy, but 2.5 times larger.

Comparison of the radio emission of these two spiral nebulae shows that their properties are very similar. On 3.7 m the galaxy emits 2×10^{21} watts per cycle per second, and the Andromeda nebula 1.8×10^{21}. The flux density of the latter varies approximately as the -0.7 power of the frequency. This spectrum is like that of the nonthermal component of galactic radiation, which confirms that the role of thermal emission from ionized hydrogen in galaxies is quite limited, at least at long wavelengths. Because of its rapid decrease of flux density when the wavelength decreases, the

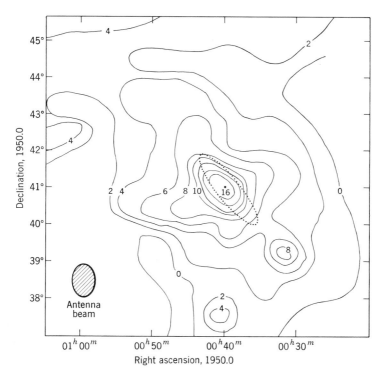

Fig. 11-1 Contour map of the Andromeda nebula on 73 cm. Note the existence of a central emission region essentially coinciding with the optical galaxy, whose shape is shown by the broken line, and the vastly extended halo. Like the halo of our galaxy, this halo emits approximately 90 percent of the total flux on meter wavelengths. The contour unit is 1°K. *(Large, Mathewson, and Haslam.)*

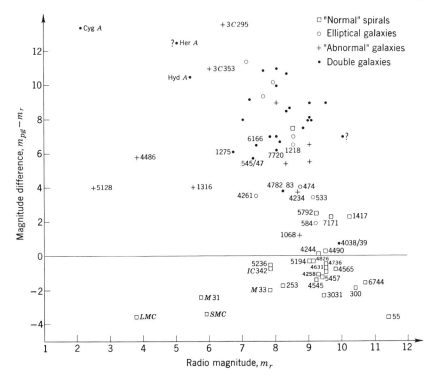

Fig. 11-2 Comparison between optical and radio emissions of radio sources identifiable with galaxies. The numbers are those of the Messier catalogue, the New General Catalogue, and the third Cambridge catalogue. The optical magnitudes (m_{pg}) are corrected for interstellar absorption.

Andromeda nebula has not yet been observed at wavelengths less than 75 cm. Later, Hanbury Brown and Hazard detected emission from other nearby galaxies, such as M 33, M 51, and M 81. In the Southern Hemisphere, Mills investigated the continuous emission of the Magellanic clouds and of several other galaxies.

The data are now numerous enough to make it profitable to compare the intensity of the radio emission of galaxies with their visible emission. For this purpose, it is convenient to express the flux density received from a radio source by its radio magnitude m_r, which is defined by the relation

$$m_r = -54.4 - 2.5 \log S_r$$

where S_r is the flux density in watts per square meter per cycle-per-second on a wavelength of 1.9 m. The constant in this equation was chosen so that the radio magnitude of a normal galaxy would be essentially the same as its optical magnitude. As in optics, the magnitude increases as the flux density decreases.

Let us plot the magnitude difference $m_{pg} - m_r$ (Fig. 11-2) against the radio magnitude. The most powerful sources appear on the left-hand side of the figure. The greater the ordinate of a point representing a galaxy, the greater the radio emission for a given optical luminosity.

We notice that the points representing most of the normal spiral galaxies are grouped together in the lower part of the diagram. This means that for all these galaxies the ratio of the energy emitted in the form of radio waves to the optical energy is essentially the same.

Apart from these spiral galaxies, three irregular Magellanic-type galaxies give measurable radio emission which is relatively weaker than that of the spirals, since they have $m_{pg} - m_r$ around -3.

With these exceptions, the radio-frequency behavior of these galaxies is in no way surprising and resembles that of our galaxy. But many other galaxies, some of which are not at all different in their optical appearance from the former, are identified with much more powerful radio sources. They are generally referred to as *radio galaxies,* although this term is not entirely satisfactory. Investigations of these mysterious objects will be the subject of another part of this chapter.

THE 21-CM LINE IN EXTERNAL GALAXIES

Outside our galaxy the neutral-hydrogen emission line has been detected in several distant nebulae. The first observation of this kind concerns the Magellanic clouds, dwarf galaxies very close to our galaxy, whose 21-cm radiation was detected in 1953 by Kerr and Hindman in Australia with a 36-foot paraboloid. The 21-cm contour map published by these authors shows that the neutral hydrogen extends well beyond the stellar concentration. Detailed study of the line profiles at different points of the clouds shows that they rotate about each other (Fig. 11-3). The rotation at each

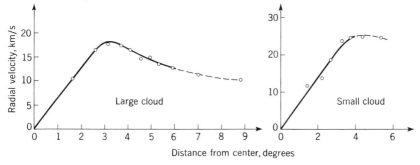

Fig. 11-3 Rotation curve for the Magellanic clouds. As the inclination of these galaxies with respect to the line of sight is not accurately known, only radial velocities are given. The distance of the two clouds is about 50,000 parsecs. *(Kerr and de Vaucouleurs.)*

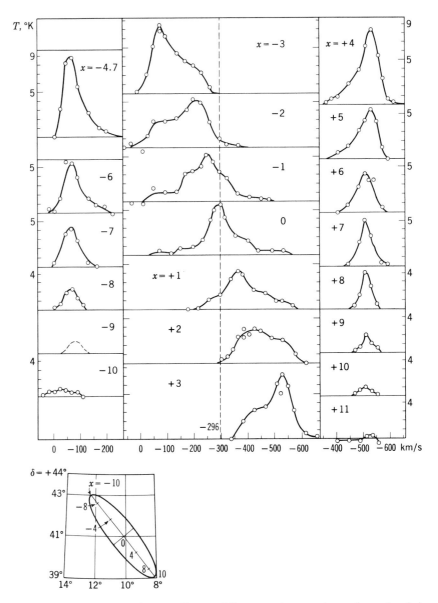

Fig. 11-4 Some 21-cm line profiles at different points on the major axis of the Andromeda nebula. The coordinates of these points were chosen as indicated on the small sketch. Note the displacement of the line as one runs along the major axis. This reveals the rotation. *(Van de Hulst, Raimond, and van Woerden.)*

point is controlled by the law of universal gravitation, and it is in principle possible to deduce the total mass of each cloud from the rotation curve. Kerr and de Vaucouleurs find 10^9 solar masses for the large cloud and 1.3×10^9 for the small cloud. Comparison of these figures with the mass of neutral hydrogen determined by measuring the total intensity of 21-cm emission is particularly interesting. For the large cloud, they get more than 0.6×10^9 solar masses, or a proportion of neutral hydrogen reaching 70 percent. The small cloud is not so rich in neutral hydrogen (about 40 percent of the total mass).[1] These figures essentially give the proportion of the interstellar matter contained in these galaxies, because it is agreed that the neutral hydrogen is the principal constituent of the interstellar medium. Only a very small proportion is ionized by radiation from hot stars, and the interstellar dust responsible for optical absorption has an extremely low density. However, an unknown quantity of hydrogen might be present in the form of H_2 molecules, which cannot be detected by conventional means.

By way of comparison, we may recall that our galaxy has only 1.5 percent of its mass in the form of neutral hydrogen. The Magellanic-type spirals are thus very rich in interstellar matter. They represent a particularly young type of galaxy, at least if it is assumed that stars are formed from interstellar matter.

Three galaxies farther off than the Magellanic clouds have now been carefully investigated on 21 cm by Heeschen and Mrs. Dieter at Harvard and especially by Raimond, van de Hulst, van Woerden, and Louise Volders with the 25-meter reflector at Dwingeloo. These are M 31 (the Andromeda nebula), M 33, and M 101. The Dutch radio astronomers measured the 21-cm line profile for a certain number of carefully chosen points in the galaxy under investigation. For certain other galaxies only the total 21-cm emission has been measured.

Figure 11-4 shows the line profiles in different parts of the Andromeda nebula from which the rotation curve can be deduced. The result does not agree very well with the optical observations of Schwarzschild deduced from observations of Doppler shifts in spectral lines (Fig. 11-5). Several authors agree in thinking that the rotation curve measured by means of the 21-cm line corresponds better to reality. More recently, the Dutch radio astronomers have measured the rotation curve of M 33. This curve is shown in Fig. 11-5 together with the rotation curve of our galaxy.

As with the Magellanic clouds, the 21-cm line profiles lead to an estimate of the mass distribution of neutral hydrogen at different distances from the center of the nebula. The curves representing this distribution for

[1] The values given for the masses of the Magellanic clouds are rather uncertain and in course of revision. The mass of the large cloud could be much greater than indicated here.

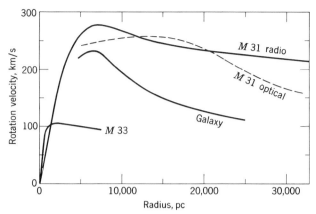

Fig. 11-5 Rotation curves for our galaxy, M 31, and M 33. The broken curve is the interpretation given by Schwarzschild to the optical observations of radial velocities in the Andromeda nebula. The other curves are deduced from radio astronomical observations. The distances of the Andromeda nebula and M 33 have been roughly estimated at 630 parsecs. (Van de Hulst, Volders, et al.)

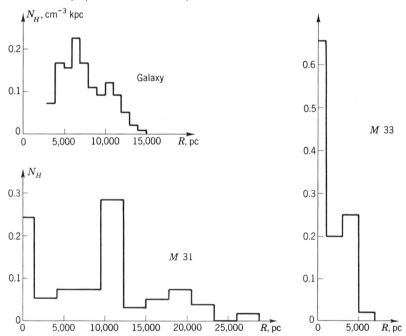

Fig. 11-6 Distribution of neutral hydrogen in our galaxy, M 31, and M 33 as a function of distance from the center. As nothing is known of the thickness of the galactic disk in M 31 and M 33, the densities N_{II} are those that would obtain if the hydrogen were distributed in a disk of thickness equal to 1,000 parsecs. In our own galaxy, where the actual thickness is about 200 parsecs, the actual density of neutral hydrogen is five times greater than the values indicated here. (Van de Hulst, Volders, et al.)

our galaxy, M 31, and M 33 are graphed on Fig. 11-6. From this point of view, important differences exist among these three galaxies. In particular, the neutral hydrogen extends much farther from the center in the Andromeda nebula than in our galaxy, and the run of the two distribution curves is quite different.

Table 11-1 summarizes the characteristics of the principal extragalactic nebulae observed on 21 cm, and in particular gives an estimate of the quantity of neutral hydrogen they contain. Although the observational errors are occasionally considerable, it is beyond doubt that the proportion of interstellar matter differs greatly according to the type of galaxy. From the observations made in the Netherlands, it appears that the greater the intrinsic luminosity of the galaxy, the greater the mass of neutral hydrogen.

TABLE 11-1

Total mass and mass of neutral hydrogen in a few galaxies *

Object	Distance, kpc	Type	Total mass, solar masses	Neutral-hydrogen mass, solar masses	Fraction of interstellar matter, percent
M 32	630	Elliptical	14×10^9	$<0.06 \times 10^9$	<0.4
M 31	630	Sb	380×10^9	4.5×10^9	1.2
Our galaxy	—	Sb or Sc	100×10^9	1.5×10^9	1.5
M 101	2,600	Sc	140×10^9	3×10^9	2
M 33	630	Sc	18×10^9	0.99×10^9	6
SMC	50	Magellanic	1.3×10^9	0.5×10^9	40 ?
LMC	50	Magellanic	$> 10^9$	0.7×10^9	<70 ?
IC 1613	440	Irregular	0.05×10^9	0.05×10^9	100

* From Volders and van de Hulst. The distance estimates may be subject to revision, in which case the neutral-hydrogen mass will have to be corrected.

The astrophysical and cosmological importance of this result is considerable, but its interpretation is still subject to caution. It will certainly be one of the foundations of any theory concerning the origin and evolution of the galaxies.

RADIO GALAXIES

We have just seen that only a few radio sources can be identified with galaxies that are comparable with our own in their radio-emissive behavior. But many other radio sources, generally much more powerful ones, have been identified with surprisingly faint, small, and therefore very distant galaxies. These are the radio galaxies.

For quite a long time, the number of radio sources identified with dis-

tant galaxies has remained rather limited, and it has been found that these few objects almost all exhibited important optical peculiarities. It was only a step, which was quickly taken, to conclude from this that there was a connection between the fact that a galaxy had some peculiarity (e.g., two nuclei, distortion, etc.) and that it was a powerful radio emitter. Nevertheless, doubts began to rise when it was realized how difficult it is to distinguish a peculiar or abnormal galaxy from a normal one. Indeed, the variety among galaxies is absolutely astonishing, as is obvious from an inspection of the recent photographic catalogues of galaxies, such as the Hubble Atlas, for example. Vorontsov-Velyaminov goes as far as proposing to replace the usual Hubble classification, or its derivatives, by a real morphological description of each galaxy. Thus the distinction between normal and abnormal galaxies appears to be rather arbitrary.

Then again, the numerous new identifications established in the last two years, the best of which are shown in Fig. 11-2, have revealed that radio galaxies include the most diverse objects from the optical point of view. The impression given by an examination of these identifications, which are due principally to Bolton and Matthews at the California Institute of Technology, and to Mills and Dewhirst, may be summarized in two points.

1 A wide variety of objects may be found among radio galaxies, including Sb and Sc spirals of the commonest type, with a slight predominance of elliptical or spherical galaxies without obvious structure, and perhaps double galaxies (galaxies with two nuclei or physically connected pairs); the spectra of these objects, where they have been obtained, are not in general particularly abnormal, although there are some notable exceptions.

2 The radio galaxies nevertheless seem to be galaxies with large dimensions and high intrinsic luminosity. For those whose distance can be approximately determined, the mean absolute magnitude is of the order of -20.4, which is distinctly brighter than average.

The dimensions and shape of the radio galaxies for a long time remained almost unknown, as a result of the poor resolving power of radio telescopes. Nevertheless, the few rare cases that were known up until 1958 showed clearly that the radio emission comes from a much larger volume than is occupied by the associated visible galaxy. The first high-resolution observations were those of Jennison, Das Gupta, and Rowson on Cygnus A, at Manchester. After this pioneer work, three groups studied the structure of radio sources with two-element interferometers.

The group at the California Institute of Technology, using two 90-foot reflectors at 31 cm (Fig. 4-6), observed the structure of about a hundred radio sources with a resolution of 80 seconds of arc on an east-west and north-south base line.

The Manchester group, using the big Jodrell Bank reflector in conjunction with a movable parabolic cylinder connected to it by radio links,

TABLE 11-2

Some radio sources identified with abnormal or double galaxies *

Object	α(1950) h m s	δ(1950) ° '	Distance, kpc	Optical dimensions	Radio dimensions	Flux density at 100 Mc/s, watts/m²(c/s)	Optical magnitude	Description
Cygnus A	19 57 44	+40 36	220,000	2 nuclei separated by 2"	2 nuclei 25 × 18" separated by 106"	$11{,}800 \times 10^{-26}$	17.9	double galaxy
NGC 4486 (Virgo A)	12 28 18	+12 40	11,000	halo 10' + jet 20"	halo 10' + double jet 30"	$1{,}780 \times 10^{-26}$	9.9	peculiar giant elliptical galaxy
NGC 5128 (Centaurus A)	13 22 28	−42 46	4,000	<25'	double halo 3° × 10° + double central source	$1{,}750 \times 10^{-26}$	6.5	peculiar elliptical galaxy
Hercules A	16 48 40	+05 05	610,000 ?	0.2'	2 nuclei 50" separated by 110"	580×10^{-26}	18.6	double galaxy
Hydra A	9 15 41	−11 53	210,000	0.5'	46"	400×10^{-26}	15.9	double galaxy
NGC 1316 (Fornax A)	3 19 30	−37 18	9,600 ?	<20'	2 nuclei 16' separated by 30'	240×10^{-26}	9.5	peculiar galaxy ?
3C 295	14 09 33	+52 26	1,800,000	1" ?	double, separation 4"	100×10^{-26}	20.9	emission-line galaxy
NGC 1275 (Perseus A)	3 16 15	+41 19	70,000	2.4'	10" + halo 4'	130×10^{-26}	13.3	double galaxy (collision ?)
NGC 6166	16 26 56	+39 40	8,800	1'	1.1'	100×10^{-26}	13.9	multiple elliptical

* Distances are usually estimated from the shift of spectral lines assuming that a radial velocity of 75 kilometers per second corresponds to a distance of 1 million parsecs.

have studied about 250 sources on 1.9 m, with east-west resolutions reaching 2 seconds of arc.

Finally the Nançay group, using two 7.5-meter reflectors provided with an integrating device (Fig. 4-16), obtained the detailed structure of a few strong sources at 21 cm with a resolution of 18 seconds of arc east-west and 66 seconds of arc north-south.

The result of these investigations, which were not entirely completed or published at the time of writing, is quite surprising. At least 50 percent and perhaps 70 to 80 percent of the sources investigated are double; i.e., they are composed of two main components. Of the 10 strongest radio galaxies, only one (Hydra A) does not seem to show double structure. The distance separating the two components is on the average four or five times their individual diameters, and the dimensions are in general all much greater than those of the associated galaxy. An average figure of 80 kiloparsecs can be quoted, i.e., two or three times the diameter of the halo of a galaxy. The mystery surrounding the extraordinary objects deepens even more when it is noticed that there is usually no morphological relation between the galaxy and the corresponding radio source. For example, an optically double galaxy may be a single radio source. Conversely, many double sources correspond to single galaxies.

The problem posed by the existence of these radio galaxies is one of the most mysterious in the universe. It is no doubt also one of the most important, and much effort should be devoted to it. At the present time, according to all appearances, we lack even the most elementary foundations for constructing a theory of extragalactic radio sources. The recent attempts of Shklovsky and G. R. Burbidge are certainly very interesting, but should be considered for the moment as quite utopian. We shall confine ourselves here to a purely descriptive study of a few of the best-known objects. Table 11-2 summarizes the characteristics of a few of them.

Virgo A

The astonishing peculiarity of the galaxy NGC 4486 (M 87), which forms part of the Virgo cluster, has been known for some time. Coming out of the nucleus of this nebula, which shows no definite structure elsewhere, is a sort of very brilliant blue jet (Fig. 11-7). The optical spectrum of this jet, obtained by Humason, shows a continuum without emission or absorption lines. NGC 4486 was identified by Baade and Minkowski with one of the most intense sources in the radio sky. It was tempting to connect this property with the presence of the jet and to explain the radio emission by the synchrotron mechanism as in the Crab nebula. The high-speed electrons required for this mechanism would be the source of the continuous spectrum of the jet. To verify this hypothesis and following Shklovsky's suggestion, Baade attempted to detect linear polarization in the light. He succeeded in 1956 and measured a degree of polarization reaching 30 percent. Consequently we may be certain that radiation from fast electrons in a magnetic field is responsible for both the visible and radio emissions.

We have been able to determine the radio distribution over NGC 4486 on 21 cm with the variable-spacing interferometer at Nançay. In the center of a halo 10 minutes of arc in diameter, and comparable with the optical halo, although noncircular, a very strong emission zone about 36 seconds of arc across is found. It is no doubt the radio counterpart of the visible jet, whose length is estimated to be 20 seconds of arc. By these features, and also by its very low spectral index (-0.33), this extraordinary jet is slightly reminiscent of the Crab nebula, although on a much larger scale. We have succeeded in resolving the radio-frequency jet into two components separated by 31 seconds of arc. Thus we have a double source again, but on a scale smaller than that of a galaxy.

Even if the production mechanism of radio waves in NGC 4486 is well explained, the origin of the jet (which really could be an ejection of matter) as well as the source of the magnetic field and the high-energy electrons necessary for synchrotron emission remain completely mysterious. The total kinetic energy of the particles would amount to 10^{51} joules, i.e., 10^7 times more than that dissipated in the explosion of a supernova.

Fig. 11-7 The radio source Virgo A (NGC 4486). This underexposed photograph of only the central part of the galaxy shows a kind of jet coming out from the center, which emits partially polarized light. Longer exposure brings out an extended halo that masks the jet. (Mount Wilson and Palomar Observatories photo.)

Cygnus A

The strongest radio galaxy, and the first to be discovered, was identified only in 1954, thanks to the admirable work of Baade and Minkowski with the Palomar telescope. We refer to the source Cygnus A, one only just less intense than Cassiopeia A. The object was discovered optically

Fig. 11-8   The radio source Cygnus A. *(Mount Wilson and Palomar Observatories photo.)*

only with great difficulty in a field very rich in stars and faint galaxies and only when the position of the radio source was known with good precision, thanks to the measurements of Mills and Smith. It is a peculiar object which at first sight defied classification. It is very faint, with an apparent magnitude of 17.9, and shows up in photographs taken with the 200-inch telescope in the form of two condensations separated by 2 seconds of arc, surrounded by an elliptical halo (Fig. 11-8). This appearance at first suggested that we might be dealing with a collision of two galaxies. The spectrum of this object, obtained by Baade and Minkowski, shows very intense and very wide interstellar emission lines, indicating a state of high excitation and internal motions reaching 500 kilometers per second. From the red shift of the spectral lines we find a radial velocity of 16,830 kilometers per second, which corresponds to the enormous distance of 220 megaparsecs (taking a value of 75 kilometers per second per megaparsec for the Hubble constant, as elsewhere in this work).

No difference in radial velocity can be detected between the two components of Cygnus A, and furthermore double galaxies of this type are so frequent in the sky that we are forced to abandon the rather attractive idea that they might be galaxies in collision. On the contrary, Ambartsumian considers that they are young galaxies in the course of separating, following a common origin. (Are there not also among stars a very large proportion of double systems which clearly have a common origin?) Warm supporters of the theory of galaxies in collision, like Shklovsky, have now abandoned this hypothesis. The radio source Cygnus A is the first one in which double structure was inferred (Jennison, Das Gupta, and Rowson). At the present time it is one of the best known, thanks to the work done with the Nançay interferometer at 21 cm. The components are separated by 106 seconds of arc and have a diameter of 25 seconds of arc. The axis of the system coincides approximately with the axis of symmetry of the optical system. The radio object thus seems to be a copy of the optical object but on a much larger scale. The two components are not circular, but rather elongated along the major axis of the system, and their brightness is neither uniform nor symmetrical. Figure 11-9 shows the brightness distribution in the east-west direction observed at Nançay, and an attempt at interpreting the whole of the observations. It is interesting to note that the emission bridge which connects the two components is more important on lower frequencies.

There is no doubt that the radio emission is due to synchrotron radiation, as Mayer, McCullough, and Sloanaker have detected strong polarization on 3 cm. However, it is still quite difficult to construct a theory of Cygnus A. The greatest difficulty to be overcome is to explain the enormous power that is radiated in the form of radio waves, which, of course, is not peculiar to Cygnus A. The total energy which has been radiated since the

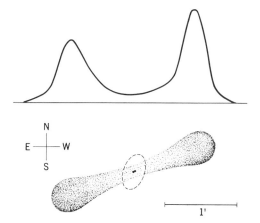

Fig. 11-9 East-west profile of the radio source Cygnus A obtained on 21 cm with the two-element interferometer at Nançay, and an attempt at restoration of the shape of the source. The optical object and its halo are shown diagrammatically in the center. (*Lequeux and Heidmann.*)

origin of the radio source, which can hardly be older than a few tens of millions of years, is about 10^{53} joules or even more. Such an energy can only be of catastrophic origin (quasi-simultaneous explosion of a large number of supernovae, large-scale thermonuclear phenomena in galactic nuclei, etc.) and is probably connected with the origin of galaxies.

NGC 1275

This galaxy, a member of the Perseus cluster, is shown in Fig. 11-10. Baade and Minkowski interpret it as two galaxies in collision. One of them seen almost edge on, with one spiral arm clearly visible, penetrates the outer parts of another galaxy, less obviously spiral, which is seen face on. The spectrum reveals that the components have a difference in radial velocity of about 3,000 kilometers per second. The collision hypothesis is thus well supported. But the associated radio source is not especially intense, and its diameter is very small, probably 10 seconds of arc, while the optical object measures 2.4 minutes of arc. If it was really due to the collision of the two galaxies, its dimensions would have to be several minutes of arc. Thus the only case where it seems that we have to do with a collision of galaxies goes counter to the theory that radio galaxies depend on collisions. In this case it could be simply a matter of emission from the nucleus of one of the galaxies, which optically shows very strong emission lines.

Centaurus A

This powerful southern source is a well-known example of a double radio galaxy and has been identified with the galaxy NGC 5128, which has a very strange appearance. A bright circular object is crossed by a dark band, which is probably the central disk appearing in absorption (Fig. 11-12). The visible spectrum, which has some emission lines, enabled

E. M. and G. R. Burbidge to discover a net rotation of the system about an axis perpendicular to the dark band. From the radio point of view, Centaurus A is remarkable for its enormous dimensions, for it extends more than 10 degrees in the direction perpendicular to the dark band. The diameter of the associated galaxy is of the order of only 20 minutes of arc. The double structure of this gigantic source was revealed by Hindman and Wade and by Bolton and Clark (Fig. 11-11). The appearance of the radio galaxy, which has been observed from 21 cm to 15 m, is practically independent of wavelength.

In the position of the optical galaxy is an intense radio source which itself possesses double structure, as shown by Little. The two components

Fig. 11-10   The radio source Perseus A, NGC 1275. (Mount Wilson and Palomar Observatories photo.)

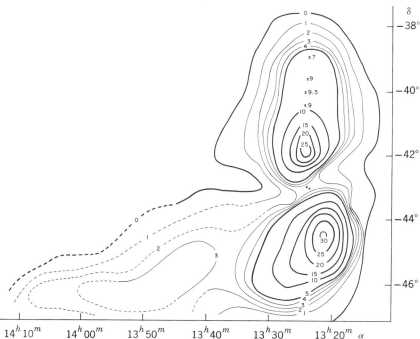

Fig. 11-11 Contour map of Centaurus A at 31 cm, contour unit 0.5°K. The tremendous extent of this source is truly remarkable when it is remembered that the associated galaxy NGC 5128 is only a few minutes of arc in diameter. *(Bolton and Clark.)*

are situated on opposite sides of the dark band (see Fig. 11-12). Using the Australian 210-foot reflector, Bracewell, Cooper, and Cousins have discovered that the northeastern component is very strongly polarized (degree of polarization 15 percent at 10 cm), and a resurvey of the extended components by Cooper and Price showed that the polarization reaches 38 percent at 20 cm wavelength in one place. Radiation is thus evidently due to synchrotron emission, and the magnetic field tends to a rather uniform orientation over the whole extent of the source. The direction of polarization varies with the observing frequency as a result of Faraday rotation in the medium between the source and the observer, and is probably due principally to the galactic halo, which gives us another way of evaluating the galactic magnetic field.

Thus we have a source which, on very different scales, is doubly double. Taking its distance to be about 4 megaparsecs, we find its overall dimension to reach almost 1 megaparsec, while the separation between the central components is only 8 kiloparsecs.

Fornax A (NGC 1316)

This is another southern source which rather resembles Centaurus A both optically and at radio wavelengths. It is also a double source, as has been shown by Wade. As with Centaurus A, the radiation from Fornax A is polarized, the degree of polarization at 20 cm being 10 and 12 percent respectively for the two components. These two radio sources and Cygnus A are far from being the only extragalactic ones in which polarization has been detected, for at least 16 are now known thanks to the Australian observations alone, and more are being reported from the Owens Valley and Jodrell Bank Observatories. The synchrotron-emission theory has thus received brilliant confirmation. Observations of the Faraday rotation of the plane of polarization as a function of frequency likewise are of enormous

Fig. 11-12 The components of the central source of Centaurus A shown superimposed on NGC 5128.

importance and it has already been observed that the rotation is stronger for radio sources which are closer to the galactic plane. This indicates a galactic origin and offers a chance of measuring the field distribution in the galactic halo.

There are still a very large number of double radio sources identified with visible galaxies among which Hercules A is one of the best known. But the variety of their properties is amazing and for the moment defies all statistics. In particular, the surface brightness of these radio galaxies varies over a range of 1,000 to 1 (some 10^5 to 10^9 °K at 1.9 m). It is obviously urgent to get at the structure of a good number of radio sources to understand their nature, a difficult and lengthy undertaking necessitating very many observations made with very large antennas and a resolving power of a few seconds of arc. For the time being, we know practically nothing about them, and the recent introduction of new observational data has only succeeded in destroying the rough ideas built up in the preceding years, a classical process in the history of the sciences, where a destructive period is often seen to precede a period of fruitfulness. The whole basis of our knowledge is now brought back into question, and some people are even wondering whether it is reasonable physically to associate a given radio source, whose components are separated by a few minutes of arc, with a minute central galaxy that is in no way peculiar. It is certain that until now no definite conclusion has been deducible from the proposed identifications and that the identification problem itself should rest on new foundations that remain to be laid. But we may be assured that a few years from now the observations which are under way or in the planning stage in many parts of the world will lead to a sound solution to the problem of radio galaxies, which is perhaps the most important and the most interesting in the whole of present-day astronomy, because we get the impression of coming to grips with the problem of the formation of the galaxies and the origin of the universe.

RADIO EMISSION FROM CLUSTERS OF GALAXIES

For a long time many astronomers thought that the space separating the galaxies was completely empty. Zwicky's observations of intergalactic bridges connecting two or three galaxies, often very remote from each other, tend to prove the contrary. These intergalactic bridges are not simply narrow filaments but luminous clouds with considerable dimensions. Zwicky succeeded in taking spectra of some of these objects which often appear to be composed of stars.

Highly rarefied gas may also exist in intergalactic space, at least in the central parts of clusters of galaxies. It is not inconceivable that the gal-

axies are formed from intergalactic matter or that, conversely, they eject matter into the external medium, the interrelations between galaxies and intergalactic matter thus resembling on a large scale the relations between stars and interstellar matter. According to Shklovsky and Burbidge, the extragalactic radio sources could represent ejections of matter by galaxies. We may thus expect to observe in clusters of galaxies, emission characteristic of interstellar matter, nonthermal emission, thermal emission, and the 21-cm line. At the present time no radiation from clusters of galaxies has been detected at 21 cm, nor any thermal emission.

On the other hand, the emission from clusters of galaxies has been observed on meter wavelengths. About 35 percent of the radio sources correspond with clusters of galaxies, whereas there should be only 10 percent if the spatial distribution of the sources were random. Several clusters have been studied in some detail. For example, members of the Jodrell Bank group, Large, Mathewson, and Haslam, have drawn a map of the Coma cluster with the 250-foot steerable paraboloid. Part of this cluster is shown in Fig. 11-13, and the radio map is shown in Fig. 11-14. Thanks to the excellent resolving power of the radio telescope on 73 cm, the cluster is clearly resolved into at least two more or less extended sources, possibly superimposed on a continuous background. Patricia Leslie and Elsmore in Cambridge have observed emission from the Perseus cluster on 1.9 and 0.75 m, a cluster that we have studied also on 21 cm. Apart from the radio galaxy NGC 1275 referred to above, this cluster contains a very wide source (40 minutes of arc) as strong as NGC 1275, and another very small one which is three times fainter. We may wonder whether these last radio sources correspond with peculiar radio galaxies in the cluster or whether we are dealing with emission from intergalactic matter. In actual fact this problem is badly put and has no very clear solution, if we agree, with Shklovsky, that the radio galaxies are masses of gas ejected by the galaxies and being progressively dispersed into intergalactic space. Under these conditions, a radio telescope would see no discontinuity between the radio galaxies of a cluster and the general radio emission of the cluster. Before deciding, it will be better to wait until the properties of radio galaxies are better understood.

The clusters of galaxies, also, show a certain tendency to cluster. Thus the small local cluster of which our galaxy is a member, and which contains only 16 objects, is only one of the members of a giant whole referred to as the supergalaxy, which includes many others, in particular the Virgo and Coma clusters, which are among the closest to us. The supergalaxy appears as a flattened system of gigantic dimensions (perhaps 20 megaparsecs in diameter), with the Virgo cluster apparently representing the central nucleus. As a result of their distribution in this ensemble, the brightest galaxies and the nearest clusters are mostly found in a zone of sky about 60 degrees

Fig. 11-13 The central part of the Coma cluster. In among the field stars, which of course belong to our galaxy, notice a large number of galaxies, which are recognizable by their misty outline. *(Mount Wilson and Palomar Observatories photo.)*

wide practically perpendicular to the galactic equator. The appearance of the supergalaxy is thus somewhat similar to that of our galaxy, and in proportion. We can philosophize to infinity on the hierarchy of the universe, whose objects, stars and galaxies, tend to concentrate in clusters or in flattened systems. This is certainly one of the most interesting puzzles posed by the structure of the universe.

As we have found radio emission from clusters of galaxies, it is natural to see whether the supergalaxy also gives detectable emission. This is indeed a very difficult undertaking, for there are few problems in our science comparable with those raised by the detection of extended areas of faint emission. So we should not be surprised if the results are very contradictory. Hanbury Brown and Hazard in Manchester, and then Kraus and Ko at Ohio State University, thought in turn to have discovered emission regions on meter wavelengths coinciding with the supergalaxy. But Baldwin and Shakeshaft in the Cambridge group, as well as Hill in Australia, find no definite association between the bright radio emission and the regions of the sky where the galaxies are particularly numerous. Consequently no conclusion can be reached on this subject.

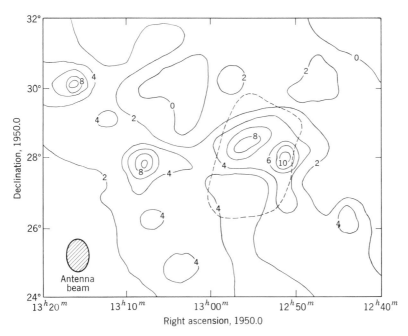

Fig. 11-14 Contour map of the region of the Coma cluster on 73 cm. This map, obtained with the Jodrell Bank radio telescope, shows two or three sources situated within the limits of the cluster of galaxies shown in broken outline. The contour unit is 1°K. *(Large, Mathewson, and Haslam.)*

RADIO ASTRONOMY AND THE STRUCTURE
OF THE UNIVERSE

Nevertheless all radio astronomers agree in thinking that no point in the sky can be found which does not emit radio waves. Many attempts have been made to measure the minimum brightness temperature of the sky at high galactic latitudes on different frequencies. It would take too long to describe the techniques used, which are often extremely sensitive and resemble those used for absolute measurements. The sky background emission may come from regions of the galaxy near the sun, situated in the local spiral arm, from the halo of the galaxy, or lastly from the background of extragalactic sources that are unresolved by the antenna. It does not seem necessary to retain the first hypothesis, although the galactic radiation can be appreciable at certain points remote from the galactic plane, as we have seen above. It is more difficult to estimate the respective contributions of the galactic halo and the extragalactic component. Mills and Shain think that in the neighborhood of the galactic poles, the brightness temperature due to the halo is still about twice as great as the continuous extragalactic background. Spectral observations cannot help us to separate the two causes of the emission. The spectrum of the two components is certainly nonthermal. Thus the study of the extragalactic components proves to be a most difficult one.

In any case, it seems that the emission from the whole of the normal galaxies in the universe cannot suffice to explain the high value of temperature in the extragalactic background (possibly 15,000°K at 15 m and 250°K at 3.5 m). It is therefore necessary to invoke the emission of the radio galaxies or of intergalactic space. Unfortunately, too few data on intergalactic space and the radio properties of galaxies are yet available to let us see whether the observed brightness temperatures can be accounted for. It is all the more regrettable because this comparison would allow us to decide among different models of the universe, assumed by cosmologists, which would lead to different values of the brightness temperature of the sky background.

Apparently more is to be expected from the statistics of extragalactic radio sources. If we succeed in determining their distribution in space, we shall be able to obtain fundamental data on the structure of the universe. This is what all the radio astronomers who have composed extensive catalogues of radio sources have tried to do. A simple graphical method introduced by Ryle permits us in principle to arrive at an answer. To begin with, let us suppose for simplicity that the universe contains on the average at each point the same number of radio sources all emitting the same power. Let S_0 be the flux density received from one of these sources situated at unit distance. At a distance R, a source produces a flux density $S(R) =$

S_0/R^2. All the $N(R)$ sources closer than this distance will give a flux density greater than $S(R)$. If they are uniformly distributed in space with a density N_0, this number is equal to $(4\pi/3)\,N_0R^3$. If we plot the logarithm of the number N of sources whose flux density is greater than a certain value S against log S, the observational points will lie on a straight line of slope -1.5 if the spatial distribution is uniform (Fig. 11-15). Any systematic departure of the observations from this straight line signifies that the density of sources varies with their distance from the galaxy. Ryle has applied this method to the sources of the second Cambridge catalogue (2C) and finds indeed that the points are distributed on a straight line of slope different from -1.5. But this result has been much under discussion, in view of the uncertainty over the flux densities and even the existence of the faint sources in this catalogue.

Nevertheless, more recent observations leading to the new catalogues of Mills and the Cambridge group (3C) still show a similar phenomenon (see Fig. 11-15). There is perhaps an excess of weak sources, and the apparent density of the universe increases with distance. Let us point out that optical observations have hitherto not revealed a phenomenon of this kind because they cannot, as we have said, detect and count galaxies whose distances are comparable with those of the faintest radio sources. We recall that the remotest galaxy whose distance is known (2,000 megaparsecs) is still a very strong radio source 3C 295, with an optical magnitude of about 21.

It is well to be very careful as to the interpretation and even the reality of this phenomenon. Even though the fact that the radio sources have very different intrinsic brightnesses does not modify the statistical law relating to the number of sources to their flux density, it nevertheless increases the dispersion of the observational points. Furthermore, it is necessary to take account of the fact that the almost entirely unknown phenomena which can take place at very great distances and the poorly determined corrections that have to be introduced (for example, the corrections for red shift) certainly upset the statistics even before the hundredth source in order of decreasing flux density is reached.

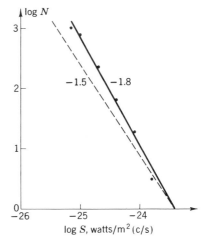

Fig. 11-15 Diagram giving the distribution of radio sources in space. The points relate to Mills's catalogue and fall approximately on a line of slope -1.8.

To clarify these points, it is necessary to accumulate identifications, angular-diameter measurements, and brightness distributions over the radio sources in order to understand their nature better and to succeed in classifying them. Thanks to the labors of the Manchester, Sydney, Cal Tech, and Nançay groups, perceptible progress has been made in this direction. No doubt many years must yet elapse before a decisive result is reached, but it is probable that the crucial experiment to reveal, at least partially, the structure of the universe will be radio astronomical.

On the line shift in the optical spectra of distant galaxies, which is generally attributed to Doppler effect due to a general expansion of the universe, radio astronomy also has its contribution to make. It would indeed be especially interesting to verify that the 21-cm line emitted or absorbed by a distant galaxy has the same shift as do the visible lines. In the case of the nearest galaxies in which 21-cm emission has been detected, the answer is in the affirmative, but this is of no interest to cosmologists because of the proximity of these objects. Much more exciting was the discovery in 1955 by Lilley and McClain of a weak absorption by neutral hydrogen in the radio source Cygnus A. The line was shifted by about 80 Mc/s, which would agree well with the optical observations of Minkowski. Unfortunately we must relax: neither Hanbury Brown in Manchester nor Muller in Dwingeloo could repeat this observation with equipment more sensitive than Lilley's and McClain's. The latter have also repeated their observations apparently without positive result. Nonetheless, we shall certainly someday manage to carry out successfully observations of this kind, in which the giant radio telescopes like the one under construction at Nançay will be a great help. It will thus be possible to evaluate the distance of the radio sources directly, even if they have not been identified. Such observations will certainly lead to progress in the identification of radio objects with distant galaxies and improve the statistics of radio sources, thus furthering our knowledge of the universe.

BIBLIOGRAPHY

Normal galaxies

Brown, R. Hanbury, and C. Hazard: *Monthly Notices Roy. Astron. Soc.,* **119:** 279 (1959) and **122:** 479 (1961).

Observations of radio galaxies

Allen, L. R., H. P. Palmer, and B. Rowson: *Nature,* **188:** 731 (1960).
Baade, W., and R. Minkowski: *Astrophys. J.,* **119:** 206, 215 (1954).
Bolton, J. G.: Obsns. Calif. Inst. Tech. Radio Obs., no. 5 (1960).
Brown, R. Hanbury: Discrete Sources of Cosmic Radio Waves, "Handbuch der Physik," vol. 53, Springer-Verlag, Berlin, 1959.

Lequeux, J., *Ann. Astrophys.*, **25:** 221 (1962).

Mills, B. Y.: Radio Frequency Radiation from External Galaxies, "Handbuch der Physik," vol. 53, Springer-Verlag, Berlin, 1959.

Mills, B. Y.: *Australian J. Phys.*, **13:** 550 (1960).

Moffet, A. T., and J. Maltby: *Nature*, **191:** 453 (1961); Obsns. Calif. Inst. Tech. Radio Obs., no. 1 (1962). See also R. N. Bracewell (ed.), "Paris Symposium on Radio Astronomy," Stanford University Press, Stanford, Calif., 1959.

Theory of radio galaxies

Burbidge, G. R.: *Nature,* **190:** 1053 (1961).

Hoyle, F.: *Monthly Notices Roy. Astron. Soc.,* **120:** 338 (1960).

Shklovsky, I. S.: *Astron. Zh.,* **37:** 945 (1960); English translation in *Soviet Astron.-AJ,* **4:** 885 (1961).

Polarization of extragalactic sources

Bracewell, R. N., B. F. C. Cooper, and T. Cousins: *Nature,* **195:** 1289 (1962).

Cooper, B. F. C., and R. M. Price: *Nature,* **195:** 1084 (1962).

Gardner, F. F., and J. B. Whiteoak: *Phys. Rev. Letters,* **9:** 197 (1962).

Mayer, C. H., T. P. McCullough, and R. M. Sloanaker: *Astrophys. J.,* **135:** 656 (1962).

CONCLUSION

12

Now that we have reached the end of our book, it seems worthwhile to us to summarize. From the multitude of often disparate or very incomplete observations mentioned in the foregoing chapters, it is not easy to disentangle the most important contributions of radio astronomy to the understanding of the universe. In our opinion, progress has been especially noticeable in three fields.

Thanks to close cooperation between astronomers, geophysicists, and radio astronomers, our knowledge of the sun has made enormous progress since the second world war. Before the work of Lyot there were only very vague ideas about the corona, which is now better understood. But the progress is concerned mainly with solar activity. Although no satisfactory theory for this activity has yet been proposed, it is now known that the magnetic field plays a fundamental role. During flares the solar atmosphere acts as an accelerator of charged particles which often reach the earth. Even though we are still far from explaining everything, we shall know in the future in what directions to bend our efforts.

Again, the discovery of the monochromatic emission of neutral hydrogen on 21 cm has brought us essential data on the galaxy, whose structure is now broadly known. The 21-cm line has also shown itself to be a powerful tool for the investigation of external galaxies.

Finally, one of the most interesting revelations of radio astronomy is the importance of synchrotron emission. Almost everywhere in the universe, there exist magnetic fields through which high-energy charged particles are moving. This fact will have to be taken into account in the development of any astrophysical or cosmological theory.

The situation is not quite so flourishing as regards extragalactic radio astronomy. Although a large number of distant radio sources have been successfully associated with optical galaxies, these identifications have not yet been susceptible of any clear interpretation, because the morphological differences between the galaxies and the radio sources with which they have been identified are extreme. The mystery of the nature and formation of the radio galaxies remains complete.

Similarly, radio astronomy has not yet made any definite contribution to cosmology. Although the agreement between the radio-source catalogues is now better than before, it is still far from being perfect. Numerous measurements of position, flux density, and dimensions of radio galaxies will have to be made before we can establish definite statistics which may serve to unravel the structure of the universe.

What direction will radio astronomy take in the coming years? From the instrumental point of view, the introduction of low-noise receivers will benefit radio astronomers by a considerable gain in sensitivity, which will be especially useful on centimeter wavelengths where hardly anything but the sun and moon can be detected without very complex and difficult equipment. Likewise, the commissioning of antennas with very large collecting areas and very high resolving power, several of which are under construction or being designed, will render invaluable services.

The study of the sun will no doubt lie dormant during the sunspot minimum occurring around 1964, but the next maximum will see the introduction of several improved instruments that will make observations of diameters, positions, altitudes, and evolution of bursts, which are still too rare today, quite commonplace. This period will also see the introduction of panoramic receivers covering the whole spectrum from decameter to millimeter wavelengths. The hectometer and kilometer wavelengths, too, will finally be opened for exploration from rockets and artificial satellites unimpeded by absorption in the terrestrial ionosphere.

We still know very little about the extragalactic radio sources, whose detailed observation demands particularly powerful equipment. Almost all the effort of radio astronomers will soon be devoted to this field, and we have the right to hope for important discoveries. But here, even more than elsewhere, radio astronomers must work in close collaboration with optical astronomers. We must not forget that radio astronomy is only one of the branches of astronomy, which, although several centuries old, is still a living science and in constant evolution.

INDEX

Numbers in **boldface** type indicate Bibliography references

Absorption, general laws, 97
  polar-cap, 158
Absorption coefficient, 16, 102, 105, 108
Active region, 131
Adler tube, 53
Agassiz station, 221
Alfvén, H., 185
Alfvén wave, 140
Allen, C. W., **9, 251**
Aller, L. H., **116**
Altenhof, W., 183, **199**
Ambartsumian, V. A., **116,** 205
Anderson, K. A., 146
Andromeda nebula, 168, 170, 171, 226, 232
  nucleus, 169, 171, 192, 197
Angular resolution, 26, 58
Antenna, 20, 24
  beam efficiency, 34
  effective area, 20, 30
  effective temperature, 22, 30, 32
  gain, 24, 30, 35
  polarized, 54
  radiation pattern, 25
  radiation resistance, 28
  reception pattern, 26
  resolution, 26
  sidelobes, 26, 33
Aperture synthesis, 58, 68, 79, 83
Array, 74, 75
Arsac, J., 70, **88**
Astrologers, 210
Atmosphere, 6
Auriga A, 207
Aurora, 157
  radar, 165
Australian National Radio Astronomy Observatory, **8**
Avignon, Y., 153, **160**

Baade, W., 182, 211, 217, **225,** 239, 251
Babcock, H. W., 136
Baldwin, J. E., 247
Barnard's ring, 222
Bay, Z., 165

Beringer, R., 161
Bertaud, C., 211
Biot, E., 210
Black body, 14
  construction, 17
Black-body emission, 115
Blaquière, A., **57**
Blum, E. J., 85, **88**
Blythe, J. H., 183
Boischot, A., **88,** 132, 144, 151, **160**
Bok, B. J., **199**
Bok, P. F., **199**
Bolton, J. G., 183, 200, 205, 234, 242, **251**
Boltzmann's constant, 14, 23
Born, M., **57**
Bracewell, R. N., **4, 57,** 70, **88,** 125, 242, **251**
Brightness, 13
  monochromatic, 14
Brightness temperature, 14
Brouw, W. N., **57, 199**
Brown, R. Hanbury, **167,** 226, 247, 250, **251**
Budden, K. G., **10**
Burbidge, E. Margaret, 241
Burbidge, G. R., 236, 241, 245, **251**
Burgess, R., **57**
Burke, B. F., 164
Bursts, type I, 149
  type II, 118, 141, 145
  type III, 118, 137, 145
  type IV, 118, 139, 141, 144, 145, 153
  type V, 118, 137, 140, 145
  U, 139, 141

Calibration, 45, 56
California Institute of Technology, 63, 205, 234
Cambridge, 83, 220, 245, 249
Carnegie Institution, 125
Carpenter, M. S., **199**
Cassiopeia A, 207, 218, 223, 225
Centaurus A, 113, 235, 240, 242, 243
Čerenkov radiation, 97, 114, 115, 147, 154

Chapman, S., 156
Christiansen, W. N., 125, 128, 129, 131, 155, **160**
Chromosphere, 119, 120
Clusters of galaxies, 244
Coates, R., 161
Cohen, M., **57**, 114
Coma cluster, 245, 246
Condensation, 131
Condon, E. U., **116**
Confusion, 86
Continuum emission, 139, 182
Continuum storm, 147
Cooper, B. F. C., 242, **251**
Corona, 119, 121, 124, 131
Correlation system, 82
Cosmic-ray event, 146, 157
Cosmic rays, 157, 186, 215
Cosmogony, 248–250
Courtès, G., 190, 194
Cousins, T. E., 242, **251**
Coutrez, R., 179
Covington, A. E., 125, 156
Crab nebula, 113, 202, 207, 209, 212, 213, 215, 224
    occultation, 126
Critical frequency, 6, 123
Cross antenna, 129
Cruvellier, P., 190, 194
CSIRO, 79, 80, 94
Cygnus A, 50, 76, 113, 200, 225, 234, 235, 238
Cygnus loop, 207, 221, 222
Cygnus X, 206

D layer, 155
Danjon, A., vi, **9**
Dapto, 94
Das Gupta, M. K., 234, 239
Davies, R. D., 224
Declination, 61
    of extragalactic sources, 235
    of galactic sources, 206, 207
de Jager, C., **159**
Delannoy, J., **57**
Delcroix, J. L., **116**
Denisse, J. F., **57, 116,** 126, 147, 154, 156
Detailed balancing, 31
Detection, 40
de Vaucouleurs, G., 185, 229
Dewhirst, D. W., 234
DeWitt, J. H., 165
Dicke, R. H., 29, 47, 161
Dieter, Nannielou, 231
Differential rotation, 175, 177, 179
Disk, galactic, 169, 180, 185

Dombrovsky, K., 213
Drake, F., 192, 193
Duffieux, P. M., 70
Dust, galactic, 172, 176, 223
Dwingeloo, 92, 223
Dynamic spectrum, 139, 145

E layer, 156
Eclipse, 125
Effective area, 20, 30
Effective temperature, 22, 30, 32
Einstein, A., 99, 112
Elsmore, B., 245
Emission, black-body, 14, 115
    Čerenkov, 97, 114, 115, 147
    general laws, 97
    gyromagnetic, 97, 111, 115
    induced, 48, 98, 152
    mechanisms, 96
    spontaneous, 48, 98
    stimulated, 98, 152
    synchrotron, 97, 111, 115, 147, 165, 189, 220
    thermal (see Thermal emission)
    (See also Solar radio emission)
Excitation temperature, 100
Extragalactic sources, 226, 235, 248

F layer, 156
Faculae, 119
Faraday rotation, 113, 242, 243
Ferraro, V. C. A., 156
Field, G. B., 105, **116**
Findlay, J., 220
Firor, J., 132, 151
Flare, 132, 136, 137, 145, 147, 157
Flather, E., **225**
Fleurs, 79
Flux, 11
Flux density, 12
    of extragalactic sources, 235
    of galactic sources, 206, 207
    monochromatic, 14
Forbush effect, 158
Fornax A, 235, 243
Fourier transform, 69, 73
Franklin, K. L., 164

Gabor, D., 100
Gain measurement, 35
Galactic center, 189, 191, 193
    latitude, 177
    longitude, 177
    radio emission, 168
    ridge, 186
    rotation, 178, 195
    sources, 200

Galactic center, structure, 169
Galaxy, 168
  external, 226, 233, 248
  normal, 226
Galileo, 168
Gardner, F. F., **251**
Gas discharge tube, 56
Gaseous nebula, 205
Gibson, J. E., 161, 163
Ginat, M., **88**
Giordmaine, J. A., **167**
Giovanelli, R. G., 134, 137, 140, 142
Globular cluster, 170
Goldberg, L,. **159**
Goodman, J., **95**
Gradual rise and fall, 132
Grating, 74, 80, 129, 131
Gray body, 15
Grivet, P., **57**
Gyromagnetic emission, 97, 110, 115

Haddock, F. T., **5, 95**, 143–145
Hagen, J. P., 223
Hall, J. S., 173
Halo, 170, 186
Harmonic, 139
Harvard College Observatory, 221
Haslam, C. G. T., **199**, 227, 247
Haute-Provence Observatory, 174, 203
Hazard, C., 226, 247, **251**
Heeschen, D. S., 231
Hercules A, 235, 244
Herlofson, N., 185
Herschel, W., 117, 168
Hey, J. S., 2, 149, 200
Higgins, C. S., 183, **199**
HII region, 173
Hill, E. R., 184, **199**, 247
Hiltner, W. A., 173
Hindman, J. V., 180, **199**
Högbom, J., 220
Horn, 36
Horse's head nebula, 206
Hour angle, 61
Hoyle, F., **251**
Hydra A., 235, 236
Hydrogen line, 89, 97, 104, 115, 179, 194, 221, 229
Hyperfine transition, 105

IC 443, 207
IC 1613, 233
Infrared, 117
Integrator, 85
Interferometer, 58
  multielement, 74, 80, 129, 131
  phase-switching, 64
  two-antenna, 59

Intergalactic space, 182, 244, 248
Intermediate frequency, 40
International Geophysical Year, 159
Ionized hydrogen, 173, 186, 192, 203
Ionosphere, 7, 123, 154

Jaeger, J. C., 124
Jansky, K. G., 1, 169
Jelley, J. V., **116**
Jennison, R. C., 234, 239
Jet, 134
Jodrell Bank, 224, 226, 234, 243, 245, 247
Jupiter, 161, 163, 164

Kastler, A., **9**
Kepler's supernova, 207, 217
Kerr, F. J., 93, 180, 182, **199**, 229
Kiepenheuer, K. O., 149
Kirchhoff's law, 16
Ko, H. C., 126, 183, 247
Komesaroff, M. N., 183, **199**
Kraus, J. D., 87, **88,** 126, 164, 183, 247
Kron, G. E., 190
Kuiper, G. P., **159**
Kundu, M. R., 131, 153, 156, **160**

Lagoon nebula, 206
Lallemand, A., 194
Lampland, C. O., 210
Large, M. I., 183, **199**, 227, 247
Lebenbaum, M., **95**
Leiden, 92
Lequeux, J., **251**
Le Roux, E., **57, 116**
Leslie, Patricia, 245
Lilley, A. E., 223
Lincoln Laboratory, 167
Line profiles, 89
Little, A. G., 65, 241
Lloyd's mirror, 67
Local oscillator, 40
Lovell, A. C. B., **167**
Lyot, B., 119, 133

M 1, 207, 209
M 8, 206
M 16, 206
M 17, 206
M 20, 202
M 31, 231, 233
M 32, 233
M 33, 228, 231, 233
M 42, 206, 222
M 51, 228
M 81, 228

M 87, 236
M 101, 231, 233
McCabe, Marie, 134
McClain, E. F., 163, 223
McCready, L. L., 66, **95**
McCullough, T. P., 163, 213, 239, **251**
McLean, D., 147
Magellanic clouds, 168, 231, 233
  rotation, 229
Magnetic bottle, 149, 154, 158
Magnetic field, 131, 133, 152, 158, 185, 224, 242
Magnetic storm, 156
Magnitude, radio, 228
Maltby, J., **251**
Maréchal, A., 70
Mars, 163
Martyn, D. F., 110
Maser, 47, 49, 100, 163
Mathewson, D. S., **199**, 227, 247
Matthews, T. A., 234
Maxwell, A., 95, 144
Mayall, N. U., 190, 209
Mayer, C. H., 163, **167**, 213, 239, **251**
Mechanisms of emission, 96
Menon, T. K., 221
Mercury, 163
Messier, C., 209
Meteor trails, 165, 167
Meudon, v, 120, 133, 211
Michigan, University of, 13, 95
Milky Way, 2, 168, 171
Mills, B. Y., 183, 184, 196, **199**, 201, 228, 234, 239, **251**
Mills cross, 78–81, 129
Minkowski, R., 217, **225**, 239, **251**
Minnaert, M. J. M., 131
Minnett, H. C., 161
Mixer, 40
Moffet, A. T., **251**
Monochromatic brightness, 14
Monochromatic flux density, 14
Moon, radar, 165
  thermal radiation, 161
Morgan, W. W., 182
Morlet, B., **57**
Mount Wilson and Mount Palomar Observatories, 212, 214, 217, 218, 237, 241, 246
Moutot, M., **160**
Mullard Observatory, 83
Muller, C. A., **57, 95,** 178, 180, 223, 250
Multichannel spectrograph, 90, 93

Nançay, 65, 66, 71, 76, 125, 127, 131, 138, 150
Naval Research Laboratory, 27, 49

Nebula, Andromeda, 168, 170, 192, 227, 232
  Crab, 113, 126, 202, 207, 209, 212, 213, 215, 224
  Horse's head, 206
  Lagoon, 206
  North America, 206
  Omega, 202, 204, 206
  Orion, 202, 204, 206
  Rosette, 204, 206
Neutral hydrogen, 104, 115, 181, 194, 221, 229
Neutral points, 134
NGC 1275, 235, 240, 241, 245
NGC 1316, 243
NGC 1952, 207
NGC 1976, 206
NGC 2024, 206
NGC 2244, 206
NGC 4486, 235–237
NGC 4565, 172
NGC 5128, 235, 240, 242
NGC 5146, 174
NGC 5364, 197–198
NGC 5668, 211
NGC 6166, 235
NGC 6523, 206
NGC 6611, 206
NGC 6618, 206
NGC 6960, 207
NGC 6992, 207
NGC 6995, 207
NGC 7000, 206
Nicholson, S. B., 162
Noise, 21, 23, 37
  measurement, 37
  receiver, 42
  thermal, 23
Noise factor, 42
Noise storms, 118, 149
Noise temperature, 42
Nonthermal sources, 207
Normal galaxy, 226
North America nebula, 206
Nyquist's formula, 21, 28

Omega nebula, 202, 204, 206
Oort, J. H., **95, 116,** 176, 178, 180, 181, **199,** 213, **225**
Optical depth, 103
Optical thickness, 102
Orion nebula, 202, 204, 206, 222
Osterbrock, D., **225**

Palmer, H. P., **251**
Panoramic receiver, 95, 138, 142
Parametric amplifier, 51
Pariiskii, Yu. N., 192

Parkes, 8
Parsons, S. J., 200
Particle belt, 157
Pawsey, J. L., **4,** 66
Payne-Scott, Ruby, 65, 66
Permittivity of free space, 107
Perseus A, 235, 241
Perseus cluster, 240
Pettit, E., 161
Phillips, J. W., 200
Photosphere, 119
Pick-Gutmann, Monique, 127, 153, **160**
Piddington, J. H., 161, 183
Plage, 128, 129, 131
Planck's constant, 14
Planck's law, 14
Planets, 163
Plasma, critical frequency, 110, **123**
    oscillations, 97, 109, 115, 140, 142
    refractive index, 123
Point source, 11
Polar-cap absorption, 158
Polar diagram, 24
Polarization, 53, 131, 144, 149, 165, 189,
    214, 236, 239, 242, 243
Preamplifier, 77
Price, M., 242, **251**
Puff, 140
Pulkovo, 67
Puppis A, 207
Purcell, E. M., 105, **116**

Quiet sun, 118, 119

Radar, 1, 165
Radiation pattern, 24
Radiation transfer, 101
Radio condensation, 131
Radio galaxy, 229, 233
Radio link, 66, 234
Radio magnitude, 228
Radio sextant, 3
Radio spectrograph, 90
    solar, 93
Radio spot, 153
Radio telescope, 20
    California Institute of Technology (90-
        foot), 63
    Cambridge, 83
    Dapto, 94
    Dwingeloo (25-meter), 92
    Fleurs, 79, 80
    Michigan (85-foot), 13
    Nançay, 66, 71, 77
    Naval Research Laboratory (84-foot)
        27; (50-foot), 49
    Parkes (210-foot), 8
    Serpukhov (22-meter), 28

Radio telescope, Stanford, 129 (150-foot),
    166
Raimond, E., 230
Ratcliffe, J. A., **116**
Ray paths, 124
Rayleigh, Lord, 14
Reber, G., 2, 169
Reception pattern, 26
    grating, 75
Receiver, 20, 36
    calibration, 45, 56
    correlation, 82
    hydrogen line, 90
    multichannel, 90, 93
    noise, 42
    panoramic, 95, 138, 142
    superheterodyne, 40
    swept-frequency, 90, 95
    switched, 43
Refraction, 7
Refractive index, 123
Resolution, 26
Resolving power, 26, 58, 125
Right ascension of sources, 206, 207, 235
Roberts, J. A., 70, 111, **116**, 141–143, 152
Rosette nebula, 204, 206
Rosse, 169
Rotation, galaxy, 175, 178
    Jupiter, 164
    Magellanic clouds, 229
    noise storms, 150
Rougoor, G. W., **199**
Rowson, B., 234, 239, **251**
Ryle, M., 46, 64, **88,** 200, 248

Sagittarius, 169, 189
Saturn, 163
Schmidt, M., **199**
Schottky's law, 42, 56
Schwinger, J., 112, **116**
Scintillations, 7, 9
Seeger, C. L., **57,** 161, 183, **199,** 227
Serpukhov, 81
Severny, A. B., 133, 135
Shain, C. A., 164, 187, 191, **199, 225,** 236
Shakeshaft, J. R., 220, 247
Shklovsky, I. S., 104, 110, 140, 186, **199,**
    212, 219, **225,** 245, **251**
Shock wave, 142, 147, 157
Shortley, G. H., **116**
Sidelobes, 26, 33
Signal measurement, 36
Simon, P., 132, 151, 156, **160**
Slee, O. B., 184, **199**
Sloanaker, R. M., 163, 213, 239, **251**
Slowly varying component, 118, 127
Smerd, S. F., 126
Smith, F. G., **5,** 200, 239

Solar atmosphere model, 122
Solar maps, 125, 130
Solar radio emission, 117, 118
  bursts, 137, 141
  noise storm, 118, 149
  quiet sun, 118, 119
  slowly varying component, 127
Solar system, 161
Solar terrestrial relations, 154
Sources, catalogs, 200, 249
  extragalactic, 226, 235, 248
  galactic, 200
  identification, 201, 244
  nonthermal, 164, 207, 216, 233
  observable, number of, 87
  thermal, 163, 202
Southworth, G. C., 2
Spatial frequency, 69, 75
Spectral line, 89
Spectral sensitivity function, 75
Spectroheliogram, microwave, 128, 130
  optical, 128, 133
Spiral structure, 176, 181
Spontaneous emission, 48, 98
Stanford, 80, 129–130, 166, 167
Stanley, G. J., 200
Stars, radio, 201
Statistical fluctuations, 85
Statistical weights, 99
Steinberg, J. L., 131
Stellar associations, 205
Stimulated emission, 48, 98, 152
Stodola, E. K., 165
Störmer, C., 157
Strömgren, B., 203
Sunspot, 131, 133, 135
Supergalaxy, 247
Superheterodyne, 40
Supernova, 210, 215, 216
  Cassiopeia A, 207, 218, 223
  Kepler's, 207, 217
  Tycho's, 207, 217
Surge, 142
Swarup, G., 125
Swenson, G. W., Jr., 28, 81
Swept-frequency receiver, 90, 95
Synchrotron emission, 97, 111, 115, 140,
  145, 165, 189, 212, 220, 236

Taurus A (*see* Crab nebula)
Temperature, antenna, 30, 32

Temperature, excitation, 100
  noise, 42
Texas, 95
Thermal emission, 11, 16, 97, 106, 115
  galactic sources, 206
  moon, 161
  planets, 163
3C 48, 201
3C 295, 235, 249
Time constant of receiver, 38
Tinbergen, J., **57**, **199**
Transfer of radiation, 101
Trent, G. H., 183
Twiss, R. Q., 100, 111, **116**, 152, 153
Tycho's supernova, 207, 217

van de Hulst, H. C., **95**, 104, 180,
  230
van Woerden, H., 221, 223, 230
Vela X, 113, 220
Venus, 163
Vershuur, G. L., 224
Vinokur, M., 86
Virgo A, 235–237
Vitkevich, V. V., 213
Volders, Louise, 231
Vonberg, D. D., 46
von Hoerner, S., **88**
Vorontsov-Velyaminov, B. A., 234

Wade, C. M., 243
Walraven, T., 213, **225**
Warwick, Constance, **160**
Warwick, J., 164
Westerhout, G. G., **57**, 178, 183, **199**,
  205
Westfold, K. C., 124, 142
Whiteoak, J. B., **251**
Wild, J. P., 94, **95**, **116**, 137, 138, 140–
  143, 145
Wild, P. A. T., 224
Wilson, R. W., 205
Winckler, J. R., 146
Wittke, J. P., 57
Wolf, E., **57**
Woltjer, L., 182, 215, **225**

X rays, 133, 154

Zeeman splitting, 136, 143, 224
Zwicky, F., 244